Creating Choice

Palgrave Studies in Oral History

Series Editors: Linda Shopes and Bruce M. Stave

Creating Choice

A Community Responds to the Need for Abortion and Birth Control, 1961–1973

David P. Cline

First published in 2006 by
PALGRAVE MACMILLAN™
175 Fifth Avenue, New York, N.Y. 10010 and
Houndmills, Basingstoke, Hampshire, England RG21 6XS
Companies and representatives throughout the world.

PALGRAVE MACMILLAN is the global academic imprint of the Palgrave Macmillan division of St. Martin's Press, LLC and of Palgrave Macmillan Ltd. Macmillan® is a registered trademark in the United States, United Kingdom and other countries. Palgrave is a registered trademark in the European Union and other countries.

ISBN 1–4039–6813–6
ISBN 1–4039–6814–4

Library of Congress Cataloging-in-Publication Data

Cline, David P., 1969–
    Creating choice : a community responds to the need for abortion and birth control, 1961–1973 / by David P. Cline.
       p. cm.—(Palgrave studies in oral history)
    Includes bibliographical references and index.
    ISBN 1–4039–6813–6—ISBN 1–4039–6814–4
    1. Birth control—Massachusetts—Pioneer Valley—History—
20th century. 2. Abortion—Massachusetts—Pioneer Valley—History—
20th century. 3. Feminism—United States. I. Title. II. Series.

HQ766.5.U5C46 2005
363.9′6′0974409046—dc22   2005047593

A catalogue record for this book is available from the British Library.

Design by Newgen Imaging Systems (P) Ltd., Chennai, India.

First edition: February 2006

10 9 8 7 6 5 4 3 2 1

Printed in the United States of America.

Transferred to digital printing in 2007.

Contents

Series Editors' Foreword

Oral history as a disciplined practice began over a half-century ago in an effort to create, for the record, accounts of the past unavailable from any other source. It burgeoned in the 1970s and beyond as a means of incorporating into our collective knowledge of the past stories of those excluded from more traditional histories. David P. Cline's *Creating Choice: A Community Responds to the Need for Abortion and Birth Control, 1961–1973* falls squarely within this tradition: this remarkable collection of interviews with clergy, medical personnel, feminists, and social activists in Western Massachusetts documents, in the words of one of the narrators, "an amazing web" of people committed to providing women access to birth control and safe abortions at a time when both were illegal in that state, as well as most of the rest of the United States. For obvious reasons, the activities of this network were confidential, often covert, and largely undocumented. We are thus indebted to Cline and his colleagues in the Valley Women's History Collaborative Oral History Project for making this history known.

At their best, oral history interviews also open up new interpretive perspectives, and here too Cline's work is exemplary. At a time when those who oppose abortion have claimed the moral high ground, these interviews make clear that many who have supported legal abortion also act on the basis of high ethical principles, as well as deep social and professional concerns. And, suggesting another way to think about the "right to life," the chilling interviews of women who survived abortions in the pre-Roe era included in this volume remind us that many women literally owe their lives to legal—and safe—abortion.

For both the history it brings into view and the contemporary relevance of that history, we are pleased to include *Creating Choice* in Palgrave's *Studies in Oral History* series, designed to bring oral history interviews out of the archives and into the hands of students, educators, scholars, and the reading public. Volumes in the series are deeply grounded in interviews and also present those interviews in ways that aid readers to more fully appreciate their historical significance and cultural meaning. The series also includes work that approaches oral history more theoretically, as a point of departure for an exploration of broad questions of cultural production and representation.

Linda Shopes
Pennsylvania Historical and Museum Commission
Bruce M. Stave
University of Connecticut

Preface

Ask educated people to explain what led to the momentous U.S. Supreme Court decision on *Roe v. Wade* on January 22, 1973, and most will say that the force of second wave feminism in tandem with the post-1950s sexual revolution swayed the Court majority as too, the nation at large. Standard histories of the late twentieth century, including major accounts of the legalization of abortion, uphold such a link. Despite its merits, this commonplace view woefully ignores multiple sources of change that converged dramatically to expand women's reproductive rights at that time. David P. Cline's edited volume of oral histories, *Creating Choice*, challenges reigning causal assumptions as he directs the reader not only to pertinent feminist individuals and groups but also to those who, while not necessarily allied with the broad feminist agenda, were no less crucial players in the reproductive rights revolution.

The rich array of voices that gather in this informed and provocative book epitomizes one of the most significant developments in the discipline of history in the United States during the past several decades—the rise of oral history as fundamental to the reconstruction and interpretation of the past. By attending to the experience of ordinary people, not just those our media selects for public gaze, we learn the daily work of social change—complicated practical details of organization, political obstacles and possibilities, spiritual and moral dilemmas, and the personal and societal insights activists gained from their struggle. Often, as in the case of the decade preceding *Roe v. Wade*, traditional documents were destroyed, particularly when relevant to activity illegal at the time. Groups that labored in secrecy were understandably not aware of kindred groups. Oral history becomes indispensable to offset the purposely unwritten and to build a treasury of documentation about groups and individuals who risked so much to grant women avenues to abortion and, in Massachusetts, access simply to contraceptives, which were not legalized for married women until 1965 and single women until 1972.

Oral history also forms an essential component of modern local history. For generations, historians have recognized that certain locales cast in relief key contours in national history, highlighting place-specific variables that often deviate from dominant patterns elsewhere and prompt revision of customary historical narratives. *Creating Choice*'s focus on Western Massachusetts during the decade preceding and years immediately following *Roe v. Wade* permits us to see close-up the crisscrossing threads of individual and group resistance and conformity to dominant legal, political, economic, and cultural realities of the national history of reproductive rights. The story of reproductive rights activism in Western Massachusetts cities, towns, and rural communities disabuses us of the notion, for example, of a central sunburst of activism—in New York City or other metropolis—that radiates out into peripheral communities less intensely. Instead, we find a more reciprocal dynamic, in which rural and suburban areas spark as well as are shaped by upheavals in major cities. While the colorful chips in the kaleidoscope of changing public sentiment about abortion in Western Massachusetts are similar to those in other regions, the number of chips of a specific color and their particular configurations shift from place to place, and offer much promise for scholars' analysis of cross regional influences and the entwined relationships between individuals and their cultural context.

Unique features of the Pioneer Valley made the region especially conducive to the growth of reproductive rights activism. As is widely known, the sexual revolution that gained momentum throughout the United States during the 1960s enjoyed a vigorous following among college students. As the hub of 13 postsecondary educational institutions, among them some of the country's most competitive colleges, the Pioneer Valley had a disproportionately high percentage of young people within its total populations. With these institutions not located in large cities, most of these students lived on campus at a distance from family oversight, and the need for birth control was predictably urgent. Numbers of college and university faculty and administrators, as well as doctors, nurses, and clergy involved in campus affairs, helped students gain contraceptives and/or abortions. Crucially, the presence in the area of several single-sex women's colleges increased the level of faculty and student interest in women's issues, especially those filling the agenda of second wave feminism. For all these reasons, the Pioneer Valley also became home to a populous community of bisexual and lesbian women, who, together with heterosexual women, were deeply invested in promoting women's bodily autonomy. Distinctive of Massachusetts and Connecticut, prohibitions against the sale of contraceptives to unmarried women until 1972 intensified anger among many of the state's residents, with articulate champions in academia who were ready to mount a struggle for women's full reproductive freedom.

Although rural, the Pioneer Valley was close enough to New York City for easy intellectual exchange with trailblazing reproductive rights activists there. The Massachusetts clergy and doctors who became allies of women seeking contraception and abortion and saw a moral necessity to resort to illegal aid found support in newly formed organizations, such as the Clergy Consultation Service on Abortion, originating in 1967 in New York City. Similarly, indicative of widespread national protest against abortion prohibitions, the underground services for women seeking abortion in Western Massachusetts had counterparts in other regions, such as the legendary abortion providers of "Jane" in Chicago. As elsewhere, the Pioneer Valley movement for reproductive freedom brought together women and men from myriad walks of life, sexualities, and political and religious persuasions. The stories of these local activists enable us more palpably to feel the voltage of history in the making.

A paramount lesson of the past several decades is the appalling ease with which the experience and deeds of ordinary people and especially marginalized populations fail to enter historical writing, teaching, and archival collecting. Individual and group records, like personal memory, fade, fray, or are discarded and lost. Public memory is fickle and prone to amnesia or blur, not to mention political manipulation! Determined to find and preserve valuable records and through oral history to generate others, librarians, archivists, and scholars have launched, over the past several decades, numerous local initiatives of documentation.

David Cline's edited volume is in part the product of just such a community initiative. In September 1997 at the 25th Women's Activist Reunion at the University of Massachusetts in Amherst, celebrating the birth of the Women's Studies Program at the University of Massachusetts in 1972, Joyce Avrech Berkman, Professor of History at the University of Massachusetts at Amherst, who specializes in U.S. and European women's history, discussed with Kaymarion Raymond, longtime feminist and lesbian activist, the formation of a women's history collaborative that would preserve the history of second wave feminism and lesbian experience in the three counties—Hampshire, Hampden, and Franklin Counties—comprising Western Massachusetts' Pioneer Valley. Knowing that Susan Tracy, Professor of U.S. History at Hampshire College, partook in their interest, they enlisted her efforts in founding the Valley Women's History Collaborative (VWHC). Tracy, currently Dean of Humanities and Fine Arts at Hampshire College, was eager to spearhead oral history work for the Collaborative. Having already taught a course on oral history Berkman readily shared Tracy's enthusiasm and approach.

Crucially, in April, 1998 Tracy received funding for the VWHC Oral History Project from the MacArthur Fund at Hampshire College for recording equipment, volunteer training, and transcription of interview tapes. During July, 1998 Tracy attended the Columbia University Oral History Training program, directed by Ronald Grele, assisted by Mary Marshall Clark. Tracy returned to the Valley prepared to supervise the training of community volunteers in the theory, ethics, and technical demands of a professional oral history program. Drawing on previous work by Raymond, Tracy and Raymond, and Berkman created a 20-foot Pioneer Valley timeline graphic, stenciling onto a scroll an incomplete chronology of feminist and lesbian events and individuals associated with the events from the late 1960s to 1984 in the Pioneer Valley. This chronology became a booklet, "The Her story Chronology," and together with the timeline, inspired additions and corrections by volunteers.

Feminist politics shaped VWHC's organizational structure and permeated the Oral History Project. Seeking to include community activists on an equal basis with scholars, the three VWHC founders worked with volunteers to design an organization in which all aspects of work—research, oral history, documentation, and public sharing of documents—were collaboratively decided upon and developed. Initially beginning with roughly eight volunteers, by Fall 2004, the VWHC had trained 43 women and men, including active and retired professionals, straight and gay people, married and single people, employed teachers and unemployed manual laborers, and university and college students, staff, and faculty. Tracy, Berkman, and Raymond together and in discussion with volunteers agreed that the women whose history they were documenting would not only share decision-making roles in the organization but could be both informants and investigators. Rather than view their compiling of information as studies of "the other," VWHC members were intellectually and politically motivated to document their own history and preserve their voices and other activists' voices for future generations of reformers and researchers. As the organization expanded, some volunteers felt uneasy with the label "feminist" but still engaged in progressive efforts to promote female equality and social justice and/or identified along a spectrum of gender and sexual orientations. The Collaborative revised its mission to encompass the history of those who shared a feminist mission but who did not strictly identify themselves as feminists and lesbians.

Certain procedures were set in place, reflecting feminist politics and professional methods. Interviewers actively chose their own interviewees, and the coordinators assured each informant pervasive control over her/his interview. After reviewing their transcript, informants were free to correct errors of spelling and fact to delete sections and names that they preferred to keep confidential. They could also add a clarifying addendum. Guiding this process was the coordinators' aim to balance the integrity and rights of individual informants to own their story with the need of VWHC volunteers to record events and experiences as wholly as possible. Through regular bimonthly meetings, the coordinators assured that research and oral history volunteers adhered to professional scholarly standards.

In 1999, the VWHC was awarded a modest Massachusetts Foundation for the Humanities grant. Subsequent highly focused grants from other agencies, such as a grant for transcribing tapes from the Women's Fund of Western Massachusetts, helped sustain the VWHC mission. Most important was a grant from the Massachusetts Historical Records and Archives Board, which enabled the VWHC to conduct a series of public brainstorming sessions (yielding names of over five hundred groups active at one time or another in promoting feminist and/or lesbian goals from the late 1960s to the 1990s) and to survey various Valley libraries, archives, and repositories for extant and future holdings relating to our region's feminist and lesbian history since the early 1960s. This survey led to the development of library and archival finding aids, a list of potential donors of papers, photographs, tapes, and so on, and a Donor Guide to available repositories and to the practical parameters of donation. We also received invaluable support from Lorna Peterson, Director of Five Colleges Inc., without which we would not have been able to achieve many of our early goals.

From 1999 to 2002 Marla Miller, Assistant Professor of History at the University of Massachusetts at Amherst, who specializes in Public History, coordinated the documentation realm of the Collaborative's mission. Although spheres of activity interconnected and coordinators often worked on joint projects, Berkman took on the development of a Research Guide, while Tracy issued various guidelines and technical development for the Oral History project. Initially, two subcommittees formed to focus separately on research and oral history, but after several years the symbiotic nature of research and oral history led to a merger of the two. Likewise, Miller met regularly not only with area archivists and librarians but also with Raymond, whose charge was the major administrative tasks of the documentation project. After Raymond's departure from the organization in Fall 2000 and Miller's withdrawal from administrative activity in 2002, Tracy and Berkman remained sole coordinators until Laura Lovett, hired in 2003 as Assistant Professor of U.S. History at the University of Massachusetts, joined them in directing the organization.

Professors Miller, Tracy, and Berkman actively promoted VWHC participation between their undergraduate and graduate students who could earn academic credit for their work with the Collaborative. With Honors students and Graduate students proving particularly reliable and skilled in scholarly research and oral history, most of the Valley's student volunteers came from the University of Massachusetts. Additionally, unlike community volunteers who often had families and full-time jobs compete for focus with their assignments, graduate students' primary academic responsibilities better meshed with the Collaborative's goals, enabling graduate students to more easily and effectively combine research and oral history tasks. Inspired and trained by his University of Massachusetts professors, David Cline was among those graduate students whose work demonstrated outstanding dedication and acuity.

David Cline entered the VWHC Oral History Project with gusto, completing 11 interviews while at the university. The origins and nature of his contributions exemplify the feminist and collaborative dynamics discussed here. When Cline began his Master's Degree program in History at the University of Massachusetts, he was already eager to extend his knowledge of women's history and he quickly expressed a desire to understand the experience of the doctors and ministers who were instrumental in providing abortion services before *Roe v. Wade* and active in pressing for abortion's decriminalization. These were the figures whom scholars in their accounts had sidelined. For this reason, most people assume women seeking abortion during the era before *Roe v. Wade* went to back-alley abortionists or resorted to self-induced methods of terminating their pregnancies. Cline discovered active networks of clergy, doctors, and nurses in Western Massachusetts who bent and/or defied the law to aid women deprived of abortion rights. These individuals in combination with feminists of myriad perspectives and with myriad priorities were vital to the changing landscape of reproductive choice in the years surrounding *Roe v. Wade*.

In his pursuit of this oft-obscured history Cline worked closely with another enterprising and talented graduate student, Kris Woll. Manifesting exceptional tact, insight and skills, Cline and Woll's research projects took the path Susan Tracy,

Joyce Berkman, and community volunteer Judi Fonsh had recently traveled; other VWHC volunteers, drawing on their own friendship ties with reproductive rights activists, had also conducted interviews with important participants in the reproductive rights movement. These friendship ties were vital in securing the cooperation of individuals ordinarily reluctant to discuss this phase of their past. Cline built steadily on such networks and soon became an accomplished detective, ferreting out his own sources and leads.

Cline's passion for the project spurred him to continue his work, work that revealed an unusual ability to establish rapport and trust from interviewees unlikely to extend openness, for example, lesbian activists, ordinarily suspicious of male academics. No less impressive is Cline's success in digesting substantial relevant historical scholarship and primary documents. The outcome of his insightfulness, collaborative spirit, drive, deep sense of moral and political purpose, and his historical expertise as researcher and oral historian is this critical and path breaking volume. *Creating Choice* answers a call that captures the voices of those unheralded souls, each of whom had a part in advancing the reproductive rights revolution.

—Joyce Avrech Berkman
Professor of History, University of Massachusetts at Amherst

—Susan Tracy
Dean of Humanities, Arts and Cultural Studies
Professor of American Studies and History, Hampshire College

Note: As our Preface sets forth the historical background that led to the worthy collection you now have in hand, we find that for the sake of historical precision we must resort to third-person rendering of what for both of us is emphatically first-person experience and regard. How else to keep you apprised, in our delineation of the role that the VWHC plays in the formation of *Creating Choice* as to which "I" is Berkman or Tracy, and even which "we" is the two of us or the two of us plus others?

Introduction

Could he have driven any faster? On September 10, 1970, William Day, a senior premed student at the University of Massachusetts at Amherst (UMass Amherst), drove as fast as he could to Holyoke Hospital. Earlier that day he and his 21 year-old girlfriend Nancy Kierzek had finally decided that they had to do something about her pregnancy, then at three months. They were both students and couldn't imagine having and raising a child. Nancy would start showing soon and they knew they had to do something now. William had taken basic anatomy classes at UMass and had been studying the limited materials he could find on performing an abortion. Plus, they didn't know where else to turn.

One of the crude methods practiced in the illegal abortion underground was the insertion of a catheter, a hollow tube, into the uterus. Trying to reject the foreign body, the uterus would contract and expel the fetus along with the catheter. William had access to catheters at the science labs at school, but not to an operating room or any kind of anesthesia. Their station wagon would serve as an operating theater, an empty parking lot as their hospital. Nancy gritted her teeth against the pain and William did his best with the unfamiliar instruments, but something went terribly wrong. Day must have inserted the catheter too deeply or at the wrong angle for he unwittingly punctured the uterus and Nancy began to bleed uncontrollably. Panicked, William jumped into the driver's seat and sped to Holyoke Hospital. After medical staff rushed to the car with a gurney and wheeled Nancy away, William Day waited anxiously in the hall. It was there that Holyoke police arrested him. As was required at the time in cases of suspected illegal abortion, emergency room doctors had notified the authorities. Day was already in custody when Kierzek died, some six hours after she reached the hospital. He was charged with performing an "abortion resulting in death"; the charges were later changed to "attempting to procure a miscarriage, with death resulting."[1]

Holyoke, where Day was arrested that night, is a small industrial city in a picturesque area of Western Massachusetts known as the Pioneer Valley. "The Valley," as most people around there call it, is about a two-hour drive from Boston to the east and four hours to New York City to the south. Holyoke lies immediately to the north of the larger city of Springfield, and just to the south of the bustling college towns of

Northampton and Amherst, home to Smith, Mount Holyoke, Amherst, and Hampshire Colleges, and to UMass Amherst, the flagship campus of the University of Massachusetts System. Scattered throughout out the Valley are other small towns and cities where, by the later 1960s and early 1970s, the once-thriving textile industry had largely collapsed and residents worked mostly in the agriculture or service industries.

By the time of Kierzek's death, thousands of women living in the Pioneer Valley had already confronted the issue of abortion. For years, local women had been asking their doctors to "help" with unwanted pregnancies. A few secretive doctors may have performed abortions for favored private patients and others may have risked referring a patient to a medical colleague out of state who was known to perform abortions, but both of these options were against the law. Some hospitals performed so-called "therapeutic" abortions for health reasons—the law allowed for these—but these were rare and difficult to procure. So most pregnant women in Western Massachusetts faced two choices: to continue the pregnancy to term (and either keep the child or put it up for adoption) or to seek an illegal abortion.

While these choices were the same for women all over the country, Pioneer Valley women faced their pregnancies within a unique community whose demographics reflected a largely Catholic heritage mixed with—and sometimes challenged by—the progressive influence of the University of Massachusetts and the colleges. Immigrants from French-speaking Canada, Ireland, and Poland came to work in the region's textile and paper mills at the turn of the century, setting much of the cultural tone of the area. During the 1960s and 1970s, increasing numbers of Latino immigrants came to take over many of the mill jobs. Many in these successive waves of immigration contributed to the local dominance of the Catholic Church. Throughout the twentieth century a diverse mix of working people, farmers, and academics was drawn to the rich agricultural land and the presence of the liberal arts colleges. As the home of two of the nation's premier women's colleges—Mount Holyoke and Smith—and, beginning in the 1970s, increasingly identified as a "lesbian-friendly" environment, the Pioneer Valley proved to be fertile soil for the development of "second wave" feminism and political activism.[2] The area gained a national reputation for its social activism in the late 1960s and early 1970s when UMass served as the site of many anti-Vietnam War protests. Amherst College and Hampshire College, although the latter did not accept its first students until 1970, also added to the mix. Even after the war, Amherst has remained a center of activism—a few local residents have been gathering at the town common every Sunday at noon for the "Amherst Vigil for a Nuclear Free World" since 1979. The town's liberal, activist reputation was reinforced in 2001 when a local battle to regulate the amount of time a phalanx of American flags could line Main Street (a battle that unfortunately erupted right around the September 11, 2001 attacks, although the original complaint far preceeded that date) became fodder for national news reports on Amherst's over-the-top liberalism.

Creating Choice at the Community Level:
An Amazing Web

Within this unique Pioneer Valley environment, women who faced daunting or unwanted pregnancies were not as alone as they may have immediately felt. A little digging for information, a couple of conversations with friends, neighbors, or fellow church members, could reveal a network of birth control and abortion information, counseling services, and referrals to providers. These networks were composed of local health professionals, clergy members, and feminist activists, many with differing motivations, but all of them providing information about, and access to, methods of birth control and abortion. Their work was done in defiance of the law, sometimes in secret, but often surprisingly openly. Although each of these groups mainly worked in isolation from one another, they came together around key events and also overlapped in significant ways.

In August 1966, Massachusetts and Connecticut became the last states in the country to legalize contraception for married women. Six years later, on March 22, 1972, Massachusetts was the battleground for the *Eisenstadt v. Baird* case, in which the Supreme Court finally legalized birth control for all women regardless of marital status.[3] Massachusetts, then, was an important battleground in the fight for reproductive laws and makes for an excellent case study. By studying the activities that took place in one Massachusetts community, we can see how struggles for access to birth control and abortion were particularly linked. Without access to legal birth control, many women had trouble preventing unplanned pregnancies and consequently sought illegal abortions. Physicians and health educators were therefore sometimes faced with the choice of breaking the laws against prescribing or transmitting information about birth control, or breaking other laws against abortion and abortion referrals. There were doctors who were willing to break these laws, but they did so at the risk of their licenses and their practices. And when they did take these risks, they often met with support from surprising places, such as university administrations and church leaders.

According to historian Linda Gordon in her history of American birth control politics, *The Moral Property of Women*, legalizing birth control did not stimulate greater use of birth control. Likewise, the Roe decision did not create a massive increase in the number of abortions sought or performed. The legislatures and judiciary simply confirmed a social reality. Gordon goes on to say that the legislators and the Supreme Court were responding to "pressure for abortion legalization from two groups: professionals, particularly physicians, and feminists."[4] This volume introduces two more categories, clergy members and women who were both feminists *and* working within the professional health-care system to create access and reform. This latter group I term "The Connectors," since their roles overlapped with those of the clergy, the health-care providers, and the women from feminist collectives.

Massachusetts provides a unique lens through which to view the links between the histories of birth control and abortion. Contraception remained illegal in Massachusetts longer than anywhere else and those who were trying to help women find safe abortions were at many times also trying to find illegal birth control for them so as to prevent another pregnancy. By the mid-1960s, only Massachusetts and Connecticut forbid the use or distribution of contraception for married women. Item 53: 939, "Offenses Against the Person," of Connecticut's legal code, revised in 1958, defined as a crime the "use of drugs or instruments to prevent conception" and applied it to "any person who uses any drug, medicinal article or instrument for the purpose of preventing conception." It further stipulated that "any person who assists, abets, counsels, causes, hires, or commands another to commit any offense may be prosecuted and punished as if he were the principal offender." The penalty was a minimum fine of $50 and or a minimum of 60 days in jail.[5] Massachusetts' law 1: 272, "Crimes Against Chastity, Morality, Decency and Good Order," was adopted in 1879 (and revised in 1956) and specifically linked contraception and abortion. It defined as a criminal "anyone who sells, lends, gives away, exhibits, or offers to sell, lend, or give away any instrument or other article intended to be used for self-abuse, or any drug, medicine, instrument, or article whatever for the prevention of conception or for causing unlawful abortion" and further prohibited any advertising or giving of advice related to birth control and abortion. Punishment included a minimum fine of $100 or a maximum prison sentence of five years.[6]

In June 1965, the U.S. Supreme Court, in *Griswold v. Connecticut*, finally made birth control legal for married women in that state. In 1966, Massachusetts also legalized contraception for married people. After one failed attempt and two amendments, on August 8 of that year, the Massachusetts legislature passed the Reid/Rutstein bill allowing doctors to prescribe contraception for married (but not unmarried) people and licensed pharmacists to sell it. Furthermore, information about contraception could now be legally distributed, but only by a public health agency, a registered nurse, or an accredited hospital. Advertising birth control was still illegal in Massachusetts.[7] It wasn't until the U.S. Supreme Court decided *Baird v. Eisenstadt* on March 22, 1972, that birth control became legal for all Massachusetts women regardless of marital status.

Of course, despite the unusual case of Massachusetts birth control laws, Pioneer Valley women facing difficult choices about contraception and abortion were not alone; estimates of the number of women across the United States who picked the harrowing and sometimes fatal choice of seeking an illegal abortion during the late 1960s and early 1970s range from 200,000 to 1 million annually.[8] Wealthier women with private doctors often could receive a discrete abortion at the doctor's office or a referral to another safe practitioner. But the majority of women had to resort to an underground network of abortion referrals and to practitioners who were often untrained, and sometimes unsanitary and unscrupulous. So it was within this broader climate, in combination with the more unique social and legislative environment of Massachusetts, that the people of the Pioneer Valley—academics, working people, homemakers, community organizers, radical feminists, ministers— united in complex and powerful ways to push for social and legislative change.

The medical professionals were probably first to start addressing issues of birth control and abortion. Because Massachusetts was so late in legalizing birth control, contraception was frequently requested of doctors by their sexually active female patients, and Pioneer Valley doctors responded to their patients' pleas for birth control in various ways. Dr. Merritt Garland, Jr., who began practicing in the northern Valley town of Greenfield in 1953, never saw any moral conflict posed by recommending birth control. He also found a way around the law. Since it was illegal to prescribe diaphragms but not to sell them, he would measure a woman for the device, write the measurements on a desk pad rather than a prescription pad, and have the woman take this "note" to the pharmacy. That way she got properly fitting contraception but he had not technically "prescribed" it. Dr. Robert Gage who practiced in Amherst before taking over the reins of the University Health Services at UMass, similarly believed that women should not be denied access to birth control. He quietly fitted and provided women with diaphragms in defiance of the law, and once he became director of UMass's University Health Services, he did the same for undergraduate and graduate students as well. Eventually he established family planning clinics at the University Health Services (UHS), with the full approval of the university administration, even though doing so was against state law.

Although a few physicians were willing to assist in matters relating to birth control, the termination of pregnancy was quite another matter. It was illegal to provide information about abortion or to refer patients to physicians practicing in states where abortion was legal. Some local doctors broke the law and sent their patients to private physicians they knew out of state or to clinics overseas. But these referrals were generally provided quietly behind closed doors. It is also probable that a few private doctors in the Pioneer Valley performed illegal abortions for private patients, but even to this day no one is naming names. But this situation was not immutable and slowly, over the years, the closed doors began to swing open, first allowing access to contraception and ultimately to the right to request abortion. In 1961 the University of Massachusetts built a new health center on campus, which for the first time provided examining rooms that allowed private conversations and physical examinations. When Dr. Robert Gage began working at UMass in 1960, his venue changed from a private practice to a state university and his patients were now students rather than paying private patients, but his underlying principles were unaltered. Dr. Gage was aware of both the legal and social pressures and he did not heedlessly flaunt the law, but he felt that the university students deserved the same consideration as his private patients. He sought and (surprisingly) received the support of the top administrators for his efforts provide information on and access to birth control at the university.

Next into the fray were clergymen. Since abortion, and to some extent the decision to use birth control, represented a major life crisis for many women, they often turned to their ministers, priests, or rabbis for assistance. For most clergy members, all each could provide was compassion and a shoulder to lean on, but beginning in New York City in 1967, a group of clergy members decided that they had to do more and the Clergy Consultation Service on Abortion (CCS) officially launched in May of that year. Convinced that abortion was a woman's right and that there were safe and scrupulous abortion practitioners, the clergy decided they had no choice but to help these women get to the safest possible abortion providers. Since local doctors usually wouldn't take the risk, this meant finding and assessing doctors in other states and countries who would.

A New York journalist named Lawrence Lader had found some of these reliable abortionists while researching his 1966 book, *Abortion*, a revealing account of the tremendous real demand for abortion, the legal obstacles, and the underground market for terminations. Women who read his book wrote to Lader desperately asking to be put in contact with the abortion providers he depicted. Lader vowed to answer every one of the dozen requests he received per day even though merely providing this information violated New York's law against Conspiracy to Commit Abortion. Lader recruited key coconspirators during a 1966 lunch with several prominent clergymen, who were hoping to provide women with more than words. Lader said he would give the clergy the names of a few trustworthy abortionists and within a year, the clergy, led by Reverend Howard Moody of Judson Memorial Church in New York City's Greenwich Village, began to organize CCS chapters.

Clergy members were trained in "problem pregnancy" counseling, in discussing options from motherhood to adoption, and in how to describe to women basic abortion procedures they may face. They also did extensive interviews and reviews of abortion providers, selecting only those they felt were safe and trustworthy. They chose some abortionists overseas in countries where it was either legal or not prosecuted, as well as a few providers in the United States. For U.S. referrals, they would only send women to providers out of state, since they felt that interstate prosecutions would be far less likely. Beginning with a splashy article in the *New York Times*, CCS operated very publicly. The clergy had agreed that if they were arrested, they would argue that they were "answerable to a higher law" than any the government might impose. CCS would grow to some 40 chapters in some two dozen states with 1,400 to 2,000 clergy members nationwide by the time the *Roe v. Wade* decision went into effect in July of 1973. Nationally, CCS estimated that in the six years they operated, they had made 100,000 referrals to abortion providers. It is not known exactly how many women received CCS abortion referrals from the two Pioneer Valley chapters, but estimates based on daily appointment books of CCS clergy indicate an average of about 400–600 annually during the busiest years. By the end of CCS activities in 1973, nationally only two clergy members had been arrested for their abortion referral work and neither of these cases were prosecuted.

CCS chapters were formed in cities across the country and in 1968 the first of two chapters was created in the Pioneer Valley by Reverend Richard Unsworth, the chaplain of Smith College in Northampton. Not long afterwards, a second chapter was created by the ministers of the United Christian Foundation (UCF), a campus ministry group located at UMass Amherst. Together, the two chapters had as many as 16 ministers, priests, and rabbis on call. A CCS clergy counsellor would typically meet privately with a woman for an hour, discuss a complete range of options from adoption to abortion, and if, requested, make an appropriate referral.

Not all women, of course, knew about the clergy counselors and even if they did, not all were comfortable confiding in a religious cleric. And so a third group entered the reproductive rights battle. To fill what they perceived as a gap in birth control and problem pregnancy counseling, members of two Pioneer Valley feminist organizations—Amherst Women's Liberation's Abortion and Birth Control Group and the Springfield Women's Health Collective—organized to provide additional counseling and information. Both groups came out of feminist consciousness-raising groups whose goals were to create safe spaces in which women could share concerns, frustrations, and information about the burgeoning women's movement. Women's bodies and health care quickly became major interests for both the Springfield and Amherst groups, and abortion and birth control were identified as areas on which to focus. Both groups organized counseling wings, trained counselors, vetted abortionists, and provided referrals for pregnant women.

Over time, members of these once very separate spheres—health care, the church, and feminist activism—began to interact as they worked toward common goals: clergy counselors were hired by the University Health Services to continue their abortion referral work under university auspices; university social workers advised clergy; a feminist birth control clinic organizer served on the Clergy Consultation board; and feminist abortion counselors, who initially provided illegal services, went to work for legal abortion providers after the *Roe v. Wade* decision. The ways in which these disparate groups encouraged each other's efforts and occasionally worked together or shared individual members made for what one former member of the CCS now calls "an amazing web" of activists, motivated by different factors but all working toward similar goals of providing safe and legal birth control and abortion services.

A few principal individuals were responsible for much of the networking between the clergy, medical, and feminist groups. Leslie Laurie arrived in the Pioneer Valley in the summer of 1971 from the Philadelphia area, where she had been Education Coordinator for one of the country's largest Planned Parenthood affiliates. She also held a degree in community organizing from Columbia University. Astounded by the lack of family planning services in Western Massachusetts, she made it her mission to change this situation and convinced the Planned Parenthood League of Massachusetts (PPLM) to hire her as an organizer for the Pioneer Valley and areas to the west. PPLM was primarily a Boston organization but liked the idea of fulfilling its image as a statewide organization. However, PPLM wanted to have an educational presence in Western Massachusetts only and was not interested in providing programs. In order to do that, Leslie Laurie had to partner with existing organizations. This she did over the next two years, establishing contacts, stimulating new programs, and applying for grants. In July of 1973, several of these partner organizations shed their separate identities and merged into a new organization, the Family Planning Council of Western Massachusetts, which Laurie was hired to head.

Like others in the Pioneer Valley, Laurie saw birth control and abortion as two linked reproductive health care issues. In addition to her work organizing family planning programs, Laurie also put her community organizer training to use in uniting those in the Pioneer Valley working on abortion referrals. She formed the Western Massachusetts Counselors' Cooperative in 1971, which soon expanded so much that it was renamed the Western New England Counselors' Cooperative (WNECC) a year later. Laurie's health clinics, the feminist counseling groups, and both CCS chapters all joined. They used the WNECC as a place to exchange information about providers and techniques. After abortion was legalized in New York State, and later in Massachusetts, the WNECC also used its mass referral power to negotiate free and reduced rate abortions for women in financial need. While Leslie Laurie was the initial fire beneath the engine of the health clinics and the cooperative, she was joined by a large group of coworkers and allies. Together, Leslie and her comrades formed the group that I have dubbed as "The Connectors" because of their roles in uniting the two issues of abortion and birth control and for their abilities to unite those other disparate groups of people—health care workers, clergymen, and feminist activists—who had previously been working in relative isolation.

Creating Choice, Creating Change

The Pioneer Valley groups that worked to create access to birth control and abortion may have had significant differences in background, philosophy, and strategy but they were synergistic in their resistance to antiabortion legislation. Their story shows how ordinary people became agents for social changes that reverberate through American society.[9]

Each of the people in this book became such an agent for change; however, the paths they took to their goals were fascinatingly unique. Jane Zapka was raised by a conservative onion farmer in Western Massachusetts, but a formative experience teaching middle schoolers in the New York State system convinced her that mental health education needed to be a priority. Later that commitment grew to other aspects of public health, most notably sex education, and she is now a medical school professor. Dr. Robert Gage decided to illegally prescribe birth control for the simple reason that his patients wanted it and he deemed it in the best interest of their health. Reverend Richard Unsworth had personally experienced the deaths of pregnant women whom he had tried to counsel. He decided that the Bible was clear that abortion was not a sin, and so he set out to make sure that women could obtain one if they wished. It was, he decided, a matter of life or death.

The oral histories in this volume reveal how health professionals and clergy, as forerunners and later as allies of the women's movement, supported this movement as it took on issues of women's health. As we examine the work of Pioneer Valley doctors, clergy, and counselors in the pre-Roe period, we begin to understand how grassroots pressure and underground networks helped to create a society that could throw off the shackles of the past and legalize abortion.[10] We also see how the women's movement of the 1960s and 1970s was intimately tied to the local communities within which it was fostered.

When the Supreme Court legalized abortion, most of the groups and individuals that had been involved in reproductive rights work turned to other pursuits. Confident that the Court had settled the issue once and for all, they returned to their private lives, their congregations, to other social change work. Most of those who had labored to procure or provide illegal abortions chose to remain silent about such private matters. The story of their work—the difficulties and risks they faced, the importance of their challenge to restrictive and unpopular legislation, and the complexity of the issues—have all but vanished from both our cultural consciousness and the historic record.[11] The web of activists who risked their freedom, reputations, and careers to provide birth control and abortion for thousands of women has remained largely invisible. This volume uses first person oral histories of some of those individuals who made up the "amazing web" to finally bring their stories to light.

Notes on Methodology

When in 2002, I set out to interview men and women who were involved in reproductive health issues in the Pioneer Valley during the 1960s and 1970s, I did not realize what a journey I was undertaking. The personal and sensitive nature of the subject matter dictates a few notes about the methods I used and the biases I brought to the work.

Many of the groups involved in reproductive rights activities in the latter part of the 1960s and early 1970s, out of fear of prosecution, did not keep many written records. Those who did keep records were rightly concerned about preserving the confidentiality of women who had had illegal abortions, and often destroyed these records after the fact. (One of those I interviewed had actually just burned the last of his confidential files only a few months before I first spoke with him.) Consequently, oral histories were critical to recovering and exploring this subject and era. In the process of research, however, I did find many documents that had not gone up in smoke, more than I ever at first dreamed of locating, and these enabled me to check and double-check the oral histories against other sources. These written records in some cases bore out the story as told in the interviews, in other cases they provided contrasting shades of interpretation, and in some few other cases they contrasted sharply with the stories as recounted 30 years later. Of course, written records are fallible too and one of the reasons I am drawn to oral histories is as a check against those very written records. Ideally, sources of historical information can be used in combination, triangulating toward a fuller version of a given time or event. In the introductory chapters that precede each group of narratives, I have used many other primary and secondary sources to contextualize and, in some cases, complicate the oral histories. By using these traditional sources to compliment the engaging and personal accounts, I hope I have provided a rich and nuanced inroad to a subject that is otherwise little known or understood.

As an oral historian, I have been fascinated not only with the history unearthed but also with the "construction" of the interview and how that influences the nature of the story being recorded. I have also been fascinated with memory and mediated recall; that is how a person's memories are filtered and altered through time and retelling. These issues came into sharp focus in the compilation of this material. Some individuals had set stories they wanted to tell and would not deviate into other areas. In some cases they denied knowledge of stories in which other sources, including newspaper accounts and other written records, clearly placed them. Since all the subjects spoke about a time 30 years distant, their stories were necessarily colored by intervening personal, social, cultural, and political changes, as well as by, in some cases, repeated retelling. I found that the interviews contain revelations not just about the historical events covered, but also point to intruiging questions about oral history methods and memory. Among these are questions of how stories change over time, why and how stories differ in separate tellings, what we can learn from ways in which oral history accounts contain deviations from the written records, and how the circumstances of the interview influence the story told and the history thus recorded.

One of the fascinating aspects of the oral history process is the dynamic between interviewer and interviewee, or as is the case in several of the oral histories in this book, interviewees. These dynamics are created and informed by such factors as the relationship between interviewer and interviewee(s), the ages of the participants, and varying understandings of a given subject, as well as the location of the interview and even the time of day when it was conducted. My general feeling is that if one shifts any of the variables—moving the meeting from Saturday to Tuesday, having a female instead of a male interviewer, conducting the interview in a person's home rather than their office or your office—one will often obtain a different oral history. By doing multiple interviews and/or reviewing and editing the transcripts together, both parties have time to reconsider, add new material, and continue the collaborative relationship begun in the initial interview.

The interviewees sometimes disagree with each other over details of events. These instances are clear examples of how perceptions of contemporary events often differ among individuals and from what is later codified as "historical truth." They also may reveal how time and subsequent events, as well as ideology and personal experiences, color an individual's memories, and in fact may represent to that person an alternate and equally valid truth from the one that history records. In his pioneering article "The Death of Luigi Trastulli," oral historian Alesandro Portelli recounts the case of an Italian town in which many different people misremembered Trastulli's death at the hands of the authorities, placing it in a time and context different than that in which it actually occurred.[12] Portelli's article is often cited in discussions both of group memory and of how memories can be transformed over time to fit into an established narrative, even of something that never happened. In my own research, I encountered my own version of the Trastulli case in the interviews with feminist collective members in Springfield. Each narrator had a different story about how many collectives existed, who the collective members were, and what the collective did. It eventually turned out that what many of the women identified as being two separate organizations, was in fact the same group at different points in time as old members left, new members joined, and the collective engaged other issues. But this documented "reality" did not always jibe with the memories of those interviewed. In the minds of some individuals who had been involved in the Springfield Women's Health Collective for only a few years of its many year history (under several different names), they had been active in it the entire time. They could not conceive of who these "others" might be who were claiming a role in their history. This does not make anyone a liar. Often just the opposite. It seems to me that often if there is a "true story" to come out of an oral history interview, it is the truth *as considered at the moment* it is delivered to the interviewer. There may indeed be many others truths.

The interviews were recorded on cassette tape and mini disk and transcribed by the interviewer or, in select cases, by a professional transcriber. With a few exceptions, the interviews were conducted one-on-one in the interviewee's home. Of the 23 interviews included here, Leslie Laurie was interviewed by Kris Woll; Elaine Fraser by Judi Fonsh; the Amherst Women's Liberation Group (in several separate interviews) by Judi Fonsh, Susan Tracy, and Marilyn Smith; and the Springfield Women's Health Collective by Susan Tracy and Joyce Berkman. I had the honor of interviewing all of the others in this collection.[13] The two group interviews—of the Amherst and Springfield women's groups—each had two interviewers and five interviewees. These interview sessions took on the dynamics of each group as they collectively told their stories. They had a body of shared memories in common, though sometimes in conflict, and the interviews ended up as a group journey over this terrain of memory.

The transcripts invite close examination and comparison and, read in sequence, unfold to reveal a previously hidden history. As different voices join the chorus of telling, nuance is added, motivations are understood, and connections between various groups and individuals become clearer.

A note on the editing: I admit to being in love with the starkness, the insightful asides, and the revealing pauses of an unedited oral history transcript, but in order to make them an interesting reading experience, I have edited each to remove my own questions, to eliminate the umms and ahhs, and to create a narrative flow. I have removed repeated phrases and false starts, and reordered the sequence of interview passages for narrative clarity. I have, however, attempted to remain as true as possible to the original tone and style of the recorded interview. For those who share my joy in the orality of an actual interview as opposed to its edited cousin, the original tapes, disks, and transcripts of all interviews are available in the Valley Women's History Collaborative archives in the Special Collections department of the W.E.B. Du Bois Library at the University of Massachusetts at Amherst.

I believe that oral histories are not monologues, they are conversations, collaborative acts created by an interviewer and interviewee. That is not to say that the playing field is always equal. By editing the transcripts, by imposing context and commentary on the interview, indeed by instigating the interview process to begin with, I have asserted a certain level of authority. To promise a true shared authority in this process is to make a false promise. However, I endeavored to work closely with the interviewees to create edited transcripts that were true to the interview experience so that the interviewees would feel that their voices had been accurately conveyed. In this spirit, each interviewee has reviewed the edited versions of their verbatim transcript, given their own editorial suggestions, in some cases added new material, and signed off on the final version as their story. Together in the post-interview process we have, in essence, continued the conversation.

A Personal Note

Given the topic of this book, I feel it is necessary to make known my personal feelings about access to abortion and birth control—in other words, to answer the inevitable questions about bias at the outset. My own feelings about legal abortion were undoubtedly influenced by the family in which I was raised. My father is a retired physician and in my family we discussed abortion openly and without moral overtones as a medical procedure, the right to which was the patient's. Following my birth as the youngest of three, my mother's birth control failed and she became pregnant. My parents, having decided that they had reached the outside limit for their family size, sought a therapeutic abortion. They lived in California and at that time according to state law a letter from a psychiatrist was sufficient means for granting a therapeutic abortion for mental health reasons. With my father's contacts in the medical community, this was easily obtained. My late mother's story thus fits the pattern, documented and attested to throughout this volume, that those with connections and money had little trouble getting access to abortion while those who did not have these advantages were often forced to carry unwanted pregnancies to term.

My family had other experiences in the realm of unwanted pregnancies as well. Several times in the late 1960s my parents provided housing to young women who came to California from out of state to live during their pregnancies. Their families had come up with some plausible reason for their daughter's long absence—a visit with a relative, a school exchange program, and so forth. After each of these girls—and they *were* girls, in their midteens—gave birth, she put her child up for adoption. My mother recalled one girl who insisted on taking the bus back home the very day after giving birth. While there were many religiously affiliated homes for unwed mothers designed to help young women in this way, my family seems to have done so as individuals motivated not by religion but by concern for the individual women.

Although I have for years believed firmly that abortion is a medical procedure that must be accessible, in doing the research for this collection and going back to a time when abortion and birth control were restricted by law, I have become more and more convinced that making abortion illegal will not in any way stop abortion. Reviewing the historic record makes it clear that making abortion illegal does not curtail its practice; it just makes it more dangerous, more restricted to the rich, and more harrowing in a multitude of ways. Does that make this a political book? Inevitably, yes, as are all acts of history making. Wherever you sit on this divisive issue, I invite you to read the oral histories that follow and to return, as I did, to a time in the not too distant past that already seems much obscured. I hope that my effort here has helped to wipe away at least a little of this fog on the lens of history.

A Moment in Time

Before proceeding to the oral histories, let's return for a moment to the City of Holyoke in the summer of 1970. Nancy Kierzek has just died as the result of a botched abortion and her boyfriend, Bill Day, who had tried to perform the procedure, sits in a Holyoke jail accused of her murder. Kierzek and Day were not alone. In addition to the thousands of others in the Pioneer Valley who faced unplanned or unwanted pregnancies, there were those who had organized to help. And still others would be organizing additional outreach efforts in the coming months. Nancy Kierzek's death stimulated a great deal of action in the Pioneer Valley. It prompted the creation of at least one problem pregnancy counseling group, the Amherst Women's Liberation's Abortion and Birth Control Group. It also sparked a number of those who had been working quietly on problem pregnancy issues to take a more public stance.

Dr. Robert Gage of the University Health Services (UHS) wrote an editorial in the *Massachusetts Daily Collegian*, the student newspaper on September 16, 1970:

> The tragic death of a coed from a nearby school as the aftermath of an attempted abortion . . . once again focused the attention of much of the University community on the problems of abortion. Again, we may predict, emotions will soar, indignation will rise, rhetoric will become sharper, and the gulf will widen between those who continue to defend time-honored standards and those who insist that all which is not new is worthless or irrelevant. Ultimately, the heat of passions may subside as

new issues take their place at center stage and we shall all find that some new light has been shed. Each time the discussion is intensified there is hope that a few more adults will have ventured from the comfort of their cherished moral strongholds and may have even dared to share with students the bold search for a code of action which is more closely related to reality and a legal framework which meets today's needs.

Change will come, as it has in the past, even in Massachusetts. Only four years ago it became legal to provide birth control information and devices to MARRIED women, and now a federal court has ruled that the Massachusetts law prohibiting similar services for unmarried women is discriminatory. Unreal and essentially punitive restrictions on abortions will almost surely have a similar fate in the near future.

In the meantime, what of the present and the couples who during this year will know personally the anguish and fear of the couple in Holyoke? It would be comforting to hope, but unreal to believe, that prevention would be uniformly successful. We as a community, therefore, must be prepared to recognize the needs of those among us who are troubled and to meet those needs effectively with resources which are available.

The especially tragic feature of the recent death is that today it didn't need to happen. Somehow the couple, whose affection was so binding that they had the will to share a bold and dangerous plan to solve their problem, should have had access to better information. Perhaps most important, they should have been able to trust in some resource in their school communities from which they could have gotten help. At some time in the future, abortion services will be more readily and openly available; in the meantime, there are adults in the University community who can be trusted and are eager to be helpful in finding answers to problems.

The staff of the health services solicits the trust and confidence of students. We aim to help anyone face a health problem and find an answer which is satisfactory, practical, and consistent with self-respect. We may not always succeed, but we are willing to try.

Dr. Gage was not the only one who wrote in the student paper about the options open to pregnant students. Reverend Ron Hardy of the Clergy Consultation Service on Abortion (CCS) chapter on campus at the United Christian Foundation wrote:

The death of Holyoke coed from an attempted abortion has hit this office in a very hard way. I share with Dr. Gage of University Health Service feelings of both remorse and some guilt. But each tragic experience is an opportunity to learn about life and love and concern, and to flee death, ignorance, distrust, and oppression.

Abortions for women should be free and available at the request of any woman. But until they are, some of us work to provide both counseling and referral services to women with problem pregnancies. Along with the Health Services, we solicit your trust and confidence. Clergy Consultation Service is a nationwide movement.

Referrals are available for in state care or clinic care in New York City where laws have recently changed. We also are able to discuss with you all the options including marriage and adoption.

Of the two responses, Dr. Gage's is perhaps the more surprising. The mission of CCS, after all, was to help women with problem pregnancies and abortion access. But the University Health Services had not previously taken any kind of public stand on abortion. Dr. Gage had worked diligently to provide access to birth control, but felt it was too medically and legally risky to attempt abortions at UHS, or even to make referrals. But Dr. Gage's letter points to a change along those lines. UHS began to refer students across campus to the CCS offices, and in 1973, hired away one of CCS's counselors, Elaine Frasier, who would later spend years working on abortion counseling at UHS. But Nancy Kierzek's death seems to be the event that pushed Dr. Gage and UHS to take a public stance on helping women seeking abortions.

The other group that was galvanized by Day and Kierzek's fates was Amherst Women's Liberation. By the summer of 1970, the members of the collective had already identified abortion as one of the areas on which they wanted to take a more active stand in the community. One of the members had undergone her own terrifying illegal abortion experience several years earlier and the group had been talking about how they could get involved in pregnancy counseling and abortion referrals. They knew about the clergymen in Northampton and Amherst, but some members felt that "those men," as they referred to them, just couldn't possibly understand an issue that bore directly on a woman's own body.

Kierzek's death drove Amherst Women's Liberation into action. On September 22, 1970, the day the story about the incident appeared in the local *Daily Hampshire Gazette*, Amherst Women's Liberation formed the Abortion and Birth Control (ABC) committee and immediately began organizing a public forum on abortion. They held the forum on the evening of Thursday, November 19, 1970, and a standing-room only crowd witnessed the first public assemblage of the various local groups committed to providing access to birth control and legalized abortion—feminist activists, doctors, clergy, and women who had themselves survived illegal abortions.

The events calendar for that day's *Daily Collegian*, the UMass student newspaper, contained a notice of the forum, as well listings for a Delta Chi rush party and a meeting of the Campus Crusade for Christ. This list of events was followed by the engagement announcements of seven female students as well as the news that two more had been pinned by their boyfriends that week. Modern feminism was beginning to make itself felt on campus, but was for the moment it existed side-by-side with older modes of feminine experience.

Amherst Women's Liberation originally scheduled the forum at the brand new auditorium of the Amherst Junior High School, but at the last minute a school administrator denied access to the group, stating that the school could not host an event sponsored by what he called the Amherst Women's Liberation "Front," and the forum was moved to a classroom at the university's business school.

The speakers and their subjects that Thursday night provide us with a clear snapshot of the contemporaneous social contexts and the constraints—legal, social, cultural, moral—facing women who sought abortions and those who aided them. Dr. Robert Chitum of the University Health Services spoke about how antiabortion legislation prevented him "from giving the best possible medical advice." Reverend Sam Johnson, from the UCF's chapter of the Clergy Consultation Service, said that "oftentimes . . . abortion is the only moral decision a woman can make. Consider how many lives may be destroyed by the advent of an unwanted fetus?" Tim Purdee, a social worker, spoke about the correlation between unwanted children and child abuse. And then the women rose to speak.

The first to talk was a married woman who had contracted German measles from her daughter while pregnant with a second child. Exposing a fetus to German measles can often cause permanent birth defects and many states considered such exposure ample reason for a therapeutic abortion. After nine weeks and refusals by numerous doctors, she finally managed to procure a therapeutic abortion. But first the doctor made the woman and her husband write an essay entitled "Why I Want an Abortion." While she was in the hospital for the abortion, the hospital staff made derisive comments and deliberately spilled blood on her. (A few years after the forum, this woman committed suicide and members of Amherst Women's Liberation would always wonder if her humiliating abortion experience had been a contributing factor.)

Then a Smith College student stood and in a clear, strong voice recounted her experience receiving a CCS referral for an abortion by a doctor in Montreal. Her parents and her pastor were understanding, the doctor was professional, and the abortion went smoothly. What shocked her, though, was the "parochial" reaction of her Smith schoolmates. Most of her fellow classmates, she said, lived in a dream world in which they somehow pretended that making love could not possibly result in a problem pregnancy. As reporter Betsy Goldman of the *Daily Hampshire Gazette* wrote, "While making love was accepted, getting pregnant was not. The idea that pregnancy comes from making love seemed a connection that most of the girls overlooked. Her open discussion of the abortion frightened them. Their lack of knowledge was appalling. Abortion, she told the audience, is no mystery. But rather, it is a rational solution to a medical problem. And she reiterated—it is the woman's right to choose. She felt that no one had the right to tell her what she should do about what was growing in her body." This may indeed be one of the earlier uses of the phrase "right to choose."

The third "girl," as Betsy Goldman called her, was not named by the paper but was Robin Dizard of the Amherst Women's Liberation ABC group. Dizard, who was actually 31 years old at the time, began by urging the college students in the audience to use contraception. "Birth control," she said, "may not be spontaneous, but neither is sitting in your room waiting for your period." Her story, she said, was typical of those women forced to go to a "back alley abortionist." She and her husband had decided that they could not at the time raise a second child, but could not find a legitimate doctor to perform an abortion. So she had made connections through the student underground, been picked up on a Chicago street corner, charged an enormous amount of money, blindfolded, and aborted on a table in the abortionist's child's bedroom before being driven, groggy and confused, back to her apartment.

In the question and answer period that followed the panel's remarks, a woman in the audience stood up and spontaneously testified that her own abortion had given her "a new chance to live." The next morning, November 20, 1970, the *Daily Hampshire Gazette* ran a five-column story on the forum with a headline borrowed from that woman's testimony: "Abortion: A New Chance to Live." If this was a how a small-town newspaper now characterized abortion, it was because of the efforts, both covert and very public, of many of its local citizens to affect change.[14]

PART ONE

The Women

Survivors of Illegal Abortions

Before the *Roe v. Wade* decision legalized abortion on demand, most women who wanted the procedure had to go to great lengths just to find out information about it, let alone finding a reputable provider. Usually that meant going through an underground network of family and friends who had gone through the difficult and degrading process themselves. California abortion activists Patricia Maginnis and Lana Phelan captured the feeling of those prelegalization networks well: "Everyone in town of childbearing age and over has either had an abortion or knows someone immediately has." But even navigating this female underground was far from easy emotionally or psychologically. "Like the famous search for the left-handed monkey wrench, this is a social game and you must go through all the hoops while everyone snickers around you."[1]

The game was a bit easier for those with money. It was often possible for them to find a professional physician willing to secretly perform the procedure. Alternately, a woman with the plane fare could fly out of the country for a legal procedure overseas. As Carol Wall recounts in her story that follows, some wealthy Bostonians could even turn to the drink steward at their country club for quiet advice on how to get "a problem" taken care of behind closed doors. But for many others, and often for those who did have the means, getting an abortion meant subjecting oneself to a myriad of difficulties.

The oral histories collected here illustrate the lengths that women would go to in order to get an abortion, and the ordeals they faced. Their stories cover a gamut of situations, from out of country abortions in Puerto Rico and Cuba, to legal therapeutic abortions, to cloak and dagger tales of backstreets and blindfolds. But in order to fully appreciate the circumstances under which women sought such abortions, it is necessary to look first at the legal history of abortion in America that forced these women to go to such lengths.

Legislation and the National Climate

Abortion has likely been practiced throughout human history, but the history of abortion as a legal issue in the United States is relatively short. Colonial and Post-Colonial Common Law dictated that fetal movement, known as "quickening," determined the point when human life began. Before quickening occurred, women were thought to simply have an obstruction of their normal menstruation and it was legally permissible to remove the blockage through the use of poisons or herbal cures. The commonly held belief, both in medical and moral terms, was that a fetus was not a human being until after quickening, usually in the beginning of the second trimester of pregnancy. Abortionists and entrepreneurs hawking various herbal abortifacients openly advertised in U.S. newspapers throughout the first half of the nineteenth century. In many of the advertisements for abortive services, pregnancies were termed "blockage of the menses" or "interruption of menses" and induced abortion was considered just another variety of spontaneous termination, or miscarriage. These ads promised "ladies' relief" or the return of "regularity." Carter's Relief for Women, manufactured by the Carter Medical Company of East Hampston, Connecticut, claimed to be "safe and always reliable; better than ergot, oxide, tansy or pennyroyal pills. Insures regularity."[2]

For years the only kinds of abortions that concerned lawmakers were those resulting from medical malpractice, but in 1821, the medical community entered the fray, pushing to outlaw non-licensed practitioners (and their "medicines") that cut into the doctors' profits.[3] The first U.S. law prohibiting abortion before quickening was passed in Connecticut and laws banning abortion after quickening followed in Connecticut and New York between 1828 and 1830, but appeared to have very little actual impact on stemming the practice. The laws made quickened abortion a felony act and unquickened abortion a misdemeanor, creating a dual medical and legal authority system that provided opportunities for both legal and illegal entrepreneurs. This duality made abortion into a market product, with medically controlled and high quality services available to the affluent while lower quality, often dangerous services were the only options open to the poor.[4] This duality would remain true until abortion was legalized one hundred and forty years later.

The two decades following the Civil War witnessed an increased emphasis on public decency and morality. In this new climate, stricter laws banning abortion after quickening became the notion throughout the country. At the federal level, the Comstock Act of 1873 suppressed "trade in and circulation of obscene literature and articles of immoral use," prohibited the selling of pills and other devices used as abortifacients, and outlawed the use of artificial contraception as "obscene."[5] Advertisements for contraceptives or abortions were deemed obscene material and any written referrals for such services were also made illegal. Gone were the newspapers ads for "French Periodical Pills" or for "Madame Drunette, Female Physician."[6] The Commonwealth of Massachusetts passed its own version of a Comstock Act, the charmingly titled "Crimes Against Chastity, Morality, Decency, and Good Order" law, in 1879. By the end of that year elective abortion was illegal in all states.

Most antiabortion laws contained an exception that permitted abortions to be performed in order to save the life of the mother. An 1861 law that made it a felony to abort a child "capable of being born alive," contained such a provision for abortions "done in good faith for the purpose only of preserving the health of the mother." These kinds of medically endorsed terminations came to be known as "therapeutic abortions." Sociologist Nanette Davis characterizes the 1861 law as marking a new epoch in the social control of abortion, one in which "murky canon law [gave] way to an ambitious medical profession. After this point the "quickened/unquickened" distinction faded and was replaced by the "therapeutic/criminal" demarcation.[7] Therapeutic abortions could be performed under a variety of circumstances, including cases in which the mother had contracted a life-threatening disease like tuberculosis, had a serious heart condition, or had a psychiatric disorder that would prevent her from delivering or caring for the child.[8] The term "psychosis of pregnancy" was frequently used to justify abortions in the first half of the century. This diagnosis eventually gave way to "depressive neuroses" and finally to "transient situational disturbance." The term most often used by doctors at Northampton's Cooley Dickinson Hospital in the 1960s and early 1970s was "acute situational anxiety of pregnancy."[9]

Early twentieth-century popular culture reinforced the antiabortion legislation. Native-born Anglo-American groups spread fear of the "immigrant hordes" of Irish and German workers and their impending broods and stigmatized abortion as potentially contributing to the "race suicide" of native-born Americans with smaller family sizes. Industrialized America's need for more workers added to the cultural encouragement of population growth.[10] However persuasive these arguments may have been in certain communities, abortion was still sought and practiced by many women and criminalizing it certainly did not put an end to its practice. Abortion simply went underground in the 1940s, beginning a long period of pervasive silence. There was the occasional flamboyant abortionist who flouted the law, like Oregon's infamous Ruth Barnett, but for the most part the world of abortions existed behind closed doors.[11]

While the public remained largely silent on the issue of abortion in the period spanning the two World Wars, the medical practice of therapeutic abortions actually grew in that time. The major increase was in abortions for psychiatric reasons. By 1947, 20 percent of therapeutic abortions were performed for psychiatric reasons. In theory, the woman needed documentation from two psychiatrists claiming that she was psychologically unable to bear pregnancy or motherhood. In actual practice this meant that patients with the resources could essentially buy such proof from unscrupulous or sympathetic psychiatrists. One counselor in the Pioneer Valley recalled a psychiatrist who never even spoke to the pregnant women who came to him for psychiatric consults; he just pointed to where to they should leave their checks, then signed their letters.[12] Historian Leslie Reagan discovered that during the period from 1943 to 1962, 91 percent of therapeutic abortions in New York City were performed on white women who, she implies, could better afford them.[13]

Despite the general social silence, there were those, mostly with roots in the struggle for birth control, who addressed the abortion issue. The Planned Parenthood organization had been fighting for birth control in Massachusetts since 1916 and in 1958 its medical director, Dr. Mary Calderone, broke the silence on abortion by publishing *Abortion in the United States*. The Kinsey Report had recently been published, which reported that over 90 percent of the single, pregnant women in Dr. Alfred Kinsey's study had had an abortion. This gave Dr. Calderone the ammunition she needed to stress that abortion was far from the sinful aberration it had been conventionally portrayed to be.[14] Dr. Alan Guttmacher, a distinguished obstetrician-gynecologist who would become president of the Planned Parenthood Federation of America in 1962 and early 1970s and a major figure in the movement for reproductive rights, pushed the discussion of both birth control and abortion further out into the open in a series of books, including *Babies By Choice Or By Chance* in 1959 and *The Case For Legalized Abortion Now* in 1967. But Lawrence Lader provided the crucial next step, turning advocacy into action by doing early illegal abortion referrals. A journalist rather than a health care specialist, Lader came to prominence in 1955 with his book *Margaret Sanger and the Fight for Birth Control*, followed 11 years later by *Abortion*, and in 1973, by *Abortion II*.

In 1970, *Our Bodies, Ourselves* was published in newsprint by The Boston Women's Health Book Collective and furthered the revolution in access to information about a range of women's health issues, including abortion and birth control. *Our Bodies, Ourselves* was the first self-help guide to the female body written by women and it paid particular attention to self-knowledge as a path to power and self-control.[15] *Our Bodies, Ourselves* is also referred to many times in the oral histories that follow by women who saw the book as key in helping them advocate for themselves about reproductive issues, including birth control and abortion.[16] Indeed, one of the area physicians says he can recall a moment of change when women, some of them carrying copies of the book, began asking more probing and informed questions about their bodies and their reproductive lives.

Organized lobbying efforts to change abortion legislation began in the early- to mid-1960s. Most notable were Patricia Maginnis's California-based Society for Humane Abortion and the New York City-based Association for the Study of Abortion (ASA), founded in 1964 and which included both Guttmacher and Lader on its board of directors. ASA members were mostly upper-middle-class professionals of some social standing, which in the words of historian Rosemary Nossiff, significantly "legitimize[d] the public debate about abortion reform."[17] The Maginnis' group, on the other hand, was a grassroots collective of a few women devoted to guerilla street action such as standing on California street corners passing out contact information for abortionists. Other more radical groups joined the struggle through the mid-1960s and into the early 1970s, many of them coming out of the women's movement and women's consciousness-raising groups.[18] Perhaps the best known of these groups is Chicago's Jane, whose members eventually went beyond abortion referrals to actually performing the abortions themselves.[19]

Legalizing Abortion

Prior to 1970, abortions not categorized as therapeutic were against the law in all 50 states, but beginning in the late 1960s, a legal reform movement began to slowly erode these laws. Restrictions to abortion crumbled in state after state in the early 1970s, laying a path for the Roe decision. This erosion may have had its roots in the massive penal code reform project begun by the American Law Institute (ALI) in 1952. Composed of attorneys, judges, and professors of law, the ALI was attempting to modernize state criminal codes by presenting model statutes that the states could then adapt and adopt. ALI Model Penal Codes were established for crimes from bigamy to homicide, creating a sample set of statutes, definitions of crimes, and appropriate punishments. Its overall goal was the standardization of an American legal system that showed staggering variation from state to state.

In 1959, the ALI turned its attention to "Sexual Offences and Offences Against the Family," which included the crime of abortion. In charge of creating a model penal code in this area Louis B. Schwartz, a law professor at the University of Pennsylvania, suggested ALI abortion codes that were likely influenced by *The Sanctity of Life and the Criminal Law*, the published Columbia lectures of the Welsh legal expert Glanville Williams. Williams likened the ineffectiveness of banning abortion to stop abortion to banning alcohol to stop people from consuming it. Williams felt that outlawing abortion condemned women to the search for an illegal and probably unsafe abortion, and he considered this "a greater evil" than the act of abortion itself. Schwartz may have also been influenced by the well-publicized death from illegal abortion, about the time of his ALI work, of the daughter of a socially prominent Philadelphia family.

Schwartz categorized his code as permitting "a policy of cautious expansion of the categories of lawful justification of abortion." He wrote: "Abortion, at least in early pregnancy, and with the consent of the persons affected, involves considerations so different from killing of a living human being as to warrant consideration not only of the health of the mother but also of certain extremely adverse social consequences to her or the child."[20] Schwartz's draft of the ALI Model Penal Code for abortion did not go quite as far as wholesale support for legalizing abortion, but it did call for legal abortion to "prevent gravely defective offspring," in cases of pregnancy resulting from rape, and in order to "preserve the health of the mother." This final category included mental health, notoriously subjective and difficult to prove. When the entire Model Penal Code was adopted at ALI's annual meeting in 1962, it included Schwartz's original recommendations for abortion law reform, complemented only by a definition of statutory rape.[21]

It took some time, but the ALI language began to appear in bills in the state legislatures. The first to approve a revision of its existing abortion law was Colorado, which passed its law on April 25, 1967, followed quickly by North Carolina on May 8, 1967. California approved its Humane Abortion Act a month later over the objections of then governor Ronald Reagan. By the end of 1969, ten states had or were just about to approve legislation based on the ALI Model Penal Code. However, these states all placed restrictions on access to abortions. North Carolina limited abortion to state residents, Colorado required approval from notoriously difficult hospital review boards, and California demanded the recommendation of two doctors and hospitalization, making it prohibitively expensive for many women.[22] In the spring of 1970, Hawaii and Alaska adopted bills that legalized physician-performed abortion for any reason as long as the fetus was nonviable, but limited their application to state residents only.

As states began to adopt abortion reform, another political debate started: reform or repeal of existing abortion laws. Activists and medical professionals began to form organizations to press for outright legalization of abortion on demand in all states. The first to fall was New York State, which had begun debating a bill to liberally reform the New York State abortion law back in 1965. Revised and reintroduced many times over the following years, the bill originally introduced by Manhattan Assemblyman Albert Blumenthal, had been gutted of most of its promise of true reform. Constance Cook, a Republican Assemblywoman from upstate New York, felt that rather than continuing to weaken already weak legislation, a radical departure was needed. "It became clear to me [that] every time he added one of those [compromises], he was losing not gaining. And that set my mind . . . to introduce outright repeal" of New York's antiabortion legislation. Cook and Franz Leighter, an assemblyman from Manhattan, introduced their bill to repeal the existing abortion laws, and thereby make abortion legal and accessible, in 1969. It died in the committee, so they proposed it again in 1970.[23] The bill that eventually reached the floor for a vote would legalize abortion up to the twenty-fourth week of pregnancy. It also specified that terminations could only be performed by doctors. But the bill did allow for abortion "on demand" up to the twenty-fourth week and it did not have any residency requirements attached. If it passed, any U.S. citizen would be able to come to New York for a legal early-term abortion.

The Cook-Leighter bill reached the Assembly floor on April 9, 1970, and dramatically, the New York House of Representatives deadlocked in a 75–75 vote. Then

Democrat George Michaels, reportedly pale and with a tremor in his hands, asked for permission to speak. He had earlier promised Constance Cook that although he had twice voted against the bill in earlier incarnations, if it came to a tie, he would switch his vote. When he got the floor, he did just that. "I fully appreciate that this is the termination of my political career," he said, "But Mr. Speaker, what's the use of being elected or reelected if you don't stand for something? I cannot in good conscience stand here and be the vote that defeats this bill." Then he sat down, bent his head to his desk, and began to cry.[24] Thus abortion was effectively legalized in New York State. Governor Nelson Rockefeller signed the "Justifiable Abortion Act" into law on April 11, 1970. Because the new law had no residency requirements, as did the abortion laws in Alaska and Hawaii, any woman could presumably come to New York and get an abortion. This by no means meant equal access to all. For a poor woman, airplane or bus fare across the country, hotel charges, and $250 for an abortion could still present insurmountable obstacles.

After the New York law went into effect, no more states changed or revised their laws prior to July 1973, when, in a move that surprised nearly everyone in the Pioneer Valley who had been working on abortion issues, the Supreme Court effectively legalized abortion on demand with the *Roe v. Wade* decision. Justice Harry Blackmun, a United Methodist, wrote the 80-page majority opinion. Acknowledging the "sensitive and emotional nature of the abortion controversy," he sought to root the court's opinion in the history of abortion both in the United States and in general. He noted the changing nature of American attitudes and laws regarding abortion, and pointed out that most criminal abortion statues dated from the second half of the nineteenth century. He concluded that what was really at stake was the right to privacy as guaranteed in the U.S. Constitution. "The right of privacy," he wrote on behalf of the court, "is broad enough to encompass a woman's decision whether or not to terminate her pregnancy." He qualified the right to abortion, however, restricting the court's ruling to first trimester abortions and allowing the states to establish their own regulations regarding abortion facilities and procedures for second and late trimester abortions.

Abortion work in the Pioneer Valley entered a completely new phase after the Roe decision. Clinics rushed to organize. Private physicians who had formerly opposed abortions suddenly recognized the potential cash cow that Roe had fostered. Some of the feminist counselors who had earlier been sidelined by mainstream medicine were now legitimately hired as counselors by abortion providers. Though not covered in the present volume, this next phase of the abortion story is equally fascinating, especially how access to services changed over time, and historical examinations of that period will greatly add to our knowledge of reproductive health history.

Illegal Abortions

Abortion still carries a heavy stigma. Even today, most women will not talk openly about what is a personal and often shameful secret. Finding Pioneer Valley women willing to share their personal stories of illegal abortion proved to be a difficult task. Therefore, not all the women whose stories follow were residents of the Valley when they sought their abortions, though all of them now live in Massachusetts and half of them lived in the state at the time of their terminations. Susan Tracy is only one of the women whose story is truly local to the Pioneer Valley. An undergraduate at the University of Massachusetts (UMass), she found an abortion referral through the activist Bill Baird, who had recently visited campus. She traveled to New York for her abortion, but the subsequent trauma that followed, including a breakneck drive to Northampton's Cooley Dickinson hospital after she began to hemorrhage uncontrollably, unfolded in the Pioneer Valley. Her story here stands in for the silent voices of the many thousands of Pioneer Valley women who experienced the difficulties of illegal abortions.

The brave women who tell their stories here are among a small but growing number who have stepped forward to recount their experiences. Most are motivated by a fear that abortion will be made illegal once again and by a desire to share the little-known horrors of illegal abortion. Though only a few published volumes have gathered some of these women's voices, they have illuminated a shrouded past and have made clear some of the patterns that dominated the late twentieth-century illegal abortion market.[25]

One of the patterns that has emerged is the increasingly clandestine and frightening lengths that illegal abortionists went to in order to conceal their identities and their practices. After police crackdowns on illegal abortionists stepped up in the 1950s, abortionists began to blindfold women before taking them to the abortion site, use middlemen (or women) to negotiate and collect fees and transport the women, and increased their prices dramatically in reaction to both the greater risk and the growing lack of competition as other abortionists got out of the market. The stories that follow illustrate some of these clandestine arrangements and show how they changed over time. Elizabeth Meyer's first abortion was conducted within blocks of Boston's State House in 1958 at an abortionist's practice that operated, she is sure, with the complete knowledge of lawmakers. By 1964, Robin Dizard's abortion involved a complex series of phone calls, a roll of cash, an abortionist whose face she never saw, and a terrifying, blindfolded drive through the streets of Chicago in a pink Cadillac. Jean Baxter, too, had to go through several steps and middlemen and turn over a great deal of money before being picked up and delivered to the abortion site somewhere in New York City's Harlem.

Another pattern that emerges is the pervasive fear that dominated the illegal abortion experience. Beyond the blindfolds and the middlemen skulking on street corners in trench coats and hats, was the very real possibility that women would not survive their ordeal. In 1955, 45 percent of maternal deaths nationally were the result of abortion.[26] And nearly all major urban hospitals saw enormous numbers of miscarriages secondary to abortion, many of these resulting in serious infection. Jean Baxter recalls her boyfriend watching from a coffee shop as the middleman drove her away and Robin Dizard can still feel her fear that she would never see her husband or her little boy again. Other women recount humiliations and rapes at the hands of their abortionists.

Another pattern that has emerged is that illegal abortions were very expensive and therefore many poor women could not afford them. Those who had the money and the social connections had fewer problems. Meredith Michaels's story illustrates how social position and connections eased her family's search for a therapeutic hospital abortion, an abortion that she points out, went to her instead of someone poor and in perhaps more desperate straits. But even those women who had access to money and private physicians were not guaranteed easy access to abortion. Both Robin Dizard and Jean Baxter speak about being chastised by doctors who refused to help them.

Since a legal, physician-performed abortion was most preferable, those women who could afford the costs flew overseas to Japan or England where it was legal or to Mexico or Puerto Rico, where it was not legalized but where it was practiced openly. Elizabeth Dunn talks about flying to Cuba for her abortions, where the procedures were performed in a modern medical clinic. Carol Wall heard that abortions were legal in Puerto Rico, so she flew there without a referral. Her hunt for a doctor in Puerto Rico is revealing of the difficulties and humiliations women faced even when choosing one of the supposedly "easy" options. For Jean Baxter and Susan Tracy, both undergraduate students at the time, the financial costs of their domestic abortions were enormous. Tracy sold almost everything she owned, including her winter coat. Baxter borrowed money from family members to pay the $600 cost of her abortion. (Her first job, a few years later, paid an annual salary of $4,000.)

Another significant pattern that the stories illustrate is that many women's unwanted pregnancies were related to ineffective or illegal birth control. Carol Wall and Elizabeth Meyer both got pregnant while using diaphragms. Robin Dizard had no idea where to look for birth control—it was illegal in Massachusetts at the time—and she got pregnant the night she lost her virginity. Ruth Fessenden, who later worked for the Clergy Consultation Service on Abortion, was turned away by a doctor at the University Health Services when she asked for contraception. And it took Jean Baxter's pregnancy to reveal the underground birth control information network at her college.

Women found a way. They navigated the undergrounds, they took the grave risks. Some of them had positive outcomes but many did not. It was this unpredictability that doctors, clergy members, feminists, and everyday women would rally together to change in the decade leading up to Roe.

Elizabeth Myer

Elizabeth Myer has lived most of her eight decades in Cambridge, Massachusetts. She is the mother of three children and also had three illegal abortions. She has spent many years lobbying on behalf of reproductive rights, working with the Abortion Access Project and with the League of Women Voters.

Elizabeth Myer was interviewed by David Cline on June 21, 2004.

"Total Relief"

My name is Elizabeth Myer. I am 79 now. I was born in Boston and grew up in Cambridge. One of my earliest memories was of my mother and friends working on a ballot referendum to make contraception legal in Massachusetts. That was way back, maybe in the late 1930s. Contraceptives were available to women of means, or with access to medical care, because private doctors provided them. I remember the vituperation of the Catholic Church and the ugliness of the Catholic men to the women who were trying legitimately to hand out literature to people approaching the polls. And the Catholic Church preached from the pulpits every Sunday to their congregations to vote against this ballot referendum. At the time, the legislature was heavily Catholic. It still is. So I grew up absolutely hating the Catholic Church for what it did to women.

My abortion was in 1958 in Boston. We had three wonderful children. I was one of those women who just have to think about getting pregnant to get pregnant. God, it was terrible! We had always used condoms, but I decided I would try the diaphragm. I tried it and I got pregnant.

I was 32 or 33 and I had 3 wonderful kids, really terrific. We'd actually had our first two children when my husband was in graduate school. During the Second World War, he was in the Navy and was in the Pacific. Then he went to graduate school at Johns Hopkins and two of the children were born at Johns Hopkins. And then the third one, Liz, was born in Wilmington. The boys were three years apart and then Liz was four and half years later. They were spaced because, while the births were easy, I found pregnancy absolutely miserable. Every woman knows her limit of how many children she can raise. For some it's none, for others it's many. But for me it was three. It was actually two, but we wanted a girl. So we took another shot at having a girl and we got one.

When it was clear that I didn't want this pregnancy, my obstetrician said, "If bleeding starts I can help, but I can't do anything else." He had given me the clue about what was needed. My task was clear: to start the bleeding. He may have volunteered it or I may have asked him, I don't know. But whichever way it went, the answer was that he couldn't do an abortion. In those days, I think it took two separate concurring medical opinions that the pregnancy would jeopardize the life of the pregnant woman. You had to be practically in your grave before they would lift a finger to help you. So anyway, that was it. If the bleeding started, then he could help. That was pretty clear.

Our friend was a member of the Tennis and Racquet Club on Boylston Street in Boston. That was a very exclusive all-male club. Women could come in and maybe have a drink or have supper, but they couldn't be members. That's long since gone, of course. The steward at the Tennis and Racquet Club had multiple responsibilities besides serving drinks—getting call girls, providing abortion information, making all the sexual referrals that you needed. Our friend got my husband a referral to a place on Hancock Street, which is on the north side of Beacon Hill, right behind the State House. I cannot believe that they were operating that close to the State House and the police and that the legislators didn't know it.

We went there at the appointed hour and I went upstairs. I've since walked up and down that street of lovely old brick buildings to see if I can identify which door it was. I thought it was about halfway down but I don't know the number. But it was clearly very close to the State House. I went upstairs and there were two women there. My memory was that it was about $700 or $800, which then was a very substantial amount of money.

I didn't want any cutting—I felt that was the way infection started. They had a clean sheet on a double bed and they injected a saline solution into my uterus. Within some hours, by evening, I was feeling a little uncomfortable and during the night, why, real cramps and bleeding started. So in the morning I called the obstetrician. He admitted me to Women's Lying-In Hospital and he did the D&C. He asked me afterwards, since the material probably didn't look right, "Well, did you do anything?" and I thought to protect him, I should probably say, "Oh no, I'd didn't do anything."

Subsequently I had two more abortions, but in Cuba. That was because of the diaphragm. I had a tipped cervix and this OB-GYN had not fitted me properly and so the damned thing wasn't working. It was my own primary care physician who said that was a problem. So it wasn't really all my fault. I'm still staggered that an OB-GYN didn't understand my arrangements and fit me for the right thing. It's like having the wrong pair of shoes. That's crazy. So I was always quite miffed. I never went back to him. If he could miss something like that, what else could go wrong?

My husband and I flew to Cuba. There was a clinic down there, which did abortions for people who could get there. It was a small affair in a small office building— sort of like some of these outpatient independent clinics that operate now. This was a freestanding clinic and it may be that all they did was abortions. I remember that they spoke English.

These were surgical abortions and they seemed to go okay. I didn't feel scared. I guess I have my father's optimism by nature about this kind of thing and I just assumed everything would be all right. And it seemed to be. The first abortion I know was in 1958 and I think the two I had in Cuba would have been probably a couple of years later and were about six months apart. After the second one, I complained to my primary care physician about my diaphragm and he said, well you need one with a spring or whatever. He gave me whatever the diaphragm is that works for a tipped cervix. We probably went back to the condoms anyway, and didn't have any more problems.

A few years subsequently, a good friend came to me. They had four children and they just could not have a fifth. That was it. In fact, the fourth one had been unplanned but they handled it. She'd been going from friend to friend, and no one either knew or was willing to talk to her. I was the first person who was willing to tell her about Cuba. Every year for a few years after that, they thanked me. They thanked me for helping them when they needed it and nobody else would. It's weird that people were so unwilling to talk. I mean, this is a country of free speech.

I'm always suspicious of people saying that abortion was an agonizing choice for them. I know for my friend, it was total relief. Mine was total relief. When these people are talking about their agony and their grief and their this and their that, I feel like yelling at them, "Hey, where's the relief?" I think if you've planned a child and want one and lose it through a medical mishap, well, I suppose it does feel like a loss. But in mine and my friend's cases, my God, we were desperate, and we were relieved at ending unwanted pregnancies. I think there are a lot of married women who have experienced that in the same way.

I've been lobbying at the State House for Pro-Choice issues now for several decades. I think I was the first person [to testify] on an abortion bill [in Massachusetts]. I remember testifying on a Pro-Choice bill in the 70s, during Michael Dukakis's first or second term as governor. At the time I was the lobbyist for the National Organization for Women in Massachusetts. I was testifying and I finally decided this is ridiculous to be talking in abstractions and third persons. So I finally said, at the end of my testimony, "And I, like many other women in this room, have had an illegal abortion." And God, everybody sat up. I briefly recounted what had happened. And that night I got calls from people around the state thanking me for being willing to personalize it and not put it in the abstract. I did it because I was angry with these legislators who were so righteous and pompous.

And more recently it happened again at a judiciary committee hearing. Once again they had put all the hot button issues together—like the death penalty, lesbian and gay marriages, and abortion. We didn't come on until ten o'clock at night, dead on our feet. They hoped to wear us out so we would go home. The committee was alternating pro and con panels with a limited time for each. I came on [intending] to just say we oppose such and such bills and we supported others, but the committee had been so rude and so unpleasant to our panelists that I, coming last, was absolutely boiling. So I listed off the bills that the League of Women Voters of Massachusetts supported and those we opposed. And then I said, "And on a personal note," and I briefly told my story. I said, "This happened a half a block behind the State House on Hancock Street, where all the legislators sent their wives, daughters, and mistresses."

At that, the chair of the committee got up and stormed out.[1] And he apparently immediately began calling around various League of Women Voters [brass] to require my being excommunicated, or [to get] an apology. So the president of the Mass League of Women Voters called me and said, "I knew when I got a call from the representative that you hadn't said that as a League member." I said no, it was very clear what my testimony was and it's in print and it's on file in the office. I said it was a personal testimony. And she said, "Well, it would help if you could write a letter of apology." I couldn't do it. I could not apologize to him. I never did.[2]

TWO

Dr. Robin Dizard

Dr. Robin Dizard, Ph.D., has lived in Amherst, Massachusetts with her husband Jan for over 30 years. She has two children and was one of the founding members of the Amherst Women's Liberation collective. She spent many years working on behalf of women's issues, especially women's rights. Dizard holds the position of Professor of English at Keene State College in Keene, New Hampshire, where her primary academic interests are in African-American, Caribbean, and multiethnic U.S. literature.

Dr. Robin Dizard was interviewed by David Cline on June 12, 2004.

"No More of this Whimsy"

I'll take us back to 40 years ago when I was 25. I was living in Chicago in an apartment with my husband and my toddler of about a year old. We had a birth control failure—my diaphragm slipped. At first I wasn't sure what I wanted to do. I want to emphasize this because in so much of the antiabortion rhetoric there is the characterization of the woman or the girl as lunging for a choice and as not quite in charge of her own fate. Really, if my experience is any guide, that's not true—or not always true. When I realized I was pregnant, my husband and I talked. He was very adamant that we could not have afforded and could not make room in our lives for another baby then. I was uncertain and wavering.

I consulted my obstetrician, Herbert Mossberg.[1] I asked him, "Can't you do anything?" Which is of course the key question. And he said, "Well, you must have seen the woman outside in my waiting room." (I had not noticed her in particular.) "She comes here always certain that she's pregnant and she isn't. And you are still married to that nice Jewish man, aren't you? I could place your baby with her." I thought that idea was horrifying.

I found out more about Herbert Mossberg later when a friend of mine who was black and married to a white man said that when Dr. Mossberg discovered she was pregnant, he immediately offered to do an abortion. Another time I inadvertently opened the wrong door in his suite and saw a woman prepped and in gynecological stirrups. So from what my friend said and from what I happened to glimpse, I'm sure he did abortions. So, what I'm saying is not that there's one corrupt doctor, but that the system was one in which men like Herbert Mossberg enjoyed their power and wielded it whimsically. Whimsy governed somebody's access. And so when we struggled to make abortion safe and legal we were saying, "No more of this whimsy stuff!" It shouldn't depend on whether you thought that a Protestant minister *might* be somebody who could advise you. It never *occurred* to me to consult a Protestant minister; although I'm sure Chicago's network must have included such [people].

Anyway, my husband was a university student and so he asked around among his friends and within a day or two we had the name of someone who did abortions. There was only one obstetrician that I saw listed in the Chicago phone book that had office hours only once a week for a few hours a night. He was that one. That ad was reassuring in a way, because it meant that this guy is operating so openly that the police are certainly aware. Now, I might also have suddenly thought, oh my God, he must bribe the police! And that was a strange thing for me because I've never operated outside the law. And suddenly that's what was beginning to happen to me. I was furious with Herbert Mossberg and I was going to have this appointment with the abortionist, whoever he was.

Our friends Minnie and Sid had said that the price was $300. It had to be handed over in cash and the rules were that you could only call once. I don't remember if they called back or if somebody answered, but they gave me a date and a time and set up the way that their agent would recognize me. And that was that. I said, "You can recognize me because I will be wearing orange shoes." I was pretty sure nobody else would do that! The rendezvous was set for a drugstore on the West Side. That's the black area in Chicago. So that's when I realized not only am I going to cross the line between legal and illegal, but I'm going to cross the color line. The color line was very, very evident in Chicago.

The person I spoke to on the telephone was female and so was the person who contacted me in the drugstore on the West Side. I don't remember what month. It might have been December, it might have been January. I was loitering around trying to look inconspicuous and look at the makeup when a black woman came by and I noticed that she watched my shoes. I looked up and she didn't make any sign, but she turned her back and behind her back she made a little "follow me" gesture. So I knew, that's her.

I was clutching the money. We had decided—my husband knowing how to do this—that since it was "underworld," we had to roll the money into a roll of bills. So I was clutching that. I followed her out of the drugstore to a car that I seem to remember was a pink Cadillac. It was a big car anyway and it was pink. I got in the backseat. And I saw my husband and my little boy driving away and I really had a moment of despair because I thought, what if I don't see them ever again? I mention that because, again, I don't think this fits the narrative about a girl making a sudden choice. Instead, it was about having made a decision and having nerved oneself to do it.

The black woman drove the car to at another place in Chicago where another woman got into the backseat. She was a university coed and her money was in an envelope, flat, instead of being in a roll like mine. That's all I know about her. The driver pulled over on a deserted street and said, "Give me the money," and both of us handed it over to her in the front seat. Then in the light of a streetlight she counted it. And then she put blindfolds on our heads. And of course that was very, very frightening. I tried to keep track of the number of times she turned but it really wouldn't have made any difference. We came to a place where the houses were small and each set in a yard with a straight walkway from the street. The neighbors must have noticed something because these blindfolded white women would stagger into this house and would come out later. I don't know if they did all of their procedures at night, but mine was at nighttime. When I came into the house, I noticed that the living room was occupied by still another woman—so they were doing three that night. That's $900 that one night. The woman who drove the car immediately went into the kitchen and began boiling instruments, which was a relief. At least they were being clean. And there were other people in the house. Somehow they decided what was going to be the order and I think I volunteered to be last. Anyway, the woman gave each of us a shot. A relaxing and somewhat confusing shot. That was another terrifying thing, but it would have been no good to protest at that point. I didn't know where I was. I had still not seen the man who was going to do the procedure.

When I was led into the room where they had the operating table I saw that it was their child's bedroom, so they must have sent the child to Grandma once a week and then set up their business. I saw the abortionist for the first time with the mask already on his face. They were taking a lot of precautions against us being able to identify him. I was kind of wobbly by then. He had another man with him who he introduced as his brother who was learning how to do abortions so that he could support himself in Paris where he was a medical student. He observed.

The doctor said, "Look, this one's a mother," gesturing to my episiotomy scar. [Given that attitude], you can imagine the level of fear and hatred and dislike was about as extreme as it's going to get.

It was a D&C.[2] I'd never had one before. I don't remember how long it took; I would imagine 20 minutes at the outside. I don't know if he gave me an antibiotic or not. He may have. I did have infection afterwards and called them against their directions. They would do nothing. The person who did give me medical care after that was not Herbert Mossberg, but our wonderful pediatrician, who didn't ask any questions, but gave me an antibiotic dose that cleared up the infection.

The brother drove me home through the dark of Chicago and dropped me off at my apartment building. It was after midnight by the time I was deposited back at my own door. I walked up the stairs and said, honey, I'm home. And that closed that chapter.

What I learned later was this system obviously thrived on secrecy. By making the people who got abortions so nervous and guilty, they insured we were not likely to go and tell what they had done or expose this man. The silence extended to the legitimate doctors like Dr. Herbert Mossberg. It also extended to the hospital people because they must have normally dealt with the aftermaths of abortions that were not as hygienic as mine was.

Some of the analysts now are saying—and I think they're right—that it wasn't our women's movement pressure alone, but the pressure from doctors and nurses saying, "Don't make us keep up with this charade any longer. Why should we be compelled in this one medical procedure into all this fraud?" There was fraud on every hand: how it was reported, how it was talked about, how it was not talked about, the secret recommendations you had to get. You had to know the right phone number. Other people talk about blindfolds or secret knocks or being driven into the underground parking garage and then taken up. So there were various kinds of concealments, but they were not all that concealed. The secrecy served a potent social agenda, which was to keep the clients helpless. And that's why I've talked about the abortion since. Because I don't want people to be that helpless.

THREE

Jean Baxter

Jean Baxter has lived in the Pioneer Valley for over 20 years and works as the Production Coordinator for the Five College Dance Department in Amherst and Northampton, Massachusetts. She is married and has two children.

Jean Baxter was interviewed by David Cline on June 12, 2004.

"Cloak and Dagger"

I'm Jean. I was born in 1948 and I graduated from college in 1970. It was an interesting time. I had two freshmen-year roommates in college and by the time I graduated, all three of us had had abortions. We were from very different backgrounds. I was from a suburban, white, Connecticut background, well brought up. Another girl was from a university background in Madison, Wisconsin. And the third girl was from a highly educated, private-school black family in Manhattan. We all went to a good college, Cornell, so we were all of a certain educational bracket.

I started college in 1966. At the time, birth control was illegal for women. Unless you had your parents' or your husband's permission or it was a medical necessity, you couldn't get birth control under the age of 21. And I didn't find out how to get birth control until after my abortion. But then I did find out that there were routes for that too.

I got pregnant my freshman year in college. I was stupid. There was no birth control, but also, I was stupid. And I did not want to have a kid—it was going to really screw up my life. I mean, I had plans. The social situation was that it was still very socially unacceptable, a grave, horrible thing, if a girl got pregnant. But we took a tally when I graduated high school—there were about three hundred girls in my graduating class of six hundred—and we figured that one out of six was pregnant. We kind of tallied it up. We figured that Suzie was and Barbara was. So it was not uncommon. We snickered about it. And then *I* got pregnant first semester of freshman year.

I did not want to have a kid. So I talked to my friends, and this was where the network came in—the network that I found out about. I was exploring different ways to not have the baby. That was my goal, to end up not being pregnant and have this stigma as a pariah. So my friend Joanie who went to Sarah Lawrence had a friend whose boyfriend's best friend went out with Hilary and Hilary had had an abortion. So Joanie gave me the information that she knew about Hilary that she had gotten from her boyfriend who had gotten it from his friend. And it turned out Hilary went to Cornell and lived down the hall from me. At the time there was a network of women in the educational institutions telling each other and helping each other. So I went down to see Hilary and I said Hilary, I'm pregnant and I heard you had an abortion. And Hilary was surprised that I knew about her abortion because we were all very secretive about our abortions. But when she found out about my situation, she told all.

I'm not sure Hilary was my first exploration. We had other avenues we were following, my boyfriend and I. One was Hilary and finding out her route. The other was some professor up at Syracuse University who helped out girls. We went to the see the professor in Syracuse and it turned out he was working in some sort of black-market adoption. He would place girls in a family and you'd have your baby and sign over your baby to someone else and not even know where it was going. It sounded pretty shady to me. It did not sound like something that I wanted to get involved in. I wanted to get it over with. I didn't want to have a full-term pregnancy. What I was interested in was an abortion as professional as possible where I was pretty sure I wouldn't die. That was the bottom line.

So I got more details from Hilary. I don't remember the names of the doctors, but there was a group of doctors in New York City and they had a racket going on. It was like a mill. You went to this doctor's office in New Jersey on a Friday night and you were clearly told that the place could very well be bugged, so watch your language and what you discuss. I remember signing in, having a medical exam. It was a regular, middle-scale doctor's office—it was not a closet somewhere. There were staff, there was a nurse, there was a doctor. They looked like real doctors and nurses. I never asked to see any credentials, but they at least acted the part.

I was given some sort of indication of, yes, we can confirm your condition. I think they gave me a piece of paper with instructions to go to a certain street corner in half an hour and look for a person with a certain kind of clothing. I would receive more instructions. Okay. So I did that. I waited on the street corner for a man with a coat and a hat. And I remember thinking, am I in a movie? I don't believe this! So this guy comes up and he gave me more written instructions. I was told the cost was $600, which in 1967 was a lot. My first job was $4,000 a year, so $600 was a lot of money. But we knew going into it that it was going to be $600. I had a hundred, my boyfriend had a hundred and we borrowed a couple hundred from his sister and another couple hundred from his sister's boyfriend. So we had the money in cash.

I had the money, but then we had to pay back his sister and her boyfriend. So when my tax refund came in later that spring, it was about a hundred and fifty bucks, I just turned over the whole thing. And I remember later my parents made some comment to me. We were saving all our money from our allowances to pay back people. I was living on nothing! And my parents at some point said about my financial capabilities how I just blew my whole tax refund. Because my parents still don't know about my abortion. At this point, if my mother finds out, I can deal with it. Maybe some day she and I will share that—we're actually getting closer. But that was funny because I was working so hard to save money to pay for this thing, and my parents thought I was irresponsible about blowing money. It was exactly the opposite.

So I met the guy with the hat on a street corner in New Jersey and he gives me instructions to bring the money in cash, to bring certain supplies for bleeding, to bring a Kotex, and to be there alone. And then he gave me an address—it was in Harlem—to wait on a street corner the following morning at nine o'clock on a Saturday with the supplies and the money and that another girl might be there too. I think there were two of us, possibly three. We would be picked up and then returned between noon and two in the afternoon.

The next morning we met up, I think it was on Broadway at 120th Street or something. This other girl showed up too and we were both standing there. My boyfriend just stayed in a coffee shop across the street until we got back. I don't know who was more scared. At least I knew what I was doing, I knew where I was. I was in some sort of control. He was in no control. There he was bringing his girl-friend to a street corner and seeing some stranger pick her up, hoping that it's going to come out right at the other end. So it's a big risk to take. It took a lot of courage to do that. You had to really not want to go through with being pregnant to do this.

A guy picked us up in a sedan. And he made sure that we had our supplies and we had our money, and took us to a high-rise brick project, probably in Harlem. It was down in a valley. I don't know the address, but I think I would recognize it. We went up to an apartment that had been converted into a doctors' facility. The living room was the waiting room, the kitchen was the lab, the bathroom was a changing area. And it had two bedrooms—one of the bedrooms was surgery and the other bedroom was recovery. There were three or four beds in recovery. Except for nurses, it was all white men. All of the facilities that we were in seemed just fine and clean and everything up to snuff. I was very impressed with how up to snuff they were. But all of the logistics surrounding it were so cloak and dagger! Not only was the abortion expensive but you had to stay overnight in a motel and we had to borrow a car. It was pretty involved.

I was exhausted. I hadn't slept much the night before. We went in and they called your name. I went into the bathroom which was where you changed into a johnny and where you gave the nurse your money. That's where they wanted to make the transaction, in the bathroom. I don't know why! That's how it worked. So then I went into surgery and they explained that it was going to be a D&C. I had sodium pen-tothal, which was fine with me. I'm not sure if it was the same doctor who examined me the night before or not. It might have been. But there were at least two doctors. There was at least one nurse. There was one person operating and one person assist-ing. I had had sodium pen the year before when I had my tonsils out and they did it the same way. So I felt these people were competent and knew what they were doing. Everything was up to snuff in terms of procedures so I never felt that I needed to bail out. If I was in a situation that was really dirty or I felt my life was in danger, I think I would have bailed out and left. But they were always courteous, always very business-like. There was no huggy-kissy, there was no pampering involved, but it was never rough. There was never anything negative said about our condition, that we were pregnant. It was just like we were all in this together. I had been told that these doctors did it because they really hated that women couldn't have abortions and they wanted women to be able to have medical abortions. That was what I was told. But they were probably making a lot of money too.

I don't know if they gave me a shot of antibiotics at the time or afterwards, but he told me they were going to give me a shot of antibiotics. And then they did the surgery and I woke up in recovery quite a long time later. I slept—I was so tired—I just slept. When I woke up the doctor made sure we were okay, whatever that meant, that we weren't hemorrhaging or anything. I was okay. And they gave us a bottle of what was probably penicillin, and then I got returned to my street corner, got picked up, and went back to my dorm.

I slept on the bottom bunk and when I got back, I remember lying on the bottom bunk looking up at the top, thinking about this, whether or not what I had done was wrong. I don't remember feeling that the decision about having an abortion was right or wrong; I don't remember that even being a question when I was pregnant. The question more revolved around getting pregnant being right or wrong. That was the thing. The big wrong was getting pregnant. It didn't have to do with abortion. Abortion wasn't possible—it wasn't legal, so it wasn't discussed.

But oh, oh, the worst thing! The only thing that really bothered me happened when I found out that I was pregnant. I hadn't gotten my period so I went to the local OB clinic, had my appointment, found out I was pregnant. The first doctor I saw was so negative, condescending, critical. He made some disparaging remarks about my being pregnant. Clearly he was not interested in helping me. That was bad enough. But then after I had my abortion, one of our instructions was to go see a doctor in four to six weeks to make sure that everything was okay. So in four to six weeks I went to see the doctor at the same place that had diagnosed me. And I said, I'm not pregnant any more. I want to see that everything's okay. And did I get a lecture! I had gone in there thinking I would ask for birth control pills or some sort of birth control. And instead I got a lecture about how I better have learned from my mistake and I better not get pregnant again, how it was immoral and that women who had abortions would never be able to be normal mothers, and that this was a guilt that would stay with me for the rest of my life. And I'm thinking, well, I guess I should feel guilty. That was really what put it in my head that I'm supposed to feel guilty about this. And I remember thinking about whether or not I should feel guilty. I remember lying in my bottom bunk looking up at the top and thinking, you know what, there is nothing to be gained from feeling guilty about this. I made the best decision that I can in this point in my life for what I need to do right now. And maybe it's a wrong decision, but you know what? It's the best decision that I can make right now. And that was pretty much it.

I've come back to that discussion with myself at different times and thought, well, maybe I'd better think about what would the child be like now if I'd had the child. What would I be missing? What did I do? And I don't see any merit in going there, in thinking about it. So I don't. And for me, it's that cut and dry. It has never bugged me. I don't think it's affected my sex life. There are lots of other factors that affect us growing up that are more consequential in our sex lives and our relationships than whether or not we have a child to term.

So that was my abortion and it never ended up being a problem. I did get birth control. I joined a sorority that spring and found out that lots of other girls had had abortions too. I found my abortion from a friend to a friend to a friend, but within the sorority network—whoa!—that's where the information is! In the sorority houses! They knew where to go. It was very common. People were pretty open about it. And I found out how to get birth control from the sorority. The sorority girls said oh, Dr. So-and-so prescribes birth control for college women. All of Cornell went to this one OB, all of the women. And he would put down [that it was] to regulate our period or whatever and we could have birth control pills, no problem. And I remember I was embarrassed or I didn't want to admit that I'd done something illegal or maybe immoral in terms of this abortion. Because when I had my first appointment with him [he asked]: "Ever been pregnant?" And I lied, I said no. But he didn't push it and I had birth control pills.

Janet, my freshman roommate from New York, told me she was pregnant and asked me about my situation so I could give her information. But she was very sharp and she had a choice of going to England or Puerto Rico. Because they were legal in England and, I think, Puerto Rico.[1] She flew to one place or the other for the weekend and had her abortion. That was the choice that she made. She was black and there was a black women's network that had information just like us white girls. She lived with me the summer after our junior year in college and we had to do it in secret because she couldn't let her friends know that she had a white roommate. It was when we were living together that summer that Suzie, our Wisconsin roommate, got pregnant. She was in Wisconsin, but she called us for help. This is like three years after my abortion, so I had to re-research it. At this point, the clergy were your source. So I went downtown to the Presbyterian minister and sure enough, he had the scoop. I think he even had typed up sheets of connections and clergy throughout the United States. He gave me the name of the clergy person in her town that she could go see and who would help her. Which is what she did. She ended up going to either Madison or Chicago for her abortion. That was assisted by the ministry and that was in 1969 or 1970.

So by the time we were all seniors in college, virtually everyone was sexually active or at least sexually savvy. But that's also when drugs came in, sex came in, hippies, women's freedom. When I was a freshman in college you had to wear a skirt to dinner. There was a curfew. Women had to be in by 10:30 at night on a weekday, 12 at night on Friday, one o'clock on Saturday. You could not have men in your room except on guest days with the door open. That's how I entered college. In my sophomore year, the university women voted to have no more curfew. And the university was willing to accept that. So in 1968 there were no more curfews. I started living with my new boyfriend even though my parents thought I was living in the dorms.

I remember that by time I was a senior I had an IUD and it was all legal and the issues were gone. That was good that birth control became legal, but my first experience was that you had to get birth control through the black market, through the grapevine. And that's where women's groups were very important in terms of helping each other.

Not everybody who went to Cornell was rich, but everyone who went there was smart. We were all educated. We all knew how not to get pregnant, theoretically. And those who did—we weren't bad people, whatever that means. And there were a lot of us. So, I feel like the Pro-Lifers just don't know what they're talking about in terms of banning abortion to stop abortion. When I grew up abortion was illegal and there was a lot of it. And I was lucky. Mine was relatively not dangerous. Relatively. But I had no assurance that I wasn't going to die or be maimed. I had no assurance of that. I would not want women to have to deal with that again, and if abortion is banned that would happen again. I am 100 percent sure of that.

I was fine after my abortion. I had kids. I had one that died. It was a fluke thing. I had two that lived. When I have to write down how many pregnancies I have had, I think—how do I answer this? And you know, now that I am old, I can answer it truthfully: four. One abortion, one who died when she was an infant, and then two that grew up. So now I can be truthful about that.

My daughter knows about my abortion. I don't know that I've told my son. I consider it special information. It's useful information but it should not be used as a weapon. And it certainly shouldn't be used by teenage girls gossiping, because it's for the wrong reason. Once I knew my daughter was sleeping with her boyfriend, then I told her. So fairly soon after I was pretty sure that she was sexually active, we were in the car and abortion came up. I said, "By the way, I want to share something with you. But it's very special information and I want you to respect it and not share it with people who won't be respectful of it." And then I told her about my abortion. I'm not sure how many details I went into other than the fact that it was illegal, that it was very expensive, that I would not be critical of someone else in that situation that needed to get an abortion, and how lucky women were now to have birth control and legal abortions and options available to them.

Some of it is just my personality, but maybe it's because of my abortion experience—I want to make sure my kids do know about sex and do know their options and do know about their controls, so that they don't get stuck by somebody else's rules or judgments putting them in a position in that way. So by the time they were 12 and 14, before they were sexually active, I had told them: "By the way, I got some condoms. They're in the hall closet." And [they responded]: "Awww, Mom, what's this, geez, gross!" And I said here's two—here's one to play with and one to put in your drawer. "Cause your not going to ask me. You're not going to ask me. And the rest are in the hall closet. And if those disappear, you have to buy your own!" But it was early enough. We always talked about sex early enough that it never was personal with them—because it didn't affect their personal life.

Recently, when I was starting menopause and not having a regular period, I had my IUD out. I remember talking to my OB about what I was going to do about birth control, because we had no way of guaranteeing that I wasn't ovulating any more. We were pretty sure that I'd be completely menopausal in a couple of years and we didn't want to go through the hassle or the expense of an IUD for just a year. So, I remember talking with her about the alternatives—how do I not get pregnant or if I get pregnant what would I do? And we talked about [the fact] that abortion's always a form of birth control. If I get pregnant, I could have an abortion. I don't know if it was that appointment or the next one, but I remember saying, "You know what, I don't want to have to make that decision again." I was pretty sure I would have an abortion, but

I just don't want to have to make that decision. I don't know what I would decide at this point. Or what my guilt would be. You know, I'm at a different place in my life. So my decision would be very different and for different reasons.

I don't think I directly helped or advised any other women in terms of getting abortions, but I've certainly been an ally for young women who wanted birth control. I work with teenage girls, I like teenage girls, and they know that I'm not a usual "Mom grownup" that's going to make comments about them or have certain expectations. So often—often—this has maybe happened six times, girls will come to me and say, "I think I'm pregnant, what do I do?" Or they'll confide in me that they're sexually active and I'll be the one that says, "You need to do birth control. You need to see a doctor." [When they say], "I don't want to talk to my mother!" [I answer], "You don't need to talk your mother. Here's the information you need."

I tell the girls in girl scouts—at the point when they're in seventh and eighth grade—if you ever have issues, you can always call me up. And maybe that's a result of my abortion. I don't know. After what I went through, I'm that much more committed to other women having choices. I guess I'm pissed off that our society was in a place [back then] that that would happen. I didn't have options. The only option was to not have sex. I wasn't going to do that one.

FOUR

Carol C. Wall

Carol C. Wall is married and the mother of three. Her illegal abortion in 1966 inspired her to work on behalf of reproductive rights and she has been working in that arena ever since. She has served as director of several Planned Parenthood chapters, worked in the area of international family planning, and most recently was a staff member for Catholics for a Free Choice. She lives on Cape Cod in Massachusetts.

Carol C. Wall was interviewed by David Cline on July 13, 2004.

"I Could not have Another Child"

I was 31 years old, married, and the mother of four children. We were living in Farmington, Connecticut. Three of the children were at home. They were eight, five, and a little over two years-old. And then we had a child that had been born with a microcephalic head, who was living in a Connecticut institution. She was very profoundly affected by this small brain, and so she went into an institution when she was only eight or nine months old. We were paying part of the expense of her being in an institution. I worked part-time as a substitute teacher in the local schools and my husband was a librarian. He loved his profession, but librarians' salaries are not great. We had a very happy marriage—I am still married to the same man today and we've been together now for over 47 years—but we really did have some economic struggles. The difference between being poor and being broke though, is of course, we had the advantage of having had really wonderful educations. Even so, we still barely hung onto the middle class at that time. My husband had wanted to get a vasectomy after the last child had been born. But it was illegal in Connecticut and we really couldn't afford his time off or the money for him to go out of state to get a vasectomy.

I remember my mother was very upset when I got pregnant the first time because it was right after my husband and I were married. I was still in nursing school. I had finished college but I had had only a little over one year of nursing school. I never did get my RN, by the way. And my mother knew I really wanted to finish and was very supportive of my wanting to do that. So she had been very upset when I got pregnant. I got pregnant on our honeymoon. It was nine months and one day. And in those days, girls, particularly those of us who had the advantage of a college education, didn't want to risk having to drop out of college, most of us. So we didn't have sex. That was one of the reasons so many of us got married young in those days. We just couldn't have sex without being married.

So, after having four children, once again our contraception failed—we had a lot of failed contraception earlier but nice babies. As soon as I knew I was pregnant this time, and this was 1966, I very quickly realized that I couldn't have another child, that it wasn't possible for us either emotionally or financially. I just couldn't have this baby. And my husband fortunately was very supportive of this decision.

When I got pregnant and didn't want to be, the only thing that I knew was that there was this physician in New York who was working on trying to get the New York law liberalized. I had known of this doctor when I was a student nurse in New York. His name was Robert Hall. It seems to me that he was either at Cornell or Columbia Medical School. And he gave me the only information I had, which was: "You can go to San Juan, Puerto Rico, and get a safe, illegal abortion." That was the extent of my information. I don't know whether Robert Hall didn't have specific information or whether he was [being cautious] because he didn't know who I was on the phone. So the only information that he gave me was that I could probably find a safe albeit illegal abortion in Puerto Rico. A lot of women from the United States were going there. We also knew that women were going to England for abortions but it was cheaper to go to San Juan and that's why I chose it.

I had called my own physician first but he had no suggestions. He himself, and I knew this, was Catholic, but was not actively opposed to abortion. And what was experienced in the years since *Roe v. Wade* wasn't present in those days—there wasn't any public discussion on abortion at all. But everyone knew that Catholics in general were opposed to abortion. Well, this doctor had seen so many unwanted pregnancies, that when I called Robert Hall, and told my physician that I was going to go to Puerto Rico, he said, "Well, I would very much like to have the information when you get back so that I can give it to other women." So who knows how many times he passed on that information.

My husband and I talked about it again and realized that there were certainly risks involved, but he could see that I was determined to go in spite of those risks. I think I told one other person, a very good friend of mine, that I was going to have this abortion. I didn't tell my parents, didn't tell anyone in my family, didn't tell anyone else. We knew approximately what these illegal abortions were costing and we had to take a loan out from our credit union. I can't remember exactly how much money I took with me, but it turned out that it cost $800 and I was to bring it in cash. That was *a lot* of money in 1966.

I took off for San Juan and I'll never forget, it was the first time I had ever been in the tropics, and I left from the winter of Connecticut and arrived with the palm trees swaying. I went immediately to the hotel and got out the yellow pages of the phone book. My Spanish was practically nonexistent, but a lot of people there spoke English. I looked in the phone book for listings of OB-GYN doctors. And probably naively, I thought the University Medical School would be a positive place, even in a Catholic country. So I got in a cab and went to the university and found the OB-GYN section of the medical school and just walked into an office. And here was this waiting room—I'll never forget it—a waiting room full of women who were very pregnant and it was just jammed packed. The office nurse looked at me, realized I was an American, and she was probably suspicious of why I was there. So she ushered me into the doctor's office in front of all of these other women who were waiting. The doctor, when I told him why I was there, proceeded to scream and yell at me both in Spanish and in English, proclaiming the sins of the American women who come to Puerto Rico to murder their babies.

I said, "Look, I didn't come here to be yelled at, can you give me some information?" Well, of course, he didn't. So I left, got into another cab, and I spent the rest of the day going from address to address. And then just before the end of that day, I gave another address to the cabbie and he turned around in his seat and looked at me with this kind of knowing look. And I somehow knew that this was going to be the right place. He took me to this stucco house with no signs—it looked like a private home—and dropped me off. And inside was a room full of American women who had come seeking to end their pregnancies. It was quite a contrast to the morning.

I was examined by a Dr. Garcia, an older man with shaky hands, and I thought, My God, what am I doing? He confirmed a six-week pregnancy. I asked if he was the one who did the procedures and he said, no, his son the doctor would be performing a D&C the following day. Then the woman in the outer office said to me, "Come back in the morning with no luggage and $800 in cash." I did as I was told. I found myself in a bed next to a dentist's wife from Long Island. She was in pretty much the same situation that I was in—had already had three children and felt that they couldn't have more. I think the only time that I really was afraid was when I realized that they were going to give me general anesthesia, which was routinely done in those days for D&Cs. I had never had general anesthesia before, and I didn't like the thought of being unconscious and maybe never waking up again. But I did, obviously, and it was so wonderful to be alive!

I can remember the relief sweeping over me, just sweeping over me and just being so happy that I could go back to my life and not have to be burdened. I remember waking up from the anesthesia and thinking, this is Freedom Day, this is Freedom Day! I was euphoric. I really was euphoric. So, it was relief but it was also euphoria. It's hard to explain. When you hear of an experience like this you say, well, how could you be so happy? But it was just this wonderful relief at being able to go back to my family and pick up where I was before getting pregnant. It was really wonderful.

I was very lucky. Evidently, the abortion was done well. I didn't bleed much. I got back and resumed by life. It is amazing to think back to what women went through before Roe and all of the horrible stories of people were not lucky the way I was. I know a couple people who lost their mothers and there is nothing that will ever replace their mothers for them in their lives.

When I got back we were then determined that Duncan would get his vasectomy. So he did. He had to go to Washington, I think. I'm glad that Duncan had it done and he was glad that he contributed to contraception.

I didn't tell other people about this experience really until *Roe v. Wade*. And [then] it felt like coming out. It felt like having been in the closet for a long time. I started my Planned Parenthood job about three years later. I became director of a small new Planned Parenthood in 1969, having had my abortion in 1966. And those three years made an enormous difference.

The job at Planned Parenthood was in Canton, Ohio. I've always felt that my personal experience made me much more tolerant and patient with women's stories when they would come into Planned Parenthood and they would have had two or three unplanned pregnancies. I can remember staff saying this woman should know better, why didn't she use her birth control, and that kind of thing. But I've just always felt that we are all human, and we all make these mistakes—we may not use our contraception well, we don't have a perfect contraceptive, and so on. So, I think my own personal experience made a big difference to how I approached my work with Planned Parenthood.

I stayed in that Planned Parenthood for about six and a half years and then went on to Cleveland Planned Parenthood. After that I was Executive Director in Akron, and then my last Planned Parenthood job was eight years in Philadelphia, which was the Southeastern Pennsylvania Planned Parenthood. I stayed there for eight years or so. From that point on I decided I didn't want to take another Planned Parenthood executive job and I'd always been interested in the developing world. I got a position as Vice President of Development for Pathfinder International, an international family planning organization with a lot of AID money, for about eight or nine years. Then I went to Washington for the last three full years of my career, working for Population Action International, which is an advocacy organization trying to push the U.S. government to do the right thing as far as family planning for people in developing countries. I also did work for Catholics for a Free Choice.

My father was a Protestant minister, and interestingly enough, when I finally told my folks that I had had an abortion, they were very supportive. That was probably right around *Roe v. Wade*. I explained to them what had happened. My mother realized that it was a big financial burden for us particularly. And my father was never opposed to abortion. He was a Congregational—United Church of Christ—minister, which is about as liberal and progressive a Protestant denomination as you can get without being Unitarian, which is what I am now. My father said later that he would give people referrals to Planned Parenthood when women came to him for counseling with an unplanned pregnancy, whether it was a married or an unmarried woman. So I think there was some good ripple effect from that.

I guess I've always thought, since I've been in this work most of my life, that it feels as if there is a certain sisterhood, if you will, in women understanding each other about making this decision. But I found that when I was called upon to debate Right to Lifers that it was very hard for people—for example, the people who were moderating debates—to grasp this concept that the women who had abortions quite often are the same women who've had babies or are going to have babies in the future. And that we can love and adore our kids and at the same time feel that a given pregnancy is just an impossibility.

I think I've always found it hard to explain why I felt having an abortion when I did was the only thing to do. It didn't feel like a choice as much as it was the right thing to do. You'll find all gradations of this—women who are desperate, women who for a whole bunch of different reasons have decided not to go through a particular pregnancy—but what I found in most of the women that I saw myself during my Planned Parenthood years was just that, for them as for me, this was the *right thing* to do. Some are more desperate than others, of course. For those of us who were married it was perhaps not quite so hard as for women who were not, or were very young, or were very, very old. So quite often I feel as if the antis are making up stories about the ambivalence or about women who are saying, "I wish I didn't have an abortion." I frankly never came across a woman who said that in all the years I was with Planned Parenthood.

FIVE

Dr. Meredith W. Michaels

Dr. Meredith W. Michaels, Ph.D., had a therapeutic abortion, officially for her mental health, in 1966 at the age of 15. She is now Professor of Philosophy at Smith College in Northampton, Massachusetts. Her research and writing focus on the way that cultural changes affect understanding of reproduction, parenthood, and childhood. She is the author, with Susan J. Douglas, of The Mommy Myth: The Idealization of Motherhood and How It Has Harmed Women *(The Free Press, 2004). She and her husband, Lee Bowie, have five children and live in Amherst, Massachusetts. She says the following about the story she recounts here:*

What follows is the story of my pre-Roe abortion—that I related at an abortion speak-out when I was a philosophy professor at Hampshire College in 1989. I have spent the years since continuing to address, in so many aspects of my life, the role that reproduction plays in women's self-identity and in their political and economic situation. I will always stand behind any banner that proclaims the right to reproductive choice and I remain convinced that the criminalization of abortion is itself criminal, only profoundly so. Since 1973, there has been a relentless effort to build roadblocks between women and the possibility of abortion: clinics are attacked, clinics close, abortion training is eliminated from medical schools, bills restricting abortion pass state legislatures, costs rise, funding dries up, motherhood is hyped as heaven on earth, and everything but the Sex-Ed curriculum is sexualized. Each move further undermines women's integrity and her position as a fully functioning citizen. Each move brings us closer to the stifling pre-Roe environment that constituted my own introduction to sexuality and reproductive responsibility. I was a kid when I had my "therapeutic" abortion. My parents assumed control over my fate; their connections and their determination ensured that I would not be a mother at 15. I see no justification for agents of the state assuming analogous paternalistic control over grown women's reproductive lives.

Dr. Meredith Michaels originally recounted this story at an Abortion Speakout at Hampshire College in 1989. She and David Cline adapted it for this collection in July 2004.

"Sex and the City, ca. 1966"

I was 15 in 1966 and passionately in love with a boy two years older than I was. And as happens, one thing led to another—despite the fact that I had sneaked into my parents' bedroom at some point and read a book called *The Ideal Marriage* by Dr. Theodoor Hendrik van de Velde. The doctor explained about the reproductive cycle and how you could avoid getting pregnant if you just did "it" at the right times. So I had this great image in my head of exactly how my body worked, but of course all of this was cloaked in euphemistic language. And I got it wrong. I counted wrong. I thought you counted from the day your period stopped not from the day your period started. So there we were in my best friend's parents' bed while they were in Connecticut for the weekend, protected by nothing more than a misreading of medical wisdom.

Of course, I found myself pregnant. At first, I thought I had the flu. Then, I thought maybe I was going crazy. There were lots of options available. But pregnant? Not one of them. Finally it became clear something was very strange. I went to— I don't even remember this part at all, how I possibly got up my nerve to do this— but my boyfriend's best friend's father was an OB-GYN whom I had met many times but had taken in only in that vacant way characteristic of teenagers, and I went to him, had a pregnancy test, and sure enough, I was really quite pregnant.

Well, at that point here we were—my boyfriend and me—strolling around New York City, walking up and down the banks of the East River, talking about how we're going to have this baby. It's going to be great! We're going to go down to the Lower East Side, get an apartment. Both of us lived on the Upper East Side, we both went to private schools, we both came from families with plenty of money but we had none of our own. In our heads, it was a very romantic time. It lasted for about three days.

When my considerably older sister came back from college, I somehow got up the nerve to tell her that I was pregnant. I had said nothing to my parents. She said, "I really think you've got to talk to Mummy and Daddy." So, Saturday morning we're sitting at breakfast having bacon and eggs. My parents are reading the *New York Times*. The maid is in the kitchen. And I said, "I'm pregnant." And my mother said, "How could you be so stupid?"

Well, I thought I was pretty stupid myself—there was a way in which I thought I was really stupid. But on the other hand now, reflecting on this from the perspective of many years later, my mother had never said a word to me about birth control. I had no idea where I could have gotten it anyway—it was illegal. So the charge of stupidity I found somewhat upsetting. I told her, no, actually I'm not stupid. We've got it all figured out. We're going to have the baby.

My parents were very fond of my boyfriend. He was going to the right college and had the right literary ambitions. But no. My mother said, "You've got to be kidding. You're getting an abortion." One of the crucial things about this story,

I think, is from that moment on it was very clear there was no choice for me at all. This was not about my choice, this was about my parents deciding about my life. I was just a kid after all, right? So from that moment, the choice was taken out of my hands. There was no more talk about keeping the baby. There was no more talk about the romance of the young struggling couple in New York on the Lower East Side trying to recreate some immigrant or poor artist past. Immediately there was a frantic attempt on the part of my parents to find someone who could give me an abortion. For a while we were going to go to Sweden—a country where abortions were legal. I was not involved in any of this decision making, mind you, this was all happening around me.

Finally, the decision was made that my mother and I were going to get on the plane to Cleveland and go to Case Western Reserve Hospital, where my father's old roommate from Harvard was the head of the OB-GYN division. So off I went with my little bag, wearing my little red suit, with my Mom, speaking nothing about this at all. My mother probably asked me what I thought about some political thing that's happening and we're probably reading the obligatory *New York Times*. We got off the plane, I went to the hospital, I was put in bed. And about a half-an-hour later with a sort of clucking of nurses around me, a doctor walked in, examined me, and said, "Later this afternoon three psychiatrists are going to come in. You have to tell them that if you have this baby, you're going to kill yourself." And I said, okay. And indeed, a couple of hours later three psychiatrists came in, stood around my bed—I'm lying in bed as though I'm sick—and they said, "Hmm, you're very upset, aren't you?" Yes. "You're feeling very fragile, aren't you?" Yes. "Do you feel that you are in control of yourself?" No! "Do you feel as though you are about to go over the edge?" Yes. My mother is sitting there sort of cheering me on. The final question: "What will you do if you have this baby?" I said: I'll kill myself. They left.

That night I was prepared for surgery. Not allowed to eat, drink, all the normal things that happen to you when you are in that weird setting. Next morning I had the abortion. That afternoon my mother and I got back on the plane and went back to New York City. And three days later I was sent to spend the summer in Spain with my oldest sister, her husband, and her child. And my sister was, at that time, six months pregnant.

This story is about class privilege. It's about the availability of abortion for people who have fathers who went to Harvard, who have lots of money, who have connections that they can utilize immediately. It's also a story about restrictions. The abortion that I got, which was called a therapeutic abortion, was allowed by Ohio law. It was in fact a legal abortion, not a criminal abortion. The hospital in Cleveland where I had the abortion was allotted, if I remember correctly, five abortions a year for psychiatric reasons. Doctors could perform those abortions only if it had been determined that continuing the pregnancy put the woman's mental health at risk. In other words, if she had the baby, she'd go nuts and maybe kill herself. I don't know how or why the quota system evolved. I do know that the abortion that I had to lie to get was an abortion that some other woman couldn't get.

When abortion is criminalized, sure it's possible for some people to get safe abortions. I was very fortunate. I'm very glad that in fact I did have an abortion. I think that my mother and father were right. It was not time for me to move to the Lower East Side and raise a baby. I also realize how lucky I was under the circumstances to be able to get the abortion that I did. But it absolutely horrifies to me think of the sixth woman. Who was she and what did my abortion do to her life?

Postscript 2004

In a letter that he wrote to my parents shortly before my father died in 1991, my father's Harvard roommate said that he had come to regret performing my abortion, not because he thought that I shouldn't have had one, but because he had compromised his ability to treat patients who had no other choice. He believed, and I think he was right, that my parents would have found another option if he had declined to do them this favor.

SIX

Dr. Susan Tracy

Dr. Susan Tracy, Ph.D., had an illegal, and almost fatal, abortion during her junior year at the University of Massachusetts at Amherst (UMass). While an undergraduate, she was voted Distinguished Senior, played varsity tennis, served in the Student Senate and on the University Reform and Student Life Committees, worked for Upward Bound, and was active in the anti-Vietnam War movement and draft counseling. She went on to get her B.A. in 1969 and her M.A. in history in 1973 from UMass Amherst, and a Ph.D. in history from Rutgers University in 1983. She is Dean of Humanities, Arts, and Cultural Studies and Professor of American Studies and History at Hampshire College in Amherst, Massachusetts. Her primary interests are in American social and intellectual history, particularly labor history; Afro-American history; and women's history. She is the author of In the Master's Eye: Representations of Women, Blacks and Poor Whites in Antebellum Southern Literature *(1995). She has taught U.S. history and women's studies courses at UMass Amherst and is a cofounder of the Valley Women's History Collaborative. She lives with her partner Connie Kruger in Amherst.*

Susan Tracy originally recounted this story at an Abortion Speakout at Hampshire College in 1989. She and David Cline adapted it for this collection in July 2004.

"We Know What You've Done"

I had an illegal abortion in 1968 when I was an undergraduate at the University of Massachusetts. Those were the years when they told us to "Make Love, Not War." So, taking the phrase seriously, in the true spirit of my generation, I did. As a good Protestant Congregationalist, the first time I made love with anybody, I got pregnant. After I proceeded to throw up for about three weeks and crave oranges and Howard Johnson's hot dogs, I found out that I didn't have an ulcer—that would come ten years later—but that I was pregnant.

Now, you have to understand that in 1968, even though we talk about the women's movement as part of the Sixties, the real women's movement is actually in the 1970s. In 1968 there was a pervasive double standard about sexuality for men and for women—the Sexual Revolution was really a sexual revolution for men. It was okay for men to have sex; it was not okay, really, for women to have sex. In Amherst it was legal for men to go downtown to buy condoms, but it was completely illegal for women who were not married to have any kind of birth control. That was the double standard. That is the world we're going back to if the New Right and the Catholic Church prevail. In addition, since I had grown up in the '50s and '60s, I didn't really know anything about my body—and didn't find out anything about it until *Our Bodies, Ourselves* came out—other than, of course, very carefully studying the directions on the tampon box.[1] But other than that, there was really no information anywhere about my body, because all of the skeletons in the classrooms were males and all the drawings in the textbooks were males. And unfortunately, as I found out later, that was true in medical schools as well.

So, on a day-to-day basis, that's what the double-standard of sexuality meant. It meant that boys went around talking about scoring, and that if you were a young woman and went out and tried to live a sexual life with some measure of sexual freedom, you were still talked about. And if you found yourself pregnant, you were entirely alone.

In my own personal situation, I was especially alone because both my parents had died and a court had placed me with my mother's sister, who was a very conservative Republican on the North Shore of Boston. And since I thought I was fomenting the revolution, you can imagine things were not very comfortable on the home front. In addition to that, I had gotten involved with a 33-year-old man who was Jewish. My mother's sister and her husband wouldn't even allow him into the house. So the idea that I would go home and say that I was pregnant and they would welcome me with open arms was not a reality. What I faced was really a kind of desperate situation. I wasn't in any kind of relationship that was anything [special]. By the time I found out I was pregnant, we had been going out for six weeks. There were no parents I could turn to. So what I faced, when I looked at my options, was that I wouldn't graduate from college, which meant that I wouldn't be able to make a living in any kind of reasonable way as far as I could see. And what I thought I would be doing was consigning myself and this child to poverty. And since I had grown up in poverty, to willingly consign a child to that life I had just left was an anathema to me. Also, as a child who had just had two parents die, the idea of having a child and giving it up felt to me like an abandonment. I just couldn't do it. I knew that I couldn't go through the rest of my life knowing that some place out there, there might be my child, and that I had not taken the responsibility of taking care of that child and that life that I'd brought into the world.

And so, as I thought it out, I thought, well, I've just got to find another way. It turned out that Bill Baird had been in Massachusetts that spring and had been arrested at Boston University for holding up a Dalcon shield. He held it up to the audience and said, "This is a Dalcon shield. This will help you protect yourself from getting pregnant." And he was arrested. Later in that same trip, after he posted bail, he was out at the University of Massachusetts. I and some other people had brought him out, so I knew how to get in touch with him. He had a clinic in Hempstead, Long Island. So the man I was involved with and I went to Hempstead, Long Island, and got a "safe referral."

There is a terrible, terrible loneliness to this whole thing. I think even when abortion is legal, our society is sufficiently screwed up that women are alone in this decision. And to make abortion illegal and not to allow a woman to make what will be the most important decision in her life—*that* is criminal.

The person I was with did not want to tell his parents what was going on. He borrowed some money from them, but pretty much I had to end up by selling almost everything I owned. I sold my winter coats, I sold my books, except for my literature books which I kept. I sold my history books. I sold my stereo. I sold my skis. Because the abortion was $600, which in those days was three times my tuition. It was an enormous amount of money to raise. Today the equivalent might be $3,000 to $5,000.

So we went to this clinic in Long Island. Of course, we were New Englanders and we didn't know how to get to Long Island. We didn't know what bridges to take, and we didn't know how to get off of Long Island once we got there! So we ended up driving and driving and driving for hours looking for the place, while being frantic and scared, because what we were doing was completely illegal. We could be arrested and anybody helping us could be arrested. And so, we went to his clinic and we got the referral. The referral was to Newark, New Jersey. We took out our map and followed it to Newark, New Jersey, getting lost on the way, of course. We ended up in Westchester County and knew it wasn't Newark, New Jersey. Somehow we finally made it over the George Washington Bridge. We got to Newark, New Jersey and got lost again. The place we were sent to was a middle-class black section. It was very clear that we did not belong there. So again we were in danger, and we were putting the black doctor in danger. Our mere presence there put him in danger—put his life in danger, put his patients in danger.

I had what I thought was a safe abortion. It was in a doctor's office. He was very kind. I was knocked out and when I woke up I was in a lot of pain. We started the trip back and decided because I was pretty tired and we were both just exhausted from fright—we didn't really relax until we reached the Massachusetts border and every time we saw a police car we almost died right then and there—to stay in a motel in Holyoke. So we were staying in the motel and I was feeling very bad. I was lying on the bed and I decided I would get up and go into the bathroom. And when I stood up I had the most incredible pain I've ever felt, probably even to this day. It went right up my leg. And then suddenly I had the feeling that all of my insides had just fallen out.

I don't really remember very much after that, other than screaming and fainting and falling on the bed. What had happened was I was hemorrhaging. I was wrapped in a blanket, and my friend and the owner of the motel put me in the car and then drove me at about 80 miles an hour to Cooley Dickinson Hospital where I underwent emergency surgery. All I remember was sort of waking up in the room and seeing bright white lights and feeling very, very cold, and hearing the doctor say, "We know what you've done and we will deal with you in the morning."

I was frightened for my friend, and I was terrified for me. It crossed my mind that I shouldn't let them drug me, because I thought if they drugged me then I'd spill all like they do in the POW (Prisoner of War) camps. I tried to remember that I would just give them my name and my student ID number and nothing else! The next morning the doctor came in and he was very sarcastic. He said, "Well, I suppose you're not going to tell me where you went?" No. "I suppose you're not going to tell me who did this?" No. "And you know I could have you arrested?" Yes. And he said, "But I'm not going to. And you might as well come to see me in my office. You can get birth control pills now that you're ruined. Nobody would want to marry you anyway, so you might as well get birth control pills so you can continue your whorish ways." Something like that. So, I went and got birth control pills from him.

After that I blanked it completely out of my mind. It was one of those things that you could not talk about, because to talk about it was to endanger yourself and just too many people. And so I said nothing to anybody and just put it out of my mind like one does with a very dangerous secret. I didn't talk to anybody about it again until 1973, when *Roe v. Wade* was announced by Walter Cronkite on the CBS Evening News. I was in graduate school at that time and I was with friends. I remember standing in a friend's living room and watching that TV, and when he said that Roe had passed and abortion was legal, I can just remember crying. Tears started falling. Because all of a sudden I realized that I knew what it meant, and that other people wouldn't have to go through what I had gone through—the terror and the loneliness.

PART TWO

Providers of Reproductive Health Care

Doctors, Health Educators, and Illegal Abortionists

There are two essential pieces to the story of reproductive health care in the Pioneer Valley. One concerns the provision of birth control, the other abortion. Birth control for married women remained illegal in Massachusetts until 1966 and for unmarried women until 1972, so for many women procuring and using contraceptives meant breaking the law. Likewise, abortions—other than the few therapeutic abortions approved by hospitals—were illegal. The oral histories that follow will give some insight into what these legal blockades meant to Pioneer Valley women and to the health-care workers who served them, but first it is necessary to review the state and national contexts.

Massachusetts and the Fight for Birth Control

Advertising contraceptives was made illegal nationwide under the Comstock Act of 1873, and selling and distributing them was made illegal in Massachusetts six years later under the Crimes Against Chastity, Decency, and Good Order act. As would be the case for nearly a century, making contraception illegal simply made it inaccessible to the poorest in the society, as the well-to-do usually had few problems obtaining birth control through their physicians. A national movement to reform the Comstock Act, led by activist Margaret Sanger, grew at the beginning of the twentieth century and in Massachusetts this led to the 1916 formation of the Birth Control League of Massachusetts. Sanger would have close ties to the League and the Massachusetts reform efforts throughout their turbulent history. Suffering from arrests and difficulty in implementing their planning strategies, the League disbanded in 1920, then reappeared a few years later. In 1926, they supported Sanger after city leaders successfully banned her from delivering a speech about contraception at Boston's Ford Hall Forum. Undeterred, Sanger sat on stage with tape covering her mouth while Arthur Slesinger, Sr. read her speech. In 1928, the League hired a social worker, opened its first office, and began pursuing a joint plan of education and legislative reform lobbying that continues to this day. Between 1932 and 1937 the League opened a series of clinics throughout the state and served some 3,000 women before a state crackdown closed the clinics and their staffs were arrested under the Crimes Against Chastity law.

The League then changed its name to the Massachusetts Mothers' Health Council and began doing research, discovering that 82 percent of their survey respondents supported legalized contraception. They gathered 60,000 signatures in 1942 in support of a ballot initiative to legalize the distribution of birth control for married persons. Though the initiative was supported by a large portion of the state's medical community and such celebrities as Helen Keller, it was defeated by 16 points. A 1948 initiative was defeated by the same margin.

During the 1950s and 1960s, and now called the Planned Parenthood League of Massachusetts (PPLM), the League worked to circumvent state law by sending patients out of state to their associated clinic in New Hampshire. At the same time, the League aggressively pushed for reform through major education and outreach efforts to garner public support for family planning. The Comstock laws finally began to crumble in 1965, dealt a major blow by the Supreme Court's ruling in *Griswald v. Connecticut* that had the effect of legalizing the distribution of contraception to married persons in most states. Massachusetts would need to enact its own legislation the following year, the Reid-Rutstein Act, which passed by one vote. In 1966, married women could finally legally procure contraception in Massachusetts, the last state in the union to so legalize it. Six years later, the Supreme Court's ruling in *Eisenstadt v. Baird* legalized contraception for unmarried persons as well. Again, Massachusetts was the last state in the country to legalize.[1]

The Baird of *Eisenstadt v. Baird* was Bill Baird, a pioneering and often controversial reproductive health advocate who made more than a few trips to Massachusetts and the Pioneer Valley during the 1960s and 1970s. Baird had become committed to abortion and contraceptive legal reform after a women with a coat hanger protruding from her uterus collapsed and died in his arms in a Harlem hospital hallway in 1963. Without a medical license and untrained in community activism, he converted an old truck into a counseling center on wheels and began distributing information on family planning in the poorest of New York's neighborhoods. He was arrested for the first time in 1965 and later that same year, in open defiance of the law, opened the country's first freestanding abortion counseling clinic in Hempstead, New York.

He took his educational road show national and was arrested at Boston University in 1967 for handing a condom to a woman in the audience. Convicted under the Crimes Against Chastity law, he was sentenced to three months in prison and called "a menace to the nation" by the sentencing judge. Appealed to the U.S. Supreme Court as "*Eisenstadt v. Baird*," the Court eventually—in 1972—found in his favor, effectively legalizing contraception for all women regardless of marital status. Justice William Brennan wrote that all women had the right "to be free from unwarranted government intrusion into matters so fundamentally affecting a person as the decision whether to bear or beget a child." The Baird decision became one of the building blocks in the Roe decision, which cited it five times.[2]

Baird's presence in the Pioneer Valley did not go unnoticed by local physicians, who themselves had for years been defying the laws against providing birth control.[3] The stories of several of these doctors follow in this chapter. But again, a woman needed access to such a private physician and that cost money. The poorest of Pioneer Valley citizens, those who arguably could most ill afford additional children, had little chance of such access.

Beginning in the early 1960s, a number of young women began to get prescriptions for illegal contraception in a surprising way—through their college physicians. While college doctors throughout the state likely prescribed birth control on the sly—it was, after all, in the college's best interests to insure that their young women did not get into trouble—the story recounted here is about the University of Massachusetts flagship campus in Amherst.

Largely through the pioneering efforts of its Director of Student Health Services, Dr. Robert Gage, UMass's health clinic provided contraception to hundreds of university women. Sexual intercourse, frequently without contraception and most often premarital, was a reality on the UMass campus as it was on all college campuses, and yet it took a rare physician or administrator to acknowledge that truth. Gage was one of the rare ones, as a UMass alumna remembered: "My sense was that he was solidly rooted in the reality of people's lives, not people's lives as he wished they were when they came to see him, but solidly rooted in what the real public health issues are for people. Kind of a C. Everett Koop type."[4] Despite the illegality of providing birth control, top UMass administrators supported Gage's efforts. But even at UHS, women ran into humiliating difficulties. Each individual physician made his or her own call about whether or not to prescribe contraception and there were a handful of UHS doctors who would not take the risk or did not believe in it. One female student recounted being asked to sign a pledge that she would soon be married before the doctor would consider her request. Dr. Gage soon responded to cases like this by systemizing the birth control program, adding an educational component, and only assigning those physicians to this area who would agree to the program.

Dr. Gage and his colleagues not only did extensive family planning education and contraception provision, but they also pioneered research on sexual life on campus. The University Health Services surveyed pregnant students during 1968–1969, and estimated that 350 students, or between 5 and 6 percent of the female student body of just over 5,800 became pregnant that year.[5] One hundred and fifty-four students were diagnosed as pregnant by the UHS itself; one-third of these completed surveys. Forty percent of the surveyed students said they did not use contraception because they simply "took a chance." Twenty percent said they were using the rhythm method. Others reported that a condom had failed or been misused, that they had perhaps been unsafe because they were interested in getting pregnant, or had been under the influence of alcohol or drugs and hadn't been "fully in control of their actions." The students also answered questions about how they would proceed with their pregnancy. During their first interview, about 50 percent of the students said they would carry the pregnancy to term, with 40 percent indicating they planned to get married, and 10 percent indicating they would put the baby up for adoption. Twenty percent of students were undecided about their course of action or otherwise did not indicate it. Thirty percent of students initially indicated they would seek an abortion, however the authors noted, "it is our unverified impression that the number of patients who obtain an abortion is substantially higher than indicated by these figures." So upwards of 30 percent, perhaps as many as 50 percent, of the 350 students who became pregnant during the 1968–1969 school year sought an illegal abortion.[6] Reverend Samuel Johnson, who counseled pregnant students at the Clergy Consultation Service on Abortion (CCS) chapter on campus from 1970 to 1972, estimated that the percentage of pregnant women was closer to 25 percent of the female student body, or 1,500 individuals each year. If half of those women sought abortions, that comes to about 750 women per year on just that one campus.

Legal Abortion

If approximately 1,500 women at UMass alone got pregnant each year and up to 50 percent of them sought abortions, certainly the total number for the Pioneer Valley was much, much higher. For most of these women, their only choice was an illegal abortion but a lucky few may have been able to legally procure a therapeutic abortion for medical reasons. But most hospital abortion committees, including those in the Pioneer Valley, approved very few.

In the early part of the twentieth century, therapeutic hospital abortions required just a simple consultation between at least two physicians for approval—a doctor usually simply found a physician friend to sign off on it—but during the late 1940s this shifted to a more centralized committee-based scheme.[7] Hospitals formed Therapeutic Abortion Committees to review all requests and abortions tended only to be performed in large teaching hospitals that could justify teaching doctors the procedure for emergency situations.

The medical establishment as a whole was very conservative on the issue of abortion. Most physicians learned in their medical school training that abortion was both highly dangerous and immoral. The standard textbook in use in most medical schools was *Williams Obstetrics*, which until its 1969 revision, read: "Since therapeutic abortion entails destroying the fetus it is a grave undertaking and must never be considered unless there is imminent danger of death of the mother as the result of pregnancy, or of great bodily or mental harm. Neither the law nor medical ethics permits the procedure for sociological reasons, i.e., illegitimacy, poverty, or rape."[8] Most therapeutic abortion committees therefore took a very narrow reading of when abortions would be permitted and some hospitals even had an annual quota, as witnessed by Meredith Michaels in the previous chapter. Even under these restrictions, abortions were still available to many with the right connections or means, as doctors sitting on these committees would often quickly pass through a private patient or friend. Overall, though, hospital committees approved only about 6 percent of cases presented.[9]

A hospital abortion was also very expensive, with separate fees for consultations, the procedure, and the mandatory hospital stay adding up to $500 to $800. Hospital abortions, further, had multiple requirements, including a referral from the patient's personal physician, a performing physician who had hospital privileges, one or two letters from psychiatrists indicating the psychological damage that would be caused by a full-term pregnancy, approval by the committee, an interview with a hospital social service person to determine economic and psychological fitness, and the consent of a husband or parent.

Although a number of states sanctioned therapeutic abortions, the medical establishment itself was fairly late to the table. It wasn't until 1971 that the Annual Clinical Meeting of the American College of Obstetricians and Gynecologists approved a resolution in favor of abortion "to safeguard the patient's health or improve her family life situation."[10] By that time, of course, legal abortion on demand was already available in New York State. However as Nanette Davis points out, abortion on demand relegated doctors to the status of technicians, which rankled the members of a profession who had undertaken years of advanced training and were used to society's continuous confirmation of their wisdom in health matters. "For most medical leaders," Davis writes, "the newer concepts of abortion on 'convenience' or 'demand' circulating in the 1960s were simply not professional medicine. Specialists did not want to become known as 'the abortionist.' "[11]

While this may have been true for senior physicians in private practice or on hospital boards, a different reality faced the young doctors in large hospitals that were simply overflowing with women suffering from the effects of illegal abortions, many of them self-induced. Women used all manner of implements and potions to try to induce abortion, from pushing corrosive potassium permanganate tablets into their vaginas to inserting objects such as coat hangers or broken bottles into their uteruses. In hospitals from California to New York, special units were established simply to deal with all the women with the after effects of illegal abortions, including septicemia, an infection of the bloodstream. Dr. Sam Topal, who would later practice obstetrics in the Pioneer Valley, worked as a resident in a New York hospital with an entire wing full of such infections, a wing hospital staff dubbed "The Septic Tank." Many of the doctors in Topal's position quickly grew to understand abortions were being performed at a high rate despite their illegality and that doctors bore the burden of trying to save and care for women after unsafe abortions. Hospital studies showed that performed in a safe, antiseptic environment, abortion had a very low level of complication. By taking medical control of the practice of abortion, doctors could perform the procedure safely and save themselves and the women from undue trauma.

The reality of the emergency rooms and the septic tanks began to influence the medical community at large. "Indeed," writes historian Leslie Reagan in *When Abortion Was a Crime*, "it was physicians and lawyers who initiated the earliest efforts to rewrite the abortion laws."[12] Doctors would "medicalize" the practice of abortion, insisting that the procedure be performed by a physician rather than a nurse or technician. The desire to maintain medical and authoritative control won out over the stigma of being the abortionist, and when the *Roe v. Wade* decision was handed down, it conceded to the medical establishment by specifying that only doctors could perform terminations.

In Massachusetts, which was especially conservative when it came to abortion and birth control, hospital abortion committees were even more reticent than in most states to approve legal procedures. As the stories that follow illustrate, these were usually only approved in cases where extreme illness threatened the mother and the fetus, or in cases where the woman was older and already had a number of children. For most women who wanted an abortion then, they were forced to turn to the illegal abortion market or to attempt an abortion themselves.

Illegal Abortion

In January 1951, *Ebony* magazine ran a feature story called "The Abortion Menace" accompanied by shadowy pictures of a cramped abortion room and of police crowded around a body on a bed. The woman was depicted as the victim of a mercenary abortionist. Such images persisted in the public's understanding of illegal abortion, just as the actual history of its practice to this day remains largely in the shadows *Ebony* so graphically depicted in 1951.

That hidden world of illegal abortions had come into being only in the previous decade or so. Even though criminalized in the 1930s, abortion had continued to be practiced fairly openly by doctors and midwives. But starting in the 1940s, criminal prosecutions became much more frequent and continued until the Roe decision of 1973. Abortion went underground. In many cases, prosecutions were politically motivated and were aggressively pursued only during election years. At other times, local authorities, though fully aware of the operation of underground abortionists, let them practice unhindered. As the story of Lorraine Florio that follows illustrates, many abortionists even had deals worked out with local police officials. Even so, the practice became one associated with the criminal underworld.

The standard abortion technique used in hospital abortions was a dilation and curettage (D&C), later replaced by a suction D&C. Most illegal abortionists, however, used a variety of other means to stimulate a miscarriage. Some abortionists preferred the "packing" technique, filling the uterus with sterile gauze, but most employed a catheter, a hollow tube, inserted into the uterus. The catheter could be inserted and then quickly withdrawn, causing an infection the uterus then tried to expel. More frequently though, the abortionist would leave the catheter inside until the uterus tried to expel the foreign body, expelling the fetus along with it. Still other abortionists injected a foreign body into the uterus, causing a similar reaction. While saline injection was the most common and would even come into medical practice, Massachusetts abortionist Lorraine Florio injected a diluted solution of Ivory Soap to stimulate miscarriage.

A catheter inserted into the uterus improperly could cause a perforation of the uterus as happened to Nancy Kierzek. Many abortions resulted in infections of the bloodstream. Antibiotics could be used to treat these infections and after 1950, when their use became more common, the death rate secondary to abortion fell from 1 in every 200 women to 1 in every 316 women.[13]

Very few accounts of illegal abortionists' day-to-day activities, the methods they used, and the networks they operated within, have come to light. Lorraine Florio is one of the few who is willing to speak about her experiences. She worked in Lawrence, Massachusetts during the 1960s and performed several hundred abortions each year. Her activities were well known by Lawrence police but she was never arrested, though she was harassed. Though she provided what she saw as a necessary service to pregnant women, she was at the mercy of both local authorities and local hoodlums and in 1967, she gave up her practice to attempt to go legitimate. Though it is unknown if any women from the Pioneer Valley traveled the two or so hours to use Lorraine's services, it is quite likely.[14]

The Quiet Fight

The health professionals at UMass Amherst, private physicians who bent to the laws to provide their patients with birth control or give a quiet abortion referral, and even the illegal abortionist like Lorraine Florio were all part of the grassroots pressure that helped to create a sea change in public opinion and, eventually, change in legislation as well. They placed themselves and their organizations at legal risk because they believed that unjust laws were violating women's reproductive health rights. Even Lorraine Florio, who made money from her abortions and drove fancy cars, still saw part of her calling as helping women in desperate need.

While others lobbied the legislature, the health care providers depicted here went ahead and did the work they felt had to be done—providing care for women. Abortion was seen as a necessity but it presented difficulty as a cause. It was hard to march up and down in a parade celebrating the choice of abortion. And yet American women, at least a million a year, wanted and needed that choice. By 1973, this grass-roots activism seemed to strongly reflect public opinion; Americans favored the right to choose and the legislature was simply out of touch. The *Roe v. Wade* judicial decision brought the law into step with the nation. The activities in Amherst and Northampton reveal how a few individuals in one small community broke the law in order to create such choice. Their story is one that undoubtedly was repeated in some way in towns and cities throughout the country.

Dr. Merritt F. Garland, Jr.

Dr. Merritt F. Garland, Jr., M.D., was born and raised in Massachusetts. He was educated at Middlebury College and Tufts Medical School before spending several years in the Army, including a stint in a M.A.S.H. unit in Korea. He opened a gynecology and obstetrics practice in Greenfield, Massachusetts in 1953, and had privileges at Franklin County Public Hospital in Greenfield and Farren Memorial Hospital in Montague, Massachusetts, where he served as Chief of Obstetrics. He retired from practice in 1972 and still lives in Greenfield with his wife Sallee.

Dr. Merritt F. Garland, Jr. was interviewed by David Cline on June 12, 2004.

Medical Background

I was born in 1920 and grew up in Bradford, Massachusetts. I graduated from Haverhill High School and went to Middlebury College in Vermont. I was an Eagle Scout, played football, and sang in the choir. In my junior year at Middlebury I decided that I wanted to be a physician, so I had a lot of catching up to do with lab courses and stuff. I graduated in 1941.

I was accepted at Tufts Medical School, but about six months after I started, the Army and the Navy took over the school with something called the Specialized Training Program. You could continue to go to school and pay for it yourself, but you were eligible for the draft. Or you could join the Navy or the Army and became a private. So you really didn't have a choice—you were stuck. I joined the Army.

We were in an accelerated program, so we were through in three years. I graduated in 1946 and went into the army. Later, since I was still on active duty, I was shipped to Korea. I don't know how I decided to get into obstetrics, but for some reason that interested me. As a matter of fact I had done one delivery while I was in Korea. A civilian who was with the Army delivered at our hospital. I was the only one interested in obstetrics, so I got to sit in on the delivery. After Korea, I got a job at Santa Clara County Hospital in San Jose and spent two-and-a-half years there as rotating intern, resident in OB-GYN and chief resident in OB-GYN. I wanted to come back to New England and there was a position opening at Mary Fletcher Hospital in Burlington, Vermont. They needed a senior resident. So I got a fellowship at the University of Vermont Medical School and became chief resident in OB-GYN at Mary Fletcher Hospital.

Going into Practice

We wanted to find a place to practice in New England and so we picked out small and medium sized towns and cities and went around and visited. My wife would interview the superintendent of schools and the chief of police, and I'd interview the radiologist and the pathologist at the hospital. They didn't care who came and practiced. People who were in practice, of course, you'd be in competition with, so we figured the right people to interview were those who didn't have a personal stake in the matter. We picked Greenfield, and in 1953 I calmly set out in private practice with no money and an empty office on the second floor of a furniture store on Main Street.

We started out with office hours one day a week. My first year in practice I had 36 deliveries. Four of them were sets of twins. In those days, obstetricians delivered or helped deliver babies. Nowadays those sets of twins would be delivered by Caesarean section (c-section). In those days, if your c-section rate was more than 5 percent Joint Commission would "object strenuously." Nowadays the section rate runs around 25 percent. Anything that's a complication gets delivered by Caesarean. Not in those days. Everything was delivered, as they say, "from below," except in extreme emergencies. The practice went along and built up very nicely. I don't remember the year, but eventually I got busy enough so I was looking for some help, an associate. And then we built an office on Church Street in Greenfield.

The other significant thing that came along at that time was the Lamaze business. During my training in California, obstetrical anesthesia hadn't been invented yet and procedures were done under local anesthesia. There was no such thing really. And in New England, obstetrics at that time was dominated by Boston Lying-In Hospital— Brigham and Women's now—where everybody was delivered under general anesthesia with something called Twilight Sleep. You got Scopolamine or whatever and then you woke up the next day and said, "Did I have the baby yet?" There were a lot of women who apparently didn't go for that and it turned out there was a bunch of women around here who felt that babies were delivered by mothers and not doctors. I attracted those people and that's what built my practice. That's why I had to get an associate. I just got so busy. In those days, especially in solo practice, it was a 24-7 job. You were always on call. You get burned out eventually.

"Prescribing" Illegal Birth Control

A lot of my practice was family planning, but in medical school nothing was ever mentioned about contraception. That's right, nothing at all. Obviously, people knew about it. People managed not to get pregnant one way or another. In 1960 in Massachusetts it was illegal to provide what they called "birth control information." Now I don't know that the law was very strictly enforced, but it certainly didn't bother my practice particularly.

I started practice in the '50s and we managed to prescribe diaphragms before they were legal. The detail men, as they were called in those days, would come in from the various pharmaceutical companies and they'd bring fitting rings and anything you needed for prescribing diaphragms. All the drugstores carried them. So what you'd do is you'd examine the patient and you'd measure her for her diaphragm. I had little notepads that said, "From the Desk of Dr. Garland" on them. It wasn't a prescription blank, just a note. And I'd write the diaphragm size on it. And they'd take it to the drugstore and they'd fill it for her. It wasn't a prescription! It was as though she'd just come in and said, "I need a diaphragm," size whatever, and there was never any problem in getting one. This is before it became theoretically legal.

The vaginal diaphragm was the only contraceptive method at that time. The [birth control] Pill hadn't been invented yet. I think it was in 1963 when the Supreme Court in Massachusetts decided that a proper penalty for an unplanned pregnancy should not be a child. And on that basis, they decided that contraception was legal—but only if you were married. Interesting anecdote in that respect: I once had a patient who was 40 years old, a woman, who had been widowed for some time. She developed a new relationship and she didn't want to get pregnant, of course. So she went to one of the other doctors in town and he told her that if she came back after she got married he'd fit her with a diaphragm. And so she ended up in my office.

Actually the rules were more regularly enforced by the hospital than by the legal profession. For instance, you could not get a tubal ligation for sterilization unless you had a so-called medical reason, which required consultation with three other physicians. The other doctors at Franklin County Public Hospital, where I had privleges, were rather sticklers for the old morality. So, essentially, you couldn't get it done.

Franklin County wasn't really a public hospital. It was a nonprofit hospital, but it wasn't funded by the county or anything. There was also the [Catholic-run] Farren Memorial Hospital across the river in Montague, where of course there was no family planning whatsoever. But they were much more open to patient concerns, so eventually I became Chief of Obstetrics at Farren. We did some finagling around because at the hospital you couldn't talk about contraception. You just didn't talk about it in the hospital, that's all. In fact, the previous Chief of Obstetrics at Farren had been fired by the hospital because he very publicly complained about their policies.

I once heard someone say that they were pro-choice but antiabortion. And we had a long-time representative in Congress, Silvio O. Conti.[1] He usually ran on the Republican ticket, but sometimes he ran on both tickets! He was very popular here in Western Massachusetts. He was essentially antiabortion but his take was that he was therefore in favor of contraception. He said the only way to prevent abortions is to prevent unwanted pregnancies. And that got him into a lot of trouble with the Catholic population. But he was very popular and he never had trouble getting elected. So I sort of look at myself in that kind of way. I thought it was better to prevent pregnancies than worry about abortion. But contraception was not very reliable in those days. There used to be a standing joke about diaphragm babies. My wife claims all her babies were diaphragm babies, but it wasn't always the diaphragm's fault!

I don't remember when [the pill came out]—right in the middle of the Sixties some time. I remember they cost $13.50 cents per cycle when they first came out. That was Ovid, which had much too much estrogen in it, so it had a lot of side effects. But it obviously became very popular. I got all the students from the private girls' schools—you know, the word got around. I had a lot of patients like that, but it never was any great problem. They'd come in and most of them had never had a gynecological exam before. And we'd talk about things and I'd examine them and prescribe the pill. They all wanted prescriptions, especially when there was going to be a spring dance or something! So, I had a lot of these gals on oral contraceptives after the pill came out. But that was not a big deal, you know. Once the pill came out and contraception was legal [for married women], it sort of solved everything for me. It didn't for a lot of the other doctors. It remained against the law for unmarried women for quite a long time, but I never paid much attention to that. Except for the doctor

I mentioned who refused to fit the woman with a diaphragm because she wasn't married, I just never thought about that particularly or took it into consideration.

Abortion, Therapeutic, and Otherwise

Strictly speaking abortion was not illegal. It was only illegal for reasons other than medical reasons. There were situations where for very serious medical reasons abortions could be done at the Franklin. Not at the Farren. You couldn't do them at the Farren no matter what—although I ended up doing one once. This woman had ovarian cancer and she was pregnant. In the course of the operation [to remove the tumor] the pregnancy was terminated. The nuns were all very cooperative. All they asked was that they could baptize the fetus, which was maybe four or five months.

Another situation at the Farren was a woman who had very serious kidney problems and she was in a coma. She was referred to me. She was actually referred to a urologist because of her kidney problem and he referred her to me when he found out she was pregnant. We were allowed to do a Cesarean section on her after 26 weeks when the baby was presumably viable. After the delivery, her kidney problem didn't go away, but she came out of her coma. She went back to her old family physician who was a good Catholic doctor and all he told her [afterwards] was, "Don't get pregnant again, period." But she got pregnant again. The word got around that this gal, she was well known, was pregnant again. And one of the things that I remember so well was one of the sisters who was in charge of the record room at the Farren said to me, "Doctor, you're not going to let her have that baby are you?" And she was admitted to the Franklin and we did a therapeutic abortion. That's the only one I can remember doing.

There were obviously women who became pregnant and were unhappy about it for one reason or another. People would come in [to my office] and we'd talk about it and I would give them a phone number to call. I have no idea where I got the phone number. As far as I know, I don't think anybody locally was doing this. And of course, if they were, they weren't talking about it. Other than the phone number, I knew nothing about where the women went, or what happened, or who did it. It may have been somebody connected with Bill Baird, who was well known in those days. There was a clergy network involved back then too. I don't know what connection I may have had with them. Nothing official. Nothing was ever in writing. I was on Planned Parenthood's consulting list, so there may have been some involvement with Planned Parenthood too, but that would have been all under the table also. Anyway, there was a connection, if you knew where to go. I don't know if it was a connection through Planned Parenthood or clergy or whatever, but it wasn't just anybody doing back alley abortions. They were screened somehow. This phone number was legitimate.

It was always discussed with the patient that I didn't know about the security or the qualifications or whatever. And I didn't ask where these people went or how it was done, but they always managed to go somewhere. I would ask them to come back and see me after they'd resolved the problem in whatever way they did, whether it was continuing the pregnancy or terminating it or whatever. I have no idea how many women that was, but many of them were able to obtain abortions. Most of them did come back for a post-abortion check-up. As far as I know there were never any serious complications, although apparently they were done in hotel rooms and things. So they weren't under the most pleasant circumstances.

I do remember when I was an intern in Maine, there was a student nurse who apparently got pregnant. Everything was very hush-hush. I remember she was admitted to a private room and everything was done very secretly. I remember she was taken to the operating room—so either she had had a botched abortion or she'd had a spontaneous miscarriage. But as far as the hospital was concerned, the fact that she'd gotten pregnant was the sin and she was promptly dismissed. Those things went on. It wasn't anything new.

I remember one thing which impressed me was how many times a mother would bring in her daughter who was, say, 15 years old and 3 months pregnant. And during the conversation I would find out that the mother had had the same problem and had obtained an abortion 15 or 20 years before. I never asked too many questions except that I understood they would go to Boston. Somehow they had a way of knowing [where to go]. And this impressed me. This happened several times—mothers who had been through the same process and they just figured it was one of the normal things to do under those circumstances.

[I remember] one very unfortunate incident. Naturally, 16-year-old girls often didn't want their parents to know what was going on. Unfortunately in my office one time, there was a new receptionist and she goofed up and she sent a bill to the girl's parents. And he came—happened to be a friend of mine—storming in and wanted to know what his daughter [was doing]. The bill that she had sent was for her office visit and he wanted to know why she had come to the office. We had trouble wiggling out of that one.

One other little anecdote involved a prominent citizen who is still around. He and his wife came in with their daughter who was, I think, in community college at the time. They very adamantly said they wanted her to have an abortion—this is before they were legal. Fine, upstanding citizens. So, of course, after I talked to the parents I asked them to sit in the waiting room and I talked to the girl and she said she didn't want to have an abortion. She was five months along anyway. So I examined her and we chatted about it, and I went out and said to the parents, "She doesn't want to have an abortion." "It will ruin my reputation!" the guy says. I said, "Well, I'm sorry but it's her decision and I can't give you any other advice other than I think she ought to have prenatal care." I never heard from them again, so I don't know what happened with her, whether she continued the pregnancy. I suppose she could have had it terminated, but she was five or six months along.

After they became legal, the Franklin Hopsital did terminations, but according to the hospital rules you still had to get consultation with one or two other physicians. But fortunately we had a friendly psychiatrist. I can remember only one time that he sent a woman back to me. He said I can't recommend a therapeutic termination because she's perfectly healthy. She just doesn't want to be pregnant. So he turned her down on that basis. But most of the time, he'd come up with some kind of psychiatric diagnosis. Another interesting thing is that after abortions became legal, some of the physicians who had been adamantly against abortions were doing them because they were now legal. This must have been in the early '70s.

I had not been trained [specifically] for terminations. It was never mentioned in medical school. But pregnancy terminations at that time were simply a D&C, which is a very normal procedure for abnormal bleeding and so on. Toward the end of my practice, when I was getting so busy I couldn't manage any more, I brought in an associate, Dr. Bill Callahan, who's still in practice in Greenfield. I remember one particular patient who must have been four or five months along. Why she needed or wanted or had an abortion I don't know, but it was actually done at the Franklin [Hospital] by Dr. Callahan. I had had no experience with second trimester abortions, so he agreed to do it. He had been in the air force before he went into private practice, but I don't know where got his experience. He did a saline injection and she aborted at the Franklin Hospital. That was after they became legal, so it must have been in the early 1970s.

When I was a Resident in San Jose, at Santa Clara County Hospital there would rarely be a time when there wasn't somebody on the ward with an incomplete abortion. Of course, we had no official connection with that—we wouldn't get them until after the deed was done. And one woman that I remember died in the hospital of septic infection from an abortion. I don't remember thinking much about it at the time—there was always somebody coming in bleeding. It was sort of routine. I remember a time when there were two patients in adjoining beds in the ward and it turned that they had both been aborted by the same chiropractor. And they got to talk with each other and they were laughing that they just happened to have been to the same person. That was in California. I'm not aware that any of my patients who I referred [to that phone number] ever had any problems in that respect. Whoever we referred them to had some kind of qualifications. And as I said, most of these patients did come back for checkups afterwards and I recall no complications that I was aware of. There were channels, once you found the grapevine and the network. And they were legitimate. They weren't the so-called back alley abortions. They were apparently done by competent people, because there certainly weren't any problems like the ones I saw in California.

EIGHT

Dr. Sam Topal

Dr. Sam Topal, M.D., practiced obstetrics and gynecology in Northampton from 1970 until his retirement in 2003. He also served as Medical Director for the Family Planning Council of Western Massachusetts. He lives in Northampton with his wife Cathy who teaches at Smith College and is the father of three daughters. In his retirement, he is taking college courses, writing, volunteering, and enjoying his grandchildren.

Dr. Sam Topal was interviewed by David Cline on February 9, 2004.

Early Experiences with Abortion: The "Septic Tank"

I grew up in New York, and went to medical school at the State University of New York, Downstate Medical Center. The year after my residency I taught at a big city hospital in New York, Columbia Presbyterian Hospital. I came to the Pioneer Valley in July of 1970, and I fell in love with the Valley. I thought the medical community was quite exceptional for a small New England town—all the "Young Turks" were New York or Boston trained. For the size of the community it was amazing. I joined a solo OB-GYN practitioner at that time, Donald Freund, now retired. The group has subsequently grown over the years to a group of six doctors, three nurse practitioners, and three nurse midwives. I retired in August 2003 after 33 years in practice.

I worked for Family Planning in New York City during my residency. In New York at that time there were not many restrictions as far as birth control. In the mid- to late-Sixties, Connecticut and Massachusetts still outlawed the prescription of contraception, but New York didn't have that restriction. It had birth control clinics. The residents would rotate through various centers of Family Planning all throughout Manhattan and the Bronx. So we had a lot of exposure to "family planning" and people coming in for contraception. Even then, the Pill had become the most popular form of contraception, but the mechanical devices were still popular. The IUD was available.

At that point abortion was illegal, and Family Planning did not counsel patients on options regarding pregnancy, at least at the clinics that I recollect working at. In a sense there really were no "choices" since abortion was an illegal "choice." Sterilization was discussed and that was also really restricted in those days. When I was resident we had what we called the Sterilization Committee, which met once a week. It would be the OB-GYN residents plus a group of OB-GYN Attending Physicians and Attendings from other departments. There was an antagonistic feeling between the residents, who wanted to get many more people approved—because of the great demand for it—and the Attendings. They had this bizarre, outrageous formula of age times number of children and you'd get to a certain figure. A ward patient had to have an extraordinarily high number, or you had to have a significant medical reason, in order to get the sterilization. I remember it being somewhat discriminatory, not as far as race or anything like that, although indirectly you might say it was, since private patients had no problems getting approved, compared to the ward patients. In fact, I'm not even sure if private patients went through the committee. So if you were poor and weren't 40 and had 12 kids, you basically weren't approved. There was no such thing as an elective sterilization.

I don't recollect anyone ever having what we would call a therapeutic abortion while I was a resident. It was illegal. But, unfortunately, a large percentage of my residency was devoted to caring for women who had induced or criminal abortions. And it was just horrible. The worst infections! True Gram negative sepsis and endotoxic shock.[1] And what was even more demeaning for the patient was they were sometimes prosecuted. Police would literally come to the ward to interview the patient, more so really to find out who did it and to try to get the abortionist. And some of these abortionists were obviously extremely dangerous. But you can imagine this young woman who is really seriously ill being interviewed by the police. It was just a horrible experience! So I think what my generation saw was an absolute disaster—it was just terrible. I can think of two deaths of individuals who had complications from criminal abortions.

Every variety and means of apparatus or chemical was tried by individuals trying to induce abortion: catheters of all sorts, chemicals, knitting needles. You've heard all these stories. We saw very significant infections and perforations of the uterus. We had something called "The Septic Tank," which was literally a whole hospital wing of very serious gynecological infections secondary to criminal abortion. It was unbelievable. And the weekends! If you knew you were on call on the weekend, the weekend is when it happened. Apparently the abortionists came to town Friday evening and Saturday, or that's when people seemed to have it. And you'd have huge numbers of women showing up in the emergency room—maybe five to ten per day. And those were just the ones who had complications. The majority, thank God, would come in incompletely aborted and we spent a lot of time completing them. That was legal. God, the numbers of incomplete abortions that we completed! Not just women having spontaneous abortions, but induced ones. There were huge numbers, huge numbers. I think everyone exposed to this was obviously shocked and was in a sense "Pro-Choice," because there was no other choice. The alternative at that point was criminal abortion.

Abortion and Contraception in the Pioneer Valley

We saw the effects of criminal abortion here in the Valley too. Not in great numbers, but we did. I can't recollect any deaths, thank God, but we did have people with serious infections. Also, we were caring for people who had legal—hospital approved—terminations elsewhere. People who perhaps had had it done in Boston or New York and did not realize it could be done in the Valley or did not want the notoriety in the sense of anyone knowing. There's still a risk of complications even from just medically correct procedures, and we'd care for those. That was still a problem until abortion was legalized.[2]

When I first came to Northampton, women could get sterilized, but there had to be a medical indication. It couldn't be elective, a woman stating, "I just don't want any more children." Insurance carriers wouldn't cover it in those days, so basically we used diagnoses such as "acute situational anxiety of pregnancy." And it truly is a psychiatric diagnosis in a way; an unwanted pregnancy *would* cause significant anxiety in certain individuals. These were the diagnoses we used for women desiring sterilization, probably for the first ten or more years when I was practicing here.

Before it was legalized, any woman wanting to have a termination had to go through this series of interviews with two psychiatrists and in a sense be approved that way. The abortions were done usually for psychiatric reasons, unless there was a serious medical problem. There was a list of psychiatrists that the woman had to see and it would be arranged that way. A lot of it was arranged through Clergy Consultation, if I remember correctly. I think the clergy found a group of sympathetic psychiatrists. This network was already established before I came here. I vaguely remember attending one meeting of Clergy Consultation at the chapel at Smith College with Reverend Dick Unsworth. I was very impressed with Unsworth—an amazing kind of guy. I've heard of the Valley Women's Center too. I'm sure they did a lot of counseling and maybe they did send us patients. I'm sure they were very active, but I'm not sure if they sent patients directly to our office or through Clergy Consultation. I'm also not sure if our office sent the patients to the psychiatrists, or if we would just give them the names and they would arrange the appointments to get the letters. The women obviously had to be seen by a doctor, get blood work done, get appropriate counseling, etcetera, etcetera. I know our office had to get everything arranged to have that done.

Once abortion was legalized, a clinic was established in Springfield which did 90-plus percent of the pregnancy terminations in the community. We weren't doing a lot of abortions in my practice and the only ones that I can recollect doing [in Northampton] were women being sterilized at the same time. These tended to be older women who had had several children, who had had a contraceptive failure or whatever. Those were the ones I remember that we did—the combination of the two procedures. We mostly performed what's called a suction D&C. I think initially we did the standard D&C, then the transition occurred probably during my first year or second year here. Eventually they were almost all done by suction D&C. Back then in the Seventies, the great majority had general anesthesia. Then eventually it was done under local.

Because it was legal medically [to do therapeutic abortions] the hospital basically cooperated. There was never a problem, except for staff not wanting to participate for religious reasons and they would always provide other staff. Other than that, the hospital never opposed it.

Some patients did go to New York for an abortion instead of going through our therapeutic abortion process. I think there were some patients who didn't want anyone to know. They were concerned about someone on the nursing staff telling a family relative, that sort of thing. This is still a small town in that sense. In New York, where it was legal before here, there were known clinics, especially for later terminations. So if there was ever an issue, even with my own private patients, I would send them to New York. I knew people, colleagues that I had trained with. If this is what people wanted, I don't remember where there was great difficulty.

I was approached by Leslie Laurie and the Family Planning Council of Western Massachusetts to become Medical Director there. I think, initially, the medical community was frightened of the Council. I don't think it was viewed as competition by any means, but, in a sense, they just didn't know the record of these people. They weren't violently opposed to it, nothing like that—I don't want to give you that impression—but they weren't supportive of it initially. It was more of not really knowing who these people were, not knowing if they were qualified and feeling that family planning is still a medical issue. That was then of course. Since then they have been supportive. Leslie brought together this outstanding group of women to work there. Really amazing. I would deal mostly with the Head Nurse Coordinator and basically we would discuss protocols and that sort of thing. I was really impressed with the talent. It was really an outstanding group, and it is still an outstanding group. It developed quickly and expanded into many other things other than family planning—drugs and AIDS counseling and care, issues of sex education in the schools, and all sorts of other issues.

We never did abortions at the Family Planning Council. That may have been for a lot of reasons, including recruiting physicians to do it. But with the availability of the clinic in Springfield and other clinics, I don't think it was ever an issue. Dr. Booker was in Springfield and he was very much involved. Dr. Bettigol was very involved with the Springfield group, which was a huge group of doctors.[3] They did the terminations.

As far as contraception goes, my practice actually became the gynecological consultants for Smith College. So if any woman had a gynecological problem, they would see us. In those days Smith had an infirmary where they saw inpatients and sometimes we saw patients there. There was a black woman, Dr. Vera Josephs, who was the head of the Health Services, a wonderful physician. Students were asking for contraception and she was concerned that if we saw them in the clinic there at Smith it would be on their medical record. And she was concerned about if someone ever saw the medical record or somehow the parents were ever to see the record. So she had this two record system that she established. A record system where just areas pertaining to contraception were written down, and then the regular record covering other medical problems. In 1970, that was fairly courageous. Ultimately Mount Holyoke College followed and we became their GYN consultants. With Dr. Gage at UMass, it wasn't an issue at all—it was just right on the same standard medical record. I'm not sure if that was because one is a private as opposed to a public institution, but they were encouraging students to have the choice of contraception. It seems so strange. The evolution of this is amazing.

Cultural Issues

There is also a cultural resistance here, bizarre as it sounds, even though it's the Valley. I mean there was a chapter of the John Birch Society here then. The descendants of the early immigrant populations in the Valley are Irish, Polish, and French. And then there are the newcomers—those who have moved from Boston or New York. But otherwise, the old Yankee group predominates. It is an interesting mix. Probably the great majority are Catholic. I know when I first came I discussed trying to bring sex education into the high school. They looked at me like I was from Mars or something! But eventually the high schools, I guess it was through the state, insisted that they have some sort of health criteria. But you know sex education was a real "town and gown" issue, and it was reflective of the times, but no more so than in any other community.

You know what was interesting about this area, too, was Catholic women who would have some qualms about sterilization. Some patients said, "I just can't do this because of the Church." When patients voiced this concern to me, I would say, well speak to your priest. There were some who absolutely condemned it, and there were no priests in the community who would ever say, "It's okay, go ahead," but some priests would just say, "It's up to your conscience, it's your choice," basically allowing the patient to make the choice. These tended to be older women who had several children, that sort of thing. Some of them had severe medical problems and pregnancies that were medically contra-indicated. I was surprised to see what was not absolute support but not condemnation either—basically allowing the patient to make the choice.

And you know, except for a very, very, very small group, Catholics practice contraception, but in private. In fact, even more than some other religious groups. And we never had any [legal] problem, we always discussed this with patients, and pills or diaphragms or whatever were prescribed. I don't recollect any problem. As far as that was concerned, the medical community never had an issue with contraception or sterilization.

Reflections on Abortion

I really didn't know anything, or virtually anything, about abortion until I was exposed to all this. There was some exposure certainly as a medical student, but not that much. In medical school, everybody is trained to complete abortions because 10 to 15 percent of all pregnancies end in miscarriage or spontaneous abortion. I think as far as training with regard to therapeutic abortions, that has probably changed considerably. I'm sure the number of trained people skilled in this has probably diminished. I don't know the statistics, but you read about some Midwestern states where there is only one individual capable of doing this—not just for political and other reasons but for reasons of skill—for hundreds of miles. That's a problem.

The generations of OB-GYN residents after 1970 have not been exposed to the results of these illegal abortions and they don't have the same reactions [to them]. As far as our own group practice, two of the six are observant Catholics and will not do terminations. But they will refer patients to other physicians. In a sense, I would say they are "pro-choice" in that they will not make any judgments, but offer the patient options. But they certainly would not participate in an abortion. They do sterilizations. That's not any problem. That's not so much an issue any more.

The difficulty is really with the second trimester abortions and eventually those were mostly done at Bay State [Hospital in Springfield]. Today, almost all of them are done for genetic indications—Down's Syndrome, that sort of thing. There are still some elective late-stage abortions, but not that many. You know, when you read about this whole issue of late-term abortion, you should know that those numbers are incredibly small and almost always for serious, serious malformations that are incompatible with life. Basically in the old, old, old days if there was an intrauterine demise of the fetus, patients tended to wait until they went into labor. But that waiting carried certain risks of coagulation problems and all sorts of things.

I have also seen abuses of abortion—and that disturbs an obstetrician-gynecologist terribly. You'll see, very rarely thank God, young women who repeat and repeat and repeat and have a second and a third first trimester abortion in spite of counseling. That's disturbing to a practitioner. But it is incredibly rare. There have also been groups of lay people in the Valley trying to do these things themselves—women doing "menstrual extractions." There was a movement where they said: Why go through your menstrual period, why spend anywhere from three to seven days when you can just do this extraction? And these people were doing it! Again it was small numbers. Anyway, we would see complications from that—mostly infections. But somehow the word spread that this was not a wise thing to do and it seemed to have stopped fairly quickly.[4]

And then there were groups of women doing self-exams and exploring themselves and how to do pap smears and cultures, etcetera. This was very common in the Seventies. The doctors that I knew in our group helped participate in some clinics. I know there was a clinic in Florence one of my colleagues and I went to, but that faded because of the availability of Family Planning and, and also I think, the fact that OB-GYN had changed, especially in going from a male-dominated specialty to what essentially will be a female-dominated specialty. The great majority of residents in most programs now are women. When I was a resident there were no women in my program. And now it is almost all women. That makes a change, especially in terms of women bringing up certain issues to practitioners.

This is my take on this whole evangelical focus on the decline of family life and morality: these pro-life groups truly don't see the whole picture—the number of single parents or the fact that both parents have to work today. And I think that if the same forces that oppose abortion didn't oppose contraception, the incidence of abortion could drop dramatically. Even the need for it. Those who are mostly opposed to the so-called Morning After Pill are pretty much the same groups that oppose "choice." It is mind boggling, because that in itself would cut down the number of unwanted pregnancies. Just standard means of contraception, education, sex education in the schools—these all seem to be opposed by these groups. And you just can't legislate against that.

Western Europe must laugh at us about this, about groups actually opposing a Morning After Pill. Here you have methods of truly reducing the rate or the need for abortion, but the pro-life groups want, somehow, to legislate sexuality. I think that's the issue. It's just part of our whole political way. Not providing funding for family planning groups, even internationally, is just shocking to me. And then there's the threat on certain obstetrician's lives including a couple of murders. That's a new phenomenon. Throughout all those years when I saw all those criminal and illegal abortions, I never heard of anyone attacking one of the illegal abortionists, and now when you have somebody doing something legally . . . it's just amazing. I think these pro-life groups should really support education, certainly sex education, that sort of thing, not prevent movements that allow the use of something like the Morning After Pill.

When I first heard about the Roe decision, I don't remember celebrating or anything like that, just that sense of relief that, hopefully, we're not going to see these terrible problems or at least see less of them. It really did have an effect. When I really think back about what these women were subjected to . . . [I can't imagine what it would it be like] to have to return to some of those things.

Within the whole reproductive freedom movement, certainly the issue of abortion is a main issue. But I think—I know it sounds corny—with all the new technology, you can basically eliminate the need for abortion, for all but an extremely small number, with education and with birth control methods and better technology. And ultimately the whole issue now with RU–486 and the ability to do abortion—certainly in the first trimester, where it doesn't require hospitalization or even going to a clinic—becomes a truly private issue of a patient's choice. If a woman does not wish to have a pregnancy, she'll do anything and ultimately will resort to those methods that my generation was exposed to. I really, truly feel that will happen if we don't continue to have legalized abortion.

NINE

Dr. Robert Gage

Dr. Robert Gage, M.D., graduated in 1938 from Massachusetts State College, now the University of Massachusetts (UMass) at Amherst. He received his M.D. from Harvard Medical School in 1942 and after nearly 15 years in private practice in Pennsylvania and Massachusetts, became the director of the University Health Services (UHS) at UMass from 1960 to 1971. He oversaw the growth of UHS from a tiny operation in an old horse building into one of the country's premier college health facilities, serving over 29,000 students as well as faculty and staff. He left UHS to become Vice Chancellor for Student Affairs at UMass from 1971 to 1976, and then Chair of the Department of Public Health from 1976 until his retirement in 1986. He is the recipient of the Chancellor's Medal, the highest honor that UMass bestows.

Dr. Robert Gage was interviewed by David Cline on February 19, 2002.

A Commitment to Student Health

I graduated from Harvard Medical School in 1942, and after a time in the service, my wife and I settled in a very rural community in northern Pennsylvania. We were there for eight-and-a-half years. I was the sole physician in that area. We then moved to Amherst in 1954, where I was in private-family practice medicine until 1960. I already had a connection to Amherst in that I was a 1938 graduate of UMass.

In my practice in Amherst I saw many students, since the health service at UMass was not especially student friendly and people stayed away from the health center in droves. They went anywhere else they could. I also saw some of the house-mothers in the women's residences. So I became interested in what I saw as the students' problems, which were, of course, mainly acute medical problems. But I had also fitted diaphragms in the office here in Amherst. Matter of fact, I remember one student in particular who came in and who has been a supporter ever since. She and her boyfriend were a devoted couple and they are still together and they still live in Amherst. And she said later that she was so grateful because she knew that I was sticking my neck out in terms of the legal framework in Massachusetts.

There was a physician on campus, but—and I want to be as charitable as possible—he was weary of the job. When he left, his parting shot was, "I hope I never see another aspirin in my life." He had been the physician, incidentally, when I was in school there. In September 1960, I made a move to [become the Director of] the Health Services at UMass, where a recommendation had been made to begin better service based upon a mandatory student health fee. In that first year, there was one other full-time physician besides myself and another half-time person and a handful of nurses.

Spreading the Word

Soon after I began, one of the housemothers wanted to know if I would meet with the members of her dormitory. That was a made-to-order opportunity because what I had to do first was build a constituency for the Health Services. The university, by the way, was just beginning to grow at that time and the trustees had made a commitment to increase the student body by a thousand students every year for ten years. That's an enormous amount of growth. So, it was a great time to begin. And we began a series of meetings in the residence halls, which, as I said, was a made-to-order opportunity to lay myself open and build a constituency.

These meetings were expected to last an hour or so. It was not long before the women became a little bolder in the questions they asked. And it became very clear that a lot of the questions they had, as do all young people in their late teens, were about their sexuality. They were having new adventures and they were uncertain about this. And although I was a man they seemed to be quite open and free in their questions. Obviously, I tried to present things factually, nonjudgmentally, which was crucial. And soon these evening sessions went for three hours—not one but three.

I was having two or even three of these sessions a week. When you add that to a busy day, that was a backbreaker. My wife Peg and the children, incidentally, paid a heavy price for all this, because these were long days and long nights. But it was important. And the clientele grew. It was not long before word got around, and we had more people come to the Health Services.

We had been just in the women's dorms, and eventually the men got in on the act and we got involved in the men's dorms too. Oh, they got interesting. Now, the thrust of their interests was a little more earthy, but essentially there was a coincidence of interests.

The challenge in that first year was to meet students and have them recognize and accept the change in the way things were running at Health Services. We were almost overcome with our own success for a while, until we could amass enough staff. When you go from less than one clinic encounter per student per academic year on average to four or four-and-a-half, that's a sea change in terms of human resources.

Part of the whole thing, which isn't related to women specifically, was a vast and not easy reorientation of the nurses. They had been running the show with this one physician and he had let them do what they wanted. They were protective and they were judgmental. They had to change this idea of, "it's raining outside, what are you doing without your boots on?" Students had had enough of that sort of *in loco parentis* business. So the staff was convinced that they were all going to be fired when I went to UMass, but I laid down some no-nos and some guidelines for them, and it turned out, once they got calmed down, that we got along well. But the attitudinal change toward students was what was crucial.

Offering Birth Control: "Something Had to be Done"

There was no overt action that first year toward offering contraception services. In the first place, the facilities didn't admit of privacy. The only place to examine people was a small room in which we'd bring in three or four women. You could hear what was going on behind these little sheet partition cubicles. And you'd get some men in with some women. It was rather primitive. With a room like that with five other people, and they can all hear, you can't talk with the person just because they're behind a curtain. And there was no place where you could be private and examine somebody to fit a diaphragm. But in 1961 we moved the Health Services from the old horse barns to the new Health Center. Then we had a lot of examining rooms, places where we could talk with somebody, examine them and, to be blunt, fit diaphragms. I don't remember how much we did the first year there, but that was the way we started.

One of the crucial things that made this work was that the other full-time physician left at the end of my first year. And [because our operations were expanding so rapidly], I had the glorious opportunity to bring in and appoint a new physician every year for the next eight years. Clearly, that was crucial to the whole ethos of the thing. We were not interested in some retired navy captain who wanted to have a part-time job. They had to believe in [what we were doing]. We made a conscious effort to get primarily young physicians. The first two or three were right out of internship or right out of residency. And we did bring in some relatively young people, perhaps in their forties, who had been in private practice a while.

It was not long before the word got around, and we had quite a clientele for birth control. It became a substantial part of the business, because that's what people were interested in. But the demand increased so much that by 1963, we realized something had to be done to provide birth control in a more systematic way. One thing on which I agreed with the other physicians was that if, for example, somebody was Catholic or had an ethical or moral objection that was fine, they were not going to be forced to fit diaphragms.

In 1964, a young woman from Orchard Hill dormitories came back from Christmas vacation and appeared on our doorstep and said "I think I'm pregnant." And so I said, that's good, I guess, if that's what you want. She said that the head of residence up there wasn't too happy with it and Helen Curtis, the Dean of Women, wanted her to go home. Helen Curtis was a very stout supporter of resources for women and a wonderful old political liberal, but she did have some blinders on. One of them was that a woman who becomes pregnant doesn't belong on campus. She felt we should be presenting role models that are good examples for women, not tolerating these unfortunate deviations. This young woman said, "I don't want to go home. My parents are hostile to this. I'll lose a semester. No reason I can't study. I don't want to go home." So, we went to bat on that and she stayed.

About that time, we had a Health Educator, Bill Darity, who was, I think, the first black Ph.D. at the University of North Carolina. We had arranged a joint appointment for him between the Health Services and the Department of Public Health. He was very much interested in community health education, which meant, as he interpreted it, putting education into the hands of the community and, getting them involved in creating a community health education program. And he had a graduate student, Jane Zapka, who was interested in community health education. Bill Darity, Jane Zapka, and I quickly devised a quick and dirty research project, a survey of the attitudes of women on that student's floor toward somebody being pregnant. There were two women's and two men's dorms in the Orchard then, so we could take that floor [with the pregnant woman] and we could compare it to a matching floor in another dorm. What we wanted to find out was the students' attitudes toward her and their attitudes toward being more cautious about taking precautions. It was published, but it wasn't any earth-shaking thing. We found out the students were very understanding—only a very small number wanted her to get out—and there was very little difference over the course of that semester between that corridor where they had a live pregnant woman, and the matching one—which was gratifying. We could tell Helen Curtis that this person had not corrupted the morals of the group. Helen took defeat graciously. We're still good friends.

So that was the beginning, a tangible beginning, of health education programs on campus. We took to the students our plan to have a full-time health educator on the staff and they supported it by voting to increase the fee enough. Jane Zapka then became our full-time health educator, and she became crucial in the contraceptive education program. Let me be candid about something: physicians are good at what they do, if they are, but they can't do everything. And I'll say it bluntly: they haven't been prepared for teaching and they are not good health educators. They haven't thought in those terms. So Jane helped us.

The Family Planning Clinic

Contraceptive health had begun to take up a disproportionate amount of time. I wouldn't say it was a nuisance, but there was just too much of that one thing. We thought there ought to be a better way to do it. We realized we had to create a program to separate out the education component of family planning from any medical advice. Fitting diaphragms and prescribing birth control pills were a physician's job and could be separated from the other—saving the physician time in the interest of doing the education better. That was the crucial thing. So we set up a system whereby students would sign up for a family planning clinic. And they accepted this. There were no secrets about this, but we did it discretely. It wasn't done in the middle of the waiting room. Students had to go into this group family planning education session before, for example, they could be fitted for a diaphragm. There was also demand for the Pill but, as with any new drug, we felt there were unanswered questions. We had to be aware of the risks. That was part of the health education business. I think we used birth control pills, but we were very careful with them. In other words, the Pill wasn't a sudden panacea.

The education sessions would be done in small groups, eight or ten, and we'd have frank discussions of the issues. Then students could make an appointment with a physician. The physicians would be assured we wouldn't have to spend a lot of time on this preliminary business about rhythm and when you're fertile, and so forth. That would be dealt with on an educational basis. That took a lot of burden off the physician's backs and, equally importantly, improved the program. But some of the physicians resented the change. Physicians are interesting people. They imagine they can do most anything, and the community sort of reinforces that—"oh, you're Dr. So-and so, yeah, you must know about this and that." So, it was interesting.

Birth control was not legal for unmarried women. So we were treading on pretty thin ice. Matter of fact, you wondered if there was any ice there at all. Massachusetts, which is very liberal on political issues, is a little cautious on social issues. And here we are at a state college. What are we going to do? So I felt that President Lederle or the Dean of Students at least ought to know what was going on. But Bill Field, then the Dean of Students, to whom I reported at that time, talked with President John Lederle about it. He came back and his words were: "John said, that if Bob Gage says it's all right, it's all right with me." That was the blessing I needed; he was at least going to look the other way and let me do what I wanted to. And the staff talked about it together and we agreed that nobody would be cajoled into doing this. Everybody who did it, did it voluntarily. We all knew the risks. We could each make our own assessment of the risk and whether this was something we wanted to do as an individual.

We were off and running. It settled into a good program, and it was widely accepted. There were no secrets about it, but we didn't advertise it in the paper or anything like that. We felt we had to treat young people as adults who were able to make their own decisions. We assumed that what we did with them was between us. I was aware that something might happen but I didn't stay awake at night worrying about it. We took a chance that something would go awry, but we were fortunate and didn't have any major problems. I do remember one telephone call I had over a holiday, Thanksgiving or something. A mother called up and said, "My daughter brought home some medicine. What is it?" And my response was, well, why don't you ask her? It wasn't what she wanted to hear but that's what I wanted to tell her.

So that's the way the women's program, from a Health Center point of view, evolved. I became president of the College Health Association a few years after that, and we had a lot of contact with [other campus health centers]. However, I have to be candid, and point out that we and the University of Nebraska and the University of Colorado probably were ahead of the pack in health education in having formal, generalized, supported, acknowledged, out-in-the-open family planning programs. This College Health Association was a great experience for me, because I was immediately drawn out of this parochial little program here and saw the world as it was outside. And I think we can say modestly that we became one of the top half-dozen college health programs in the country.

Drawing the Line at Abortion

Contraception did sometimes fail. My recollection is we did not meddle with the matter of abortion. To be very blunt, the risk for that was too high. We could not, under any circumstance, do something here at the university. It would have been totally unsafe. We didn't have an anesthesiologist. We were not equipped with staff or equipment. Even if it had been legal, it would have been medically irresponsible. And we realized that. And nobody was going to do anything under the table. We all understood that. We were in fear. And since it wasn't legal, there was no referral service system. I did know somebody in New York City who performed abortions, but I don't remember referring students there. As I recall, our position had to be: it's very unfortunate, but there is nothing we can do. We are a state institution. We can defend contraception, unequivocally, but abortion is going a little too far. I think I was aware of the Clergy Consultation Service, but I never had any interaction with it as I recall, except on an individual basis. And see, the whole abortion business, came after I was out of the Health Services. I was Vice Chancellor then.

There were social strictures, too [against abortion]; not just the law but the public support of the law was too great. I don't remember any vast heavyweight women's movement that would come and negotiate with us, and say we want you to refer for abortions. I didn't know anybody around here who did them. Well, there had been people who did them quietly, but they weren't about to take on more. They weren't the sort of people I would trust for a program.

Now obviously there were failures outside of our system; people who hadn't bothered to come in. We had a baby born in the middle of the night outside in the rhododendron garden. It received no prenatal care. This big football player came in carrying this little baby, saying, "Quick, take it, I don't wanna drop it." We had another student who came down to the Health Services and had to go over to the hospital immediately. Of course, she barely got there before she delivered. I had to call her mother in the middle of the night and say, "I have interesting news for you. Your daughter just had a baby." She said: "What? How'd that happen?" Well, the usual way. This was in the late spring, and she said, "You know, when she was home for Christmas I wondered about that." This is so vivid in my recollection. I said, didn't you ask her about it. And she said: "Well, you know, there are some things you don't talk to your daughter about." And I thought, My God, what else do people talk about? It makes the tears come to think about that. What could be more crucial than an understanding between a mother and her daughter? That underlines why we had to be useful, because we couldn't count on parents. We realized there were these barricades between students and parents.

I became Vice Chancellor of Student Affairs after that, from 1971 to 1976. That was a backbreaker of a job, because of the incredible range of issues and the meagerness of the resources back then. And then I took a sabbatical year off and went to Harvard School of Public Health and got a degree there. Then I came back on campus and taught public health until I retired in 1985.

When I started at Health Services, we had a cook—a wonderful Polish woman the students used to call "the fat cook"—an assistant cook, half a dozen nurses, and a housekeeper. And we ended up with 14 physicians and a staff of 150. It was a great opportunity and it was an interesting time, a dynamic time in the sense of being filled with change—socially and medically. I think we stayed ahead of the curve pretty well. I would say we got into the business of women's health care by the backdoor but legitimately. As far as I know, the university was never put under any duress for anything that we did. I think part of that was because we did it with discretion. We did it openly but not blatantly. We didn't have a neon sign up there saying: "Contraceptives!" People could acknowledge it or turn their head aside on campus, however they wanted. It turned out to be successful. It was a very interesting segment of my life. And I think in a way, aside from our family, it may be the most important thing I did.

TEN

Dr. Jane Zapka

Dr. Jane Zapka, D.S., grew up in the Pioneer Valley in the town of Hadley. She graduated from Skidmore College, received her Master of Science degree in Public Health and Community Health Education at the University of Massachusetts at Amherst (UMass), and her Doctor of Science in Health Administration from the Harvard University School of Public Health. She served as University Health Services' Public Health Educator for 11 years. After many years working at the UMass Medical School in Worcester she is now Professor of Biostatistics, Bioinformatics, and Epidemiology at the Medical University of South Carolina in Charleston. Dr. Zapka's expertise is in primary care and prevention services, with a focus on program evaluation, quality improvement, managed care and other health services research areas. She has participated in community-based projects, involving provider, patient, and public education for improving quality of, and partici- pation in, breast, cervical, and colorectal cancer screening. She is currently involved in studies of quality of care at the end-of-life, policy analysis of state tobacco legislation and lifestyle interventions in the workplace to reduce obesity.

Dr. Jane Zapka was interviewed by David Cline on April 6, 2002.

A Commitment to Sex Education in Public Health

I was in the Public Health program at the University of Massachusetts in 1967 and 1968. It was a pretty small operation in those days. I was working on my Master's degree in Health Education with Dr. Bill Darity, Chair of the Public Health degree program, and was a teaching assistant. Master's degree candidates were encouraged to do field projects and I ended up doing mine at University Health Services with Dr. Bob Gage who had an affiliation with the School of Public Health.[1] Later, I joined the staff at Health Services as the first Health Educator. Both doctors, Darity and Gage, were committed to social programs and quality services. I did my student field training in 1968 and I took the staff position in 1969. I was there 11 years. My whole life became college health—I was just so embroiled in college health. You choose your passions where you can make a change, and I was very active in the national setting, very invested in the American College Health Association and in moving their agenda [forward]. Given my conservative background, I was more comfortable doing that than being a more vocal fighter. But I was always very comfortable in the milieu of college health. That was what consumed me and my associates.[2]

Dr. Bob Gage had to fight very hard to create the Community Health Educator position for me at Health Services. I started there doing some very basic health education work. I know that some of the clinicians were dead set against it, but when Bob gets an idea there is no stopping him. Of course, most people didn't know what health education meant except that, "Gee, this person was taking up a third of a physician's salary and what was she doing here?" But Bob was very progressive; he was way ahead of his time. He was convinced that the Health Services was not there just to sew people up and take care of their infections, but that the Health Services had a broader mission that included dealing with what we called "the crazy behavior": alcohol, drugs, sex—often together. Some of what we did was pretty traditional health education, like making sure we had information for students about various things such as vaginitis or smoking or whatever. But Bob Gage's vision was to foster more *outreach* into the community, not just do "patient education," and get students involved in building a good health service and in promoting their own health.

My job was to work within the university's residential system. In fact, I still run into alums on the street who were Heads of Residence back then and they'll shout, "Hey, I remember you!" I remember what it was like in a dormitory in 1969 or 1970, when the concept of housemother was still alive and well. We certainly helped the physicians when they needed educational materials, but it was more community focused. And I would say it was pretty clear pretty quickly that a lot of the emphasis was going to be related to issues of human sexuality.

Taking Risks for "Natural Business"

We would be invited to a group in the dormitories or in a sorority or, more rarely, a class, to talk about birth control. However, the [real] agenda was to talk about *responsible* birth control and what it meant. We were really trying to get people to look at their behavior in a social and personal context. Bob was so committed to it and it just seemed like sort of natural business. My staff and I really never viewed it as doing something illegal or even actually innovative. But we did make a joke that Jane had "the brown bag" of contraceptives, which were illegal. And Bob would make sure we had them. Did I feel I was taking a personal risk? I suppose part of it was naiveté, but it just seemed so logical to me. Here was this very charismatic, committed physician who was essentially the one who took the big risk.

We went through the birth control methods and inevitably, we would also get to talking about abortion issues. At that time, these college women were going to England and they were going to Canada for abortions. It was that reality that made us committed to making sure they were making good decisions, really thinking about what they were doing sexually, and making sure they were protected if they did it. Because the other part of it—[pregnancy]—was so real for these very desperate women. That reality made you more committed to looking at what we can do to ourselves when we don't think about sex consciously and plan for it. I was not a [problem pregnancy] counselor, but fortunately, we could use the Clergy Consultation Service.

You know, when I say I'm not a counselor, I think there's a gray area between education and counseling. And, of course, we tried our best to know who really needed more in-depth work and get [them] moved on but, you know, a lot of kids have just normal questions and dilemmas and craziness. But [for referrals for abortion counseling], I really think that CCS was *the* route. They were so valuable because they were performing a service that no one else could perform.

Elaine Fraser had been like a one-women personification of CCS. I knew who Reverend Unsworth was, but I didn't know him—it was Elaine I worked with. We were friendly and we each knew what the other was doing. She would sometimes tell people to contact me to make sure I got something going in the sorority or the dormitory, and of course she was always on our list of referrals and contacts. There was such mutual respect between us, though I always viewed her as far more necessary than I was. A lot of people could have done my job but I think very few people could have done hers. Everyone was *so* grateful for her being the kind of person that she was! Because clinicians were at a loss at the end of the day. She was, like I said, *it* personified.

Getting Organized: Creating the Family Planning "Clinic"

Some of the [UMass] doctors were prescribing birth control before 1968 in a very unorganized way. While there was no public acknowledgement of a clinic, yes, the Health Services was there to help educate and help students understand their behavior and what they wanted to do [in matters of birth control]. It was the place where they could get the help they needed. But in the early days it was piecemeal—I think that was part of Bob's frustration—if you happened to end up with the right doc, you might get the help you needed. Eventually we had to ask, what is the party line?

What are we going to tell students? How do we get out there in a systematic way? How do we make the access clear?

Change came because of Bob Gage pushing but I think the university was behind him. I think they were grateful that birth control came under the broad aegis of the University Health Services.

It was then Bob's job and [Chief of Medicine] Tom [McCabe's] job to work out a more organized system for birth control services. There was a lot of change for the staff then, too. The pharmacy staff had to be trained in such a way that when a woman came with a prescription for birth control, confidentiality would be respected. If any physician was uncomfortable with the birth control service, it was his or her right [not to participate]. We made sure it was organized enough that those clinicians who wanted to be involved were, and those who didn't want to be involved, were not. We felt that once a woman made the decision to use birth control, she shouldn't get hassled at the point of service. Before Bob got things organized, the luck of the draw wasn't always lucky.[3] Interestingly, the physicians who signed on and were willing to provide birth control were all male physicians. Neither one of the two women [physicians] participated.

Staff in my division helped educate students on what to consider when they made their birth control decisions, and instructed them on how to use the Health Services. We went through another phase where we had a formal education session at the Health Services prior to the medical appointment. If a woman wanted to get a diaphragm, she had to go to the educational session first. My staff facilitated those group sessions. The student would come to a session—I think they were on Wednesdays at 4 p.m.—and it took an hour. She then had [to fill out] the infamous pink sheet—(God knows why we chose pink!)—and then could proceed with making an appointment with a doctor.

Most women, once they got to the session, were perfectly happy and perfectly comfortable, but other women had a little attitude. It was perceived by some as an embarrassment, as a hassle. But that was okay—you know, some of them knew a lot. And some thought they knew more than we did! I think the physicians felt more confident about our sessions, particularly once they observed that we were giving correct and accurate information. They knew the decision [to use birth control] was actually informed, the choices were there.

Pregnancy Tests and Counseling

Bob made it a mission to have good gender representation, and so an increasing number of women joined the mental health staff. There were only two female physicians but there were more females on the mental health staff. The "front" of the educational program was made up of women. Elaine Fraser, who had come on to the UHS mental health staff, would go out a lot; I would go out a lot. And then I hired another part-time nurse, Anne Gross, to do a lot of the education work. She was a nurse practitioner and then came on half-time with my staff. She was a nice bridge between the community work and the clinician's work. When Elaine Fraser shifted over from CCS, pregnancy and abortion counseling was the main focus of her work. It was natural—everyone knew her, everyone worked with her. She was very well respected as an excellent counselor.

Of course, the first step in pregnancy and abortion counseling was just getting a pregnancy test done. That was sometimes a hassle—getting courteous, sensitive pregnancy testing could be as much of a hassle as getting sensitive, courteous contraception service. We had worked it out that CCS could refer clients to us for pregnancy testing. Of course many of the tests were negative, so the follow-up counseling and education was very important.

The women were often referred for counseling only to get them through this scare they had had. But the take home message was: look, if you don't want to have the scare, let's look at what you're doing. They were urged to get involved in one of the educational programs. Part of my educators' talks included a discussion of how to access services. I would also work with the heads of residences. And I would spend a lot of time preparing materials for the residence hall counselors who became the network for referrals to the right place.

I was personally out of the abortion loop, in many respects, but I would certainly hear about some of the problem cases. Some of the kids had a lot of trouble with money. But the fascinating thing is they usually got it all together. And I know a lot of time was spent—because I remember Elaine talking about this a great deal—over the important role parents ended up taking with a lot of these college women. Part of the problem for many women was the awesome fear of letting their parents know about their situation. Elaine said that it was very rewarding to see that the students often found that it worked out better than they thought it would.

Peer Counseling: Taking Health Education into the Dorms

After a few years, we got a grant for the Peer Sex Education program. It was actually one of the very few federal Title X grants that was funded in sex education. We used to call it "Nixon's Token Sex-Ed Grant." (If he knew what we were doing he would have taken our money back!) I don't know how it happened, but I wrote the grant and we got it. Amazing!!! I think that Peer Sex Education was perceived as something new. It was essentially designed to give a good curriculum in sex education to college students and promote responsible decision making. Initially, I ran the curriculum, did the training and the supervision. Most of the participating students were women. They were the ones who would then be in the dorms, living in the dorms, and doing the real hands on counseling stuff at one o'clock [in the morning]. It was tough [to give them the responsibility for that] because we were still responsible for them. What they did reflected on the Health Services. And that wasn't always easy because people have all kinds of motivations for getting involved. Bob and one of the clinical psychologists helped. We made it very clear we weren't training counselors at the undergraduate level; we were training educators. But there's a fine line there.

I wouldn't call [our approach] rigid, but it was fairly conservative because we had a public responsibility. Public Health school curricula were still not very progressive then. There were major universities that would never think of having a course in sex education unless it was in the PE [Physical Education] department. When we got the federal grant to do Peer Sex Education (PSE), Bill Darity made it happen that the students could get academic credit for this course. That was great because we wanted it made clear: "If you want to do the course it's not going to be casual." It was a three-credit course—they had tests, exams, papers, the whole business. Bill made sure that it was academically viable.

The administration hired another fellow, Ron LaFrance, maybe a year or two after me to deal with the drug issue that was just really flourishing at that time. I was far too conservative and straight-laced [to deal with it], but Ron LaFrance was into that scene and that culture and he had the experience, sensitivity, and philosophy to deal with it. The two of us had a real outreach focus and we set up the programs. Peer education really took off over the drug issue—because *nobody* knew how to deal with it and no one was going to believe a doctor or a mental health staff person talking to them about it. The peer drug counselors came a little bit later. By then our students actually set the stage for [programs in] campuses around the country.

UHS then hired another health educator, Ron Mazer. This was really important for the program because we needed to start getting guys [and not just girls] into this discussion. Ron was actually a Unitarian minister and he was great at it. One of his most popular talks was "Sex with Ethyl," meaning ethanol or alcohol. He would often get invited to the Greek houses. He had a way about him to just go into those fraternities and say, "Okay guys, you know there's reasonable behavior we've got to start thinking about." Most health educators in the field were then and still are women, so we made fun that he was our "token male."

As we grew, we became known as the Division of Community Health Education. There were also the Divisions of Medicine, Mental Health, and Environmental Health. Dr. Gage had a responsibility for that as well. We were the youngest and the newest. Later on we got more diversified and would do stress management, physical fitness, and the whole bit. But it really all started out because of the interest in issues of sexuality and birth control.

Going National

Dr. Gage became very big in the American College Health Association. He indeed became its president and raised hell in that organization. At the national level, he made sure that issues like sexual health were on the agenda. I can remember my first year at one of those meetings when he almost got into a fistfight with other college health services directors over the Vietnam War. He was just incredible. He really shook things up.

With people like Bob Gage and Tom McBride—the Chief of Medicine then—the UMass had a tremendous, tremendous national impact on college health. Dr. McBride in his calm, quiet way, would say, "This is just what we have to do." They would go together to national meetings of the American College Health Association and encourage people to hire [educators] like me. And it was really rewarding to then see our star PSE people being invited to other universities to train people [and explain]: "And this is how we got started and this is what we do." The College Health Association had no health education unit when it started, but now it has one of the biggest. They [realized that] one of the most important roles of college health services is health education. Some of our peer educators went on to be leaders in the health education profession. When I look back on that time, I certainly didn't think I was having that kind of impact. But we really made a difference!

And that was fun—to see that college health was more than "runny noses and pregnancy tests." College health became a place where excellent physicians practice; it wasn't where old physicians went to retire. And Bob deserves enormous recognition for that.

Networks

There were [other important] people who were in the larger community. I can remember Ruth Fessenden was an effective advocate and leader and many of the Heads of Residence were involved in her Everywoman's Center. The Center started around the same time as our UHS department, and we were running in parallel paths, doing similar kinds of things. We were conscious and aware of each other—kind of on the same circuit—but they were referred to as "The Feminists," and we were "The Health Educators." Seems humorous today.

I can also remember Elaine [Fraser] in those days, and Merry Boone. Leslie Laurie was one of my keenest role models. Leslie was the primary community person with whom I had contact. I was on her first board when Western Massachusetts Family Planning got started. Of course, there was also [current State Representative] Ellen Story, who worked with Leslie. I still just marvel at her. I bring my students to the State House to meet with her.

We're Still Not There

I never felt it was an issue of whether I viewed myself as a feminist or not. I just did what I thought was important to do. I was raised very, very conservatively, and

I'm sure my father was looking down on me—if he ever knew what I was doing! But it just seemed so logical to me that I never got the feeling that I was making a decision. It was just what I should do.

Today, I think there is much more openness about contraception, for which I'm grateful. But this whole notion of sexuality and alcohol just still continues to blow my mind. I mean the recent data on binge drinking and women? I just want to take them and shake them! Another concern I have is the unwillingness of medical clerkships and residency training in OB-GYN to deal with the abortion issue. No one [at my hospital] wanted to answer my question when I asked, "What do we do here?" with respect to giving physicians-in-training exposure or training in abortions. The answer, finally, was "Nothing."

I'm in my fifties, and I must say I'm disappointed that we're still where we are. It astounds me that we're still fighting. I was reminded of it again when my colleague from Harvard called me for a Kaiser Foundation study on the medical effectiveness of abortions done by physician assistants.[4] They were going to do the usual reviews of medical records. They had two clinics, one in New Hampshire and one in Vermont. One clinic is staffed by physicians; the other clinic is staffed by physician assistants. I was helping to design a survey and analyze the women's reactions to the process and their satisfaction with the medical care follow-up. It was a reminder of how hard it still is for some women to have an abortion. I would say that at least 70 percent of the New Hampshire clients were women from Massachusetts. I think they still want the anonymity. In fact, those who had covered benefits would not use the benefits. They're afraid that there's a lack of confidentiality. They go out of state and pay for it out of pocket. It's not an accepted service. I recall telling my medical students, *you* go to that clinic in Vermont and *you* go to that clinic in New Hampshire, and you see how it feels to walk through that door past the protestors and the policeman with his gun. You see what that feels like. We're still not there.

ELEVEN

Dr. Lawrence Siddall

Dr. Lawrence Siddall, Ed.D., was born in Guangshou (formerly Canton), China in 1930. He received his undergraduate degree from Oberlin College, his Master's in Social Work from the University of Connecticut, and his Doctorate in Education from the University of Massachusetts at Amherst. After working at the Holyoke Mental Health Clinic beginning in 1962, he joined the Mental Health Staff of UMass's University Student Health Services in 1967 and worked there until 1978. While at UMass he coauthored two papers on the issue of pregnancy among female students. In 1978, Siddall took a position with the Valley Health Plan, Health Management Organization in Amherst, which in time was absorbed by Kaiser Permanente. He retired from Kaiser's mental health staff in 1996. His primary interest, in addition to coordinating the group therapy program, was doing couples therapy. Siddall did not rest quietly in retirement. He joined the Peace Corps and taught high school English in Poland from 1997 to 1999. Siddall now works as a volunteer docent at the Mount Holyoke College Art Museum and has been studying Spanish. He continues to travel extensively and has taken recent trips to Honduras, Guatemala, and Mexico. In September 2004, he visited China, including his birthplace in Guangzhou.

Dr. Lawrence Siddall was interviewed by David Cline on February 10, 2004.

UMass Mental Health Service

I came to the Mental Health Service at the University of Massachusetts in 1968 and worked there for 11 years. It was a department in the University Health Services. Young women who were pregnant were part of our patient population. Most were referred by the physicians in the Health Service, though some came to us on their own. How to help these students with unwanted pregnancies was a significant concern to me and others on our staff.

What we had to offer focused primarily on helping them clarify what they saw as the best solution to their problem. The two options were to carry the pregnancy to term or have an abortion. For those who wanted to have their baby, they had to decide whether they would drop out of school. Going home was not a happy prospect for many of them. Some wanted to stay in school as long as possible. For those who hoped to get an abortion, they faced a frustrating array of obstacles: it was expensive, few practitioners were known to us, and it was illegal.

We also provided an opportunity for the student to talk about the impact of the pregnancy on her emotionally. One contributing factor was her relationship with the putative father. If he was her boyfriend and they had a positive relationship, I offered to see them together if she wished. Couples therapy was one of my special interests, so I encouraged women to come in with their boyfriends. I remember seeing one couple in great distress. The unplanned pregnancy presented a major problem for them both and at first there was strong disagreement about what to do. There was eventually a positive outcome and my seeing them together proved much more beneficial than if I had just seen the student by herself.

Sometimes the father was someone the student wanted no further contact with. Her shame and anger about having gotten pregnant by this person were often the focus of our sessions. There was also a student's concern about whether to tell her family. Especially for younger women who were still closely involved with their families, becoming pregnant caused tremendous distress. I recall one student who tearfully wailed, "My parents will kill me if they find out." In some cases I offered to see students like her together with her parents, but this never occurred.

For students wishing to stay in the area and consider the option of giving their child up for adoption, we referred them to Children's Aid and Family Service in Northampton. For those who wanted to explore having an abortion, there were only a few practitioners that we knew about during my first couple years working there. We made referrals mostly in New England, but a few women on their own even went as far as Montreal, London, and Tokyo. When you stop to think of it, it was amazing the determination of these students to resolve this issue.

Working with the Clergy Consultation Service

I then became involved with the Clergy Consultation Service. I don't remember the year exactly, probably around 1970. I began attending their monthly meetings in the office of Richard Unsworth, who was the Protestant chaplain at Smith College in Northampton. I often wondered if the college administrators were aware of these meetings. The group was made up of five to eight Protestant ministers [and one rabbi]. I got to know those who regularly attended fairly well. Others came to the meetings only periodically. I was the mental health consultant for the group, which was developing an extensive network of practitioners willing to perform safe therapeutic abortions. My primary function was to help the clergy in their efforts to deal with the emotional and psychological problems that the women experienced in dealing with unwanted pregnancy. Women came to the group from all over the region—that included the area colleges and also older, married women. I made quite a few referrals myself. I never knew exactly how many women were seen by this group per month. I don't know if anyone kept track.

To be effective the group's work had to be clandestine. It certainly wasn't listed in the newspaper. The CCS definitely became an important resource for women here in the Pioneer Valley.

Our group was highly motivated to help these women and I don't think any of us felt that it made any sense for abortions to be illegal. For me there was no inner conflict about this issue. I think we all shared the belief that each woman should be free to decide this matter for herself. Here were these women in distress and there had to be a way around the legal obstacles.

It was rewarding being able to work with the members of the CCS and see their commitment to a social part of their profession. Dick Unsworth was very helpful in leading the group, of which there were many like it around the country. A lot of people would be surprised to know how many clergy were out there working on their behalf.

University Health Services

I recall that the atmosphere at the Health Services was one of being receptive to providing birth control to students. In my view it didn't make sense not to because it was part of comprehensive health care, and I think we let women know that contraceptives were available to them.

I coauthored two papers about pregnancy on campus, taking a look at why about 5 or 6 percent of women got pregnant even though they had access to birth control. It seemed to be one of life's constants.

I think in a lot of ways the Health Services was quite forward looking. Its director, Dr. Robert Gage, certainly was progressive in his policies, and he definitely set the tone for all of us. However, some of the physicians on his staff would not prescribe contraceptives. Nevertheless, if a student were assertive enough, she could get birth control.

My own awareness of the struggle women faced in resolving the issue of problem pregnancy didn't surface until I began working at UMass. I don't recall the specific moment of the *Roe v. Wade* decision, but I do remember the relief we felt for all the young women who no longer had to come through our doors. It was unfortunate that it didn't come sooner. But with this historic decision in 1973, suddenly the landscape changed. An interesting time!

Lorraine Florio

Lorraine Florio was born in Lowell, Massachusetts in 1932 and lived for many years in Lawrence, Massachusetts. She has one son and currently lives north of Boston. From approximately 1962–1967 she performed several thousand abortions, traveling as far away as Maine and Canada. In 1971, she was arrested in a drug sweep after narcotics agents saw her car being used on drug runs. Though she protested her innocence, she sought a plea bargain rather than face a jury who she feared would look at her as an immoral abortionist. She was sentenced to three years in prison and was paroled after one year. In the years since, she has worked in a factory, at a country club, and as a barmaid. She currently works as a bookkeeper.

Lorraine Florio was interviewed by David Cline on June 13, 2004.

The Making of an Abortionist

My name is Lorraine Florio. I'm presently 71 years old. I was born in Lowell, Massachusetts. My parents were French and Italian. I grew up middle class and graduated from a Catholic grammar school and a Catholic high school, and attended two years of business college. After that I worked part-time for a doctor for a number of years in the Lawrence area and traveled back and forth to Lowell. I got married. I had one son. My marriage was sort of an arranged type of situation. My husband was 40 years older than me and it wasn't a successful marriage. I left him, and as opposed to living by myself in an apartment with a young baby, I offered to live with my parents. So my activity was a bit controlled. It was good for my son to be in a family situation growing up and my parents were very good to him.

When I was about 14 years old, my best girlfriend Kathy became pregnant. Her parents were kind of a little bit uppity and they didn't want the disgrace. We're talking more than 50 years ago—a long time ago. But that was the attitude then. I was still very young—same age as her. They shipped her to St. Margaret's Convent in Boston and those nuns were very cruel. They had those girls that were pregnant washing floors in the eighth or ninth month of pregnancy. She said they never came near her until the baby popped out and its head hit the wall. No medical attention. No semblance of any kind of kindness extended to her. She had to give up the baby for adoption because her parents didn't want to take on a child that was, you know, born out of wedlock at the time. And it kind of disturbed her life—I'm still friends with her—she's been looking at faces all her life trying to see if she recognizes [her child]. It's been a tough road for this one girl. She made a successful marriage though. She married a politician in Lawrence, and they had two children.

When I worked for this doctor in Lawrence, I was a receptionist and took the patients' temperatures and answered the telephone. Those were the years where an older doctor visited patients in their homes. And this doctor here, Dr. St. Lawrence, was an old-time French doctor from Paris. He had his practice in Lawrence, Massachusetts.

I noticed that women would come in like three, four months pregnant and they were all having miscarriages. So I just approached him one day and said, "Geez, doctor, what's going on?" I mean, I wasn't that savvy, but I figured something was going on. He says, "Well there's a way of bringing on a miscarriage that will do minimal damage to a woman and help her with whatever problem that she has." So I became wide-eyed all the time—watching and listening. And he shared how it was done and what precautions I should take. He didn't train me, but he made diagrams. And one day he called from his home—he was ill and he was quite old—and he said, "Lorraine, I feel that the few times that you watched me, I feel that you're able to do this." Bingo! I did one and it worked fine. So the doctor died about six months after that. The doctor died in 1962 and I continued until about 1967.

I never lied to any one of the ladies that come to me in the future for an abortion. I never told them I was a doctor, a medically trained person. I just sat with them for two hours and explained the good and the bad of it and what could happen. My thing was, don't wait. If you find out that you have a problem, do it. Because I wasn't quite sure at the time when life begins. Raised Catholic, I had, at times, a little bit of guilt. I felt a little, you know, guilty. And I would urge them not wait too long.

Some of them started bleeding terrible. They'd wind up in the hospital and the hospitals then would tell them, unless you tell us what went down we can't help you, we can't save your life, you're going to die. If somebody tampered or inserted any instruments or anything inside your vagina that caused this, if you tell us what happened we will know exactly what to do. Well I had ran this through with them prior, because the doctor had told me that is what they do, that is the normal practice in a hospital. And out of [more that a thousand that I did], perhaps a hundred and fifty ladies wind up in the hospital. I used to call the ambulance for them to go to a hospital if they were in harms way a bit. They never, never divulged any way that their bodies had been tampered with.

Doing the Procedure

I'd put a clean sheet in the bathtub, okay. The girl would get in the bathtub. She would be naked from the waist down. And the solution that I used, I used to boil Ivory Soap so that it would be sterile, in a clean pan. It's liquid but a little bit foamy, like body lotion. I had a solution of that soap and water. And with a syringe with a bulb about an inch big, with one piece of the little hose in the solution, with my hand well sterilized, I'd enter and go inside with the other end into the womb, and squirt just one or two squirts of that solution. And I could tell when it worked because the girl would immediately feel a sensation, like a little bit of body heat and a cramping. So I'd let her lay there for a few minutes with a pillow on her back, until she was stable enough to get up. Then I'd let her lay down for an hour or so until the initial shock was over with, give them something to eat, and start her walking. "Let's go for a walk. Let's stay active, okay?" And from within the time that that was injected in her body it took about 12 to 13 hours for anything to start happening. There was staining to start with and then there was a slow procedure over a couple of days.

I stayed in touch with every one of those girls until it was all over with. I felt good if they stayed in my house or I always had their phone numbers. And I'd go back and forth to their homes and check and see how they're doing. I always wanted them to pass the afterbirth. It's amazing how much there is even after two or three months. Because if that doesn't come through, that's what builds up and then they start hemorrhaging. I'm not sure of the medical terms for that type of infection, but that's what happens sometimes. [If there was a problem] I would certainly drive them to the hospital or let an ambulance come and get them. I never, never wanted to fool with anybody's life, you know. It wasn't to my advantage.

I'd have to say I did between twelve and fifteen hundred abortions, maybe more. I didn't keep records except of the ones that were most involved in my life as a result of doing abortions for them. And I did as many for free as I did for pay. Because some of those women, they were desperate, believe me. If I had been in anyway a person who wanted to exploit misery, I was in the position to. But I felt I had a certain affinity for these women, and I would think, if this was me, I would do anything to have an abortion. And I found it so mind boggling that they were to the point that they would crawl on the floor and eat cat shit to get an abortion.

They didn't come just from the Boston area, Andover, or Lowell. People would fly from California, people would fly from Florida. It spread by word of mouth. I charged $350. But women are conniving. If I charged $350 they would tell their boyfriends that the price had gone up to $600. My price was still $350, so they'd pocket the rest. There was an awful lot of that. Could I say it's wrong? I mean, let's face it.

Then there was an attorney who got $5,000 for his fee [to his clients who wanted helped procuring an abortion]. He had a clientele of people that stretched from Newton to Brookline to Natick because he was a very good attorney with a nice reputation. He'd charge $5,000 to his clients. I'd still charge $350, so he would pocket the rest. He would pick me up and drive me to their homes. I never had their phone numbers but they had mine to call as it progressed.

And I would make trips up to the University of Maine in Portland. And the girls there had a kitty. I had an understanding with them that if there was more than one or two girls pregnant, it would be $350 for the first one and then $50 each other. They're in school, give the kids a break. I figured I was doing them a big favor. And then they had girlfriends that had girlfriends that had girlfriends. They would set up a room for me to do them in.

I could not refuse someone. They would get hysterical, believe me. Once I had some people from Canada call me [and ask me to come up there]. I speak French and Italian. When you come to the border they kind of look through your baggage and stuff. That Ivory Soap solution that I used, when it cools down it solidifies. So when they opened my luggage they found that little container that I had. Do you know that they had it analyzed to make sure that it wasn't any kind of plastic explosive? They were just so retarded. That's what I went through at the frontier! They said, but why are your carrying Ivory Soap? I said, "Well, I have a skin condition that I can't use a bar of soap right on my skin. I have to melt it in the bathtub. So I make a little bit ahead of time." That was one little incident.

Trying to Quit

In 1967, I met this man who was a Harvard graduate, a biochemist. And he liked me. He was very scholastically intelligent, but not very street smart. And he was intrigued by the whole situation, you know, how one woman can have so much control over a group of other women. And the reason was, I was available even if you didn't have any money. The word was out: "Lorraine's a good shit, she'll help you." And then when our relationship developed he was not very comfortable with that situation. He said, "Life is life and I think that perhaps now you're young but when you get older you will have some misgivings about this situation. I would urge you to stop." But being a little bit sneaky like I was, I still snuck out and did one or two.

I didn't want to work in an office with a bunch of women. I love women, okay, but I didn't like that conventional type of woman that had to go in with a little three-piece suit. It was like a model show. I was not going to pay any attention to that phase of womanhood that lived climbing the ladder. So I started to going to barber school to hopefully establish a little clientele for myself, a little shop. And then as the relationship progressed, he said why don't you come in a few days to my factory and work in the personnel office? You'd be great at that. So I worked in his factory for a while and then I became involved in a country club that he bought. My values changed, but I was still a big advocate for women having the choice and, until *Roe v. Wade*, I still snuck out and helped anybody that was in need.

Shady Deals and Shakedowns

There were situations where women were exploitive of either their husbands, or their boyfriends, or whoever was involved with them too. I had perhaps done an abortion for some of them and they'd come to me and say, "Look, I gotta get back at this guy. He just dropped me like a hot potato. You just tell him I'm pregnant. Let him give you the money, and I'll split it with you." Well, to my sorrow now, I was a little bit loose on morals, okay. I did go for it. And it wasn't a nice thing to do, but it's said and done with now.

And the married women having affairs were notorious for giving me their charge cards. They would call and say, "Lorraine, use my credit card and as soon as you finish your purchases that one day, call me and I will call in my credit card lost or stolen so I won't be liable and have a problem with the husband." So that was some of the action at that time that went on. Again, out of desperation. It was just another example of what abortions being illegal created for the women that were involved—myself and the other person.

When my "practice" expanded, the mob guys from Boston got a hold of it. All I had to do was one of the girlfriends of one of the wise guys in Boston. That gang I was afraid of because I knew they were bad people. I wasn't St. Theresa, but they were bad people. So my experiences with that element of society were scary. It was never a shakedown for money. It was always ultimatums that "it better work" and "nothing better happen to my daughter." The shakedowns were from the local wise guys, the wannabes from the Lawrence and Lowell area.

The police in the city where I lived knew what illegal activity was going on. The first ones to know are the police. I kept a clean, not an exquisite home. But you know, everything was clean. There were no loud parties. There was no reason for the police to be involved, other than that I was doing abortions in my home. And I did their girlfriends, their wives, and their daughters for free. So I was given a lot of leeway. They never, ever bothered me. Again, the young women who ended up in the hospital were already schooled what to say and what answers to give the medical staff in the event of anything not going right.

The chief of police in the small city where I lived was a bit perverted. He always looked the other way with me. I had this friend in Boston that knew street hookers. They weren't bad girls, that's just how they made their living at the time. So, periodically, I'd call one of them. I'd give her a hundred dollars, and she'd come to my house and service this policeman. The doctor's house was set up, the front of the house was on one of the main streets and it extended on the backside of another street into an alley. I had access to the whole house. I would leave the alley bulkhead open. He'd leave his car a couple of streets away, walk down the alley, come down through the bulkhead, lock it, and walk up the stairs, down the hallway, into my apartment. So about once a month, I'd have this girl come up from Boston. That was my little price to him to stay in business.

Well, one time he comes to my home. He knew that these girls were professional hookers and one night he got a little cocked and he pulls his gun out and he goes to me, with the gun pointed at me, he goes, "Bitch, don't ever try to set me up or pull any shit with me. I'll shoot the two of you and just say that you resisted arrest." I was shocked because that was never my intent. I thought I had cultivated a friend, even though my activity was illegal. I figured he's a good Joe. He wants to get laid once in a while. Then I got a phone call a few days after. He apologized for his misbehavior and he goes, "It was a combination of things. My conscience didn't feel right that night," he said, "because I hate to think that it's come down to the fact that I can no longer enjoy myself with a young, young woman." He said, "Those hard-core whores that you get me—it doesn't interest me any more." He says, "You're in charge here. You get me one of those sixteen or seventeen year-olders whose parents leave her there or they come on their own. They'll do anything you tell them."

I said, "Okay, yeah, you're on." I hung up and I felt totally disillusioned. I said this is never going to happen in my house. So, I thought about it for a few days and I went to Boston and I saw the same woman that was procuring these women who were hookers at the time. I told her the story like I'm telling you now. I says, "Get me one that's nice and clean and young looking and not too much mileage and we'll school her." So that's what we did. He honestly thought he was having intercourse with a 17-year-old that was pregnant. She was crying and everything. And that did it for him. She got a little bonus, you know.

[There were others in the area doing abortions] but they were women that did it on the fly. They got arrested two or three times. I never, never, never made any connections with them. I figured I was breaking the law, but I was breaking it at a higher level than they were. You know, in any kind of business you always think you're the French poodle of the business!

If I had to drive in an area that I was not too sure of, I would have this young man drive me, okay. A local hoodlum. He carried a piece. Because I didn't know sometimes where I was going, so he would come along as my "boyfriend," supposedly who was giving me a ride. And every time that I used his services, out of the $350 I'd give him a hundred dollars. In those years, that was a lot more money than the hundred is now. And he continued on with his life after his time that he was of service to me. He became a psychoanalyst and he worked for the City of Lawrence. And then when my life turned around and I became a little bit more stable financially and socially, he tried to shake me down real, real bad. It was taken care of, but it wasn't a nice situation.

The One That Haunts Me

In the area where I grew up there were a lot of Lebanese and Syrian people. And in this one family, there was about six or seven boys and they weren't of the best character. One of them was married and he was a car salesman. He became involved with, I tell you, the most gorgeous girl you've ever seen in your life. Nineteen years old. She didn't have the greatest home life and here was a slick car salesman with a Thunderbird and plenty of what seemed like money. He was making her all kinds of promises. I had known him and his family since the time we were young children together. One day I got a phone call and it was him, Paul. He goes, "Oh, Lorraine, I am in a mess." I says, Well, what's a matter? "Diane is pregnant." I says, Well, how far gone is she? He says, "Oh, she missed one or two periods." I'm not a doctor, so I had to go just by feeling and asking her a few questions. But she was so thin and so young that her pregnancy didn't show. And I think that he had perhaps schooled her prior to my helping her with her problem.

So she come over and she was crying and very upset. I kept her in my home on the strength that I knew Paul. And I didn't feel good about him as a person, but in the entourage that I was involved in, I couldn't make any judgment on anybody's character really. I did it anyways for him. One day. Two days. Three days. Four days. She's just staining. I'm saying, Paul, we'd better bring her to the hospital. He says, "No, she doesn't want to go to the hospital." I didn't like it at all. On the fourth day in the middle of the night, she started screaming. I said, What's a matter, Diane? She said, "Lorraine look at the blood!"

She gave birth to a child. I would have to say from the size of her fetus, it was six to seven months. I had never, never been confronted with a situation like that in my life. I was scared. She was ash white; I thought she was going to die. I didn't let her see the baby. When I cut the chord, then there was no breathing or nothing. I was really, really messed up with that. I rolled it up in a little blanket and put it in a shoebox that I had in the closet. I made sure that all the afterbirth came out. I made her some tea. I made her as comfortable as I could under the situation. She was only then 20 and I was about 34. I was pissed at this guy. I called him and I said, Paul, get yourself down here right now. At that time she was sleeping and she was coming along, you know, because I had given her something to eat and I took care of her. I told him, I said, you know Paul, you lied to me about the time that this girl was pregnant. This is the result. I did my part. Please, for the love of God, do what's right with this, okay, and I gave him the shoebox. He left saying, "This will never happen again," and acting like he was the victim or something. She stayed with me for about a week until she recuperated and went back home to stay with her mother.

Now, a couple of months go by, another phone call from Paul: "Oh, Lorraine, we went back together, this and that happened." Well, now I knew that it couldn't be more than a month that she was along. So she goes to me, "Well, I don't like the idea, but I'm going to let you do it once more because you were so kind to me and I'm not afraid, Lorraine." She says, "I just don't want to feel that he has to be with me because I'm pregnant." And in the meantime she had found out that he was married with three grown sons. Anyways, I took care of this situation again. Another three months goes by, she calls me again. Again we did it. Two more months. I says, Diane, we cannot keep using this as a form of birth control. I said you're going to have to do something. This will be the last time. She says alright, so we did it once more.

Now she come back in another month pregnant again and she goes to me, "Lorraine, he's got to marry me, he's got to leave his wife, I'm in love with him, that's it. Make believe you're doing it and it's not working." This was the conversation. So she'd come up, we'd have a cup of tea, and talk, whatever. He'd pick her up. The next day: "Hey Lorraine, you've gotta get this bitch off my neck. What am I gonna do? You know I'm married and I got three kids. You've been my mother's friend for all these years"—now he's using the family bullshit—"you've been friends with my family for all these years. You can't leave me in this kind of trouble, this girl is crazy. She's obsessed with me. You've got to help me out." I say, "Well, I'm doing the best I can, Paul." And I was hating him every minute. And she'd come up again. Well, she come up like that five or six times and it didn't work, because I wasn't doing it. So, it was always the same conversation with me: "Gotta get that whore"—now from his lover she'd become the whore, okay—"Gotta get this whore off my back." The last time she was at my house she said, "Lorraine, I'm having this baby. He's gotta leave his wife and that's it." She says, "I want him to marry me." I knew she was making a mistake, but there was nothing I could say to convince her. So, I didn't hear from them for a long time.

One day I picked up the Lawrence paper: "WOMAN KILLS HER BABY IN THE CARRIAGE." He had given her such a hard time, he was so mean to her, he was just an animal, that this girl here went crazy. She bought a set of knives and stabbed that little baby 19 times. So, naturally they arrested her. And I was really messed up with that scene. She was sent to Danvers and at that time there was a doctor there, Dr. Hagopian, one of the head psychiatrists. I called him and I explained the situation. I said, "If this girl is guilty of murder, the whole world is guilty." And I explained to him [about Paul and the abortions]. I couldn't get too involved because I didn't want to be prosecuted in any way. This doctor was a gentleman. He always kept that conversation between he and I.

And now, another while goes by. *Roe v. Wade* comes to be and we're sitting, myself, my friend, my son, and another couple in Bishop's Restaurant in Lawrence. I was looking around and I made eye contact with her, Diane. She was back with that Paul. He'd take her out of the hospital periodically. They were trying to get her over this trauma and able to go back out into society and function. She looked at me and she went absolutely crazy. She started screaming: "Paul, Paul, that's her, that's Lorraine, that's the woman who killed all my babies!" She picked up the table and she's coming toward me. He picked her up, cradled her, and walked out with her. That was very embarrassing. I didn't feel good at all about that one.

Looking Back

I didn't always feel good about myself. It was like instant gratification. I drove big convertibles. But that wasn't the element of people that I wanted to impress. I knew that there was something else inside of me that wanted to come out and just never could. Because I had chosen. I don't care if you've got money coming out of your ears, once you choose to break the law to that extent, it's not going to do it for you. You go beyond the boundary. It's almost as if there's no return. I'm not looking for sympathy. It's what I chose to do.

But I'm sure that I have saved marriages. I have helped young women make better choices because I was there when they needed someone. I don't believe now that abortion should be really a form of birth control. In cases of rape, incest, and somebody being negligent, I think it should always be available to a woman who psychologically or physically is unable to bring a fetus to life. Yes, it should always be available for them. But there are better methods now and times have changed. And I'm happy that I was able to make a difference in some people's lives.

PART THREE

The Clergy and their Allies

Clergy and Affiliated Lay Abortion Counselors

In the 1960s and 1970s pressure at the grassroots level and from the introduction of the American Law Institute (ALI) Model Penal Code combined to induce state legislatures to institute changes to their abortion laws. It is tempting to equate social activism during the 1960s and 1970s with radicals but in the case of abortion, activists came from the foundations of society as well as from its fringes. Many members of the medical community were angered, as Robin Dizard put it in the story of her illegal abortion, at "being compelled into all this fraud." They were tired of fabricating psychiatric illness to satisfy arcane legal requirements for a therapeutic abortion, tired of performing abortions illegally, and very tired of being forced to fix the tragic consequences of illegal and self-induced abortions—abortions that physicians could have performed safely had they been legal. Doctors and lawyers began to push for change, and they found, what might seem an unlikely ally in another pillar of the community—the clergy.

In many cases a woman with an unwanted pregnancy was facing not just a medical crisis, but also a social and a moral crisis. Abortions were considered by many to be taboo for moral as well as legal reasons. This meant that the pregnant woman often felt she had no one to turn to for help or advice and was thus isolated from normal social contacts at a critical and stressful time. While many women turned to family and friends to help them work through their fears or resolve their pregnancies, some turned to their ministers or rabbis. A number of these clergy members organized the Clergy Consultation Services on Abortion (CCS) to provide referral services in a safe and methodical way, while at the same time using their prestige in the community to press for change. They were aided by journalist Lawrence Lader who advised the founders of CCS, "Start with the women. Organize the clergy to refer women to qualified doctors."[1] Reverend Howard Moody, a longtime activist in New York City and national politics, and who had been active in the Civil Rights fight in the South, welcomed the challenge. He quickly got to work figuring out a way to put Lader's urging into action, and on May 27, 1967, a front page article in the *New York Times* announced the establishment of the Clergy Consultation Service on Abortion (CCS).[2]

The announcement of the formation of CCS followed 8 months of preparation by Moody and a group of 25 clergy colleagues representing most denominations other than the Catholic. In those eight months they met with lawyers from the New York Civil Liberties Union who counseled that they conduct their services in as open a way as possible and, if asked, to answer that they were not doing anything illegal, since, as clergy, they were answerable to a higher law. Lader had used a similar justification for his referrals, but the clergy clearly had a stronger stake to this claim. The clergy also met with doctors and counselors who gave them a basic tutorial in female anatomy and abortion procedures. They established connections with fewer than a dozen abortion providers with whom they would work and set up a method of monitoring them. All of the providers were outside New York State and most were located in Puerto Rico or Japan. The clergy calculated that by referring only to doctors out of state they would make the task for law enforcement more difficult, as local District Attorneys would be less likely to pursue indictments across state lines. Only *one* arrest was associated with CCS; Reverend Robert Hare was working with a Cleveland area CCS chapter when he referred a woman to a doctor in Massachusetts. After having undergone the procedure, the woman was driving home when she began to bleed extensively and pulled over for help. She unwittingly pulled into a State Police headquarters, which prompted an investigation and charges being brought against both Hare and the doctor. All charges were eventually dismissed.

CCS's rasion d'etre was straight forward. According to Reverend Moody: "It was primarily to provide counselors to enable women to get safe, low-cost abortions with a minimum of mental anguish and emotional trauma," with a secondary goal "to change the laws that made our presence as counselors necessary."[3]

Moody and his colleagues arranged the basic procedure for CCS referrals. A central phone number with an answering machine message would provide the names and telephone numbers of clergy who were doing counseling that week. Clergy members would meet privately with each woman at their own offices and, during a counseling session, provide the referral. Counseling sessions lasted from ten minutes to one hour and the referrals were to be given orally. The woman might write the information down, but if the clergyperson did so, it would have provided evidence of breaking the law prohibiting conspiracy to commit abortion. Ruth Fessenden, a counselor who worked with one of the Massachusetts chapters later in the development of CCS, suggests another reason for the lack of written records: "People who were working around these issues worked in sort of trusted connections and were accustomed to being able to do business on a word. So the notion of a paper [trail] wasn't a part of the culture."[4]

CCS quickly spread throughout the country as satellite chapters were formed by friends of Moody and those who knew of him through the informal network of activist clergy involved in social change movements. By the time of the *Roe v. Wade* decision in 1973 there were approximately 40 loosely affiliated chapters and about 2,000 associated clergy, and parts of the larger religious community were also beginning to change.[5] In 1972, at the annual meeting of the General Conference of the United Methodist Church—at which official policies are decided and implemented—the "Social Principles" code of the church was amended to call for "the removal of abortion from the criminal code, placing it instead under the laws relating to other procedures of standard medical practice."[6] Of course not all ministers of a certain faith adhere to official policy, and by 1980, seven years after the Roe decision, United Methodist pastor Ken Unger from Ohio had formed the active Protestants Protesting Abortion.

A Clergy Consultation Service in the Pioneer Valley

In 1967 and 1968 when Howard Moody was putting out word on the jungle telegraph that he was forming the CCS, one of the first ministers to respond to the call in Massachusetts was Harvey Cox, then a professor at Harvard Divinity School. Cox in turn called up his friend and former Yale Divinity School classmate Reverend Richard "Dick" Unsworth, then a chaplain at Smith College in Northampton. Unsworth agreed to start a chapter in Western Massachusetts. That was some time in 1968, though the exact date is not clear.[7] Unsworth, who had earlier done research and writing on abortion with reproductive rights activist Dr. Alan Guttmacher, was well informed about the issues and had been paying close attention to the work Moody was doing in New York.

Among other reasons, Unsworth was driven to his involvement in CCS by two fatalities of young women he knew or had counseled. A third incident involved a young married Amherst woman who had a severe medical condition that would likely kill her if she tried to give birth to a child. Although the couple meticulously practiced birth control, it failed and she became pregnant. She was eventually able to get an abortion referral through CCS. The life or death nature of this incident has an obvious parallel to the very public 1962 Sheri Finkbine case, which had a major effect on both legislation and popular opinion about abortion nationally. Finkbine, a 29-year-old Arizona mother of four and a television personality, had been prescribed a tranquilizer to calm her nerves during her fifth pregnancy. When she discovered that the tranquilizer contained Thalidomide she was scheduled for a therapeutic abortion, but when she told her story to a local newspaper, the Arizona courts stepped in and denied her access to the procedure. She eventually obtained an abortion in Sweden.[8]

Unsworth characterizes his CCS chapter as a "spin-off of Howard Moody's effort," but no formal relationship or network existed between New York and

Western Massachusetts. When he began putting together a service in the area in 1968, he too began by calling on those fellow clergy he knew through other efforts to effect social change.[9] A couple of ministers turned him down, but most whom he approached signed on. Unsworth remembers that there were initially three clergy in Northampton and another three in the Amherst area. One of these was Unsworth's fellow chaplain at Smith College, Yechiael Lander, who served as the rabbi both there and at Amherst College.

Unsworth's office at the Smith College chapel served as the unofficial headquarters of Western Massachusetts CCS, and a telephone line and answering machine were installed there. Women would call this number and would then be referred to whichever minister or rabbi was "on duty" at the time. They would then schedule an appointment with that clergyman. (Later in the development of CCS, referrals were made through a central phone number in Boston serving CCS activities throughout the entire state.)

Unsworth and Lander were joined in their efforts by the chaplain at Mount Holyoke College, and by several Congregationalists and Methodists from Amherst and Northampton. Then there were the ministers of the United Christian Foundation (UCF), who had offices across the Connecticut River from Smith and Northampton, on the campus of UMass Amherst. The Protestant ministers at UCF were young and most had been involved in antiwar and other radical movements. They had come to the abortion issue on their own and eagerly signed on for the service. They soon realized they saw so many CCS clients that it made sense for them to form a separate chapter. By 1969, there were at least eight ministers and rabbis in Unsworth's group and three in the UCF group. By March 22, 1971, when the two chapters had a joint meeting, fourteen counselors attended and at least another three more were involved.

Abortion Counseling at the University

The UCF clergy had probably already been thinking about starting a CCS chapter, or something similar, by the time that Unsworth was looking for interested ministers to participate. Unsworth believes that the UCF clergy had borrowed the idea from Howard Moody independently, and he recalled being invited over to speak with them a handful of times and cautioning them that "they needed to be careful, because they didn't have only their own personal ministry as a congregational parson or whatever. They had an apparatus called the UCF that didn't have the standing with the university that a college chaplain would have had. They were there at the tolerance of the university, as it were."[10]

The university had tolerated UCF's presence since before it was the University of Massachusetts. In 1923, the boards of five Amherst churches—Baptist, Congregational, Episcopal, Methodist, and Unitarian—hired Reverend John B. Hanna to serve as an advisor to the Christian Association, a newly formed student group on the campus of what was then the Massachusetts Agricultural College. The Christian Association morphed into the Student Christian Association in the 1940s, and then into the UCF in 1952 to "assist in promoting and advancing the Christian religion among the students, faculty, and staff of the University of Massachusetts." UCF became independent of the university in the mid-1960s and it soon affiliated with the United Ministries in Higher Education, which provided funding for a small staff.[11] The university's only contribution was to donate office space. At the time that Unsworth was reaching out to UCF to help out with abortion counseling, the foundation was run by a board of local ministers, representatives of the six major Protestant denominations, the YMCA, the YWCA, the Massachusetts Council of Churches, the Student Christian Movement, and members of the faculty, staff, and student body at UMass.[12] In 1969–1970, UCF had a staff of three ministers and a part-time administrative assistant.

When the UCF chapter of CCS opened it did so publicly, with a press release sent to local media. Listing their address on the UMass campus, the clergymen announced that they would offer "counsel without fee to women faced with problem pregnancies." As with the other local CCS chapter, women were instructed to call a Northampton phone number where they would hear a taped message describing who was on duty and how to reach them.[13]

An article in the *University of Massachusetts Daily Collegian* from November 9, 1971, "Abortion and What to Expect," recounted one student's experience of having received an abortion referral through CCS. "Cathy Jones" said that the first step in getting an abortion was to go to CCS. She recounted that the counselors there were "helpful and handled me in a tactful, understanding way. Questions they asked are based on an emotional rather than physical level; your relationship to your parents, the man involved, and your ideas on abortion. They explained to me in details what would happen from the moment I arrived in New York, till [sic] the end."[14]

The UCF group was one of only a few CCS chapters nationally in which laywomen as well as clergy became involved in the problem pregnancy counseling.[15] The original justification for the CCS project and its defense against prosecution necessitated that the counseling be handled by clergy, who could argue that they were answerable to a higher law. The UCF counselors were actually in violation of CCS's organizing policies, as evident in a memo sent to the Western Massachusetts groups by the Boston Clergymen's Consultation Service on Problem Pregnancies some time in 1969: "LET US EMPHASIZE: Clergymen counselors must be ordained in order to be protected under the immunity laws of the Massachusetts."[16]

Elaine Fraser, who was not an ordained minister, was hired by UCF as a part-time administrative assistant in the winter of 1968 and became an important figure in reproductive counseling, both at UCF and later across campus at the University Health Services of the University of Massachusetts. According to the ministers and Fraser, the UCF clergy were just beginning to do problem pregnancy counseling when she was hired and they felt that a woman should be involved in the process.[17] She relinquished some of her secretarial duties and was trained by the ministers to counsel pregnant women. By the spring of 1970, she was working full-time at UCF and half of that time was devoted solely to counseling.

Because Fraser was devoting much of her days to counseling pregnant students, a part-time administrative assistant, Ruth Fessenden, was hired in October 1970 to cover the office duties. But soon she too became involved in CCS activities. At first she just greeted clients and tried to put them at ease. Although she had been told about the CCS activities during her job interview, she stated in her staff report in March 1971 that, "One surprising aspect of the job has been the diplomacy required in handling many situations, especially CCS [i.e., counseling services]. It is important to make the people feel comfortable, but still the necessary business has to be done." Before long, Fessenden too was doing counseling.[18]

In taking on the problem pregnancy counseling, Fraser and Fessenden perhaps put themselves and the organization at greater risk; unlike the clergy, they could not fall back on the "higher law defense." Reverend Sam Johnson says now that he would claim that Elaine and Ruth, though not ordained, were also "ministers" and were also driven to their actions by the desire to serve a higher law. This defense was never tested in court so it is unknown if it would have held up.

While Fraser maintained that her counseling sessions at CCS only involved discussing options and that she always left it to the clergy to make the actual referral to an abortion provider, Fessenden recounts that in her own sessions, it didn't always happen that way, and that she did both counseling and referrals on her own.[19]

Fessenden recalls having two to six appointments a day and seeing hundreds of women over the course of a year. Some women came to her committed to having an abortion and simply seeking a referral. Others wanted to discuss all the options available. In either case, Fessenden and her colleagues would detail each option—carrying the fetus to term and caring for the child, putting the child up for adoption, or seeking an abortion— just to make sure that the women had carefully thought through and considered all angles. The counselors worked closely with Children's Aid and Family Services in Northampton to find aid for single mothers or to set up adoptions. Other aid groups, including Catholic Charities, provided single mothers with housing, baby clothes and furniture, and other aid. Once all the options had been discussed and considered, an appropriate referral was made, either to an adoption agency, an agency that assisted unwed mothers, or to an abortion provider. The women, Fessenden recalls, were given enough information to make an informed choice. It was, she says, an "options supermarket."[20]

Changes Over Time

Staff at UCF changed substantially during the few years that the organization hosted a CCS chapter. In the fall of 1969, the staff consisted of Elaine Fraser and four ministers.

The first ministers to take on the counseling in 1968–1969 were Ron Hardy and Frank Dorman, the organization's president. An intern from the Harvard Divinity School, Sam Johnson, soon joined Hardy in doing the majority of the counseling. They were the two youngest clergy at the organization and the most radical.

Hardy worked at UCF as an intern even before his ordination as a Baptist minister in May 1968 at the age of 25.[21] He had been deeply involved in the peace and antiwar movements and was one of 25 people arrested during a 1968 takeover of the UMass administration building to protest Dow Chemical (which produced napalm and Agent Orange, dangerous chemicals used to devastating effect in the Vietnam War) recruiting on campus. He also started a draft-counseling group in one of the dorms in the fall of that year, was involved in an interracial relations working group, and coordinated a task group on low-income housing in Amherst.[22] Dorman characterizes Hardy as Amherst's "token radical."

On May 5, 1970, Ron Hardy took the minutes for a weekly staff meeting, but alongside his record of committee appointments and notes on UCF's annual retreat, are personal notes: "*Where have I been? pain—despair—reduced to a child—reading the Bible—being alone—waiting—striving to love in the midst of all that.*" Later on the same page he wrote: "*Where are we headed? Politics have snoballed [sic]; repression is near, heels are being dug in—need to keep pushing but we need to be more subtle—more careful.*"

Hardy committed suicide on November 6, 1970. He immolated himself in the woods near his home in Cummington, Massachusetts. While immolation had been used by some Buddhist monks protesting the Vietnam War, Hardy's death was portrayed in the local press as the suicide of a troubled individual.[23] Frank Dorman, president of UCF and also a CCS counselor, presided at Hardy's funeral and now says that Hardy's death inspired him to take on more radical methods in his own ministry. "I think that sort of convinced me that I should not continue to expend energy in the local church, fundraising bakers and that sort of thing. I preached against the war, frequently, but his death made me say, okay, somebody needs to pick up the standard and run with it. So I did. I resigned from my church and got heavily involved."

We shall never know whether Hardy's decision to kill himself was in part the result of stress arising from his commitments to social change. Certainly he felt that social inequities were compounded by governmental and social repression. To use Hardy's scrawled phrase, these had "snoballed."[24] Elaine Fraser recalled that "compartmentalizing" was the only way to handle the stress of her counseling work and Ruth Fessenden explicitly saw a connection between Ron Hardy's work at UCF and his death, which she characterized as reflective of the chaotic state of the world at the time. She found it understandable that someone who was dealing with the social problems of the time perhaps would have trouble handling it psychologically or emotionally. "If someone had the ability to take that all in, really, it is as though you wouldn't be able to withstand what that was all about."[25]

After Ron Hardy's death, Sam Johnson and Elaine Fraser conducted most of the CCS counseling, with Frank Dorman picking up the occasional shift. Johnson and Dorman both left UCF at the end of the 1971 academic year, and, by September 1971, UCF was down to one full-time clergy member, Tom Lindemann. Lindemann focused on curricular matters and was little involved in the CCS activities. Starting in the fall of 1971 then, two women, Elaine Fraser and Ruth Fessenden, neither of them members of the clergy, presumably did all the problem pregnancy counseling.[26]

Collaborators in the Pioneer Valley

The CCS clergy found some allies within sympathetic staff at the University Health Services, as well as in local women's rights groups. Ruth Fessenden of CCS remembers many individuals who had involvements in several of the organizations at once. "The community networks always overlapped," she said. "You can name any two groups and there was probably overlapping membership." Collaborations took the form of referrals, public gatherings, and joint staff meetings.

In the fall of 1970, shortly after UMass student William Day was arrested for double homicide following his attempt to perform an abortion on his girlfriend, Reverend Ronald Hardy of UCF made a presentation about CCS to Dr. Gage's Health Services staff. In a memo he distributed to them, Hardy provided an overview of the history of CCS, included descriptions of the major referral options used by the service, and suggested that more information on referrals was also available from Dr. Gage.[27] Though Dr. Gage himself now says in his oral history that he had no contact with the CCS ministers, the memo demonstrates the ideological—and actual—cooperation between the University Health Services and CCS on matters of abortion. Indeed, Reverend Johnson says one of the reasons he and others at UCF felt they could risk breaking the law against giving abortion referrals was that they were protected by their relationship with the University Health Services: "I think there was some actual protection, but also we felt a sense of authority about it—this must be okay, this must be right. Nobody is going to come after us because of that kind of status within the university."

Reverend Sam Johnson recalls that the United Christian Foundation ministers worked closely with the Health Services in training counselors in the Peer Sexuality program. He also recalls meeting with pregnant students who had been referred to him by both Health Services and the Everywomen's Center at UMass. Also, in October of 1972, the UCF staff sent a description of CCS to the UMass Student Senate to be included in their "Human Sexuality Handbook" for the following academic year. It read in part: "Clergy Consultation Service offers no cost counseling to people with problem pregnancies. It will counsel women on all the alternatives open to them; it is not limited to abortion referrals. This office works in cooperation with the University Health Services. All counseling is confidential of course."[28]

The female staffs of the Health Services and the United Christian Foundation also kept in close contact. Elaine Fraser of UCF reported that she got all of her medical information and some of her counseling tips from the UHS nurses and, later, from Jane Zapka, UHS's Director of Community Health Education, who ran the health center's contraception education clinics. And Zapka recalls that she and Fraser referred clients to each other and were in touch several times a week to talk about the referrals.[29] Arrangements were made so that students who visited CCS fearing they might be pregnant could go to the Health Services for pregnancy testing. In turn, students who came to the Health Services with confirmed pregnancies would be referred to CCS for counseling.

In addition to the CCS groups, the Pioneer Valley was also home to several feminist organizations that did volunteer abortion counseling. Part of their motivation was to provide an alternative route for pregnant women who did not want to seek counseling from a religious person or from a man (as the common perception was that all the CCS counselors were male). But Elaine Fraser and Ruth Fessenden served as bridges between CCS and the feminist counselors. Lorna Peterson and Robin Dizard of the Amherst Women's Liberation Abortion and Birth Control Committee both credit Fraser with having trained them in the basics of problem pregnancy counseling, and Fraser conceded that while the two women had good skills, she "taught them the nitty-gritty."

Reverend Richard Unsworth recalls working closely with Planned Parenthood and that Leslie Laurie and others at Planned Parenthood would refer pregnant women to him and others in Western Massachusetts CCS for counseling. He remembers that his problem pregnancy counseling volume went up after Planned Parenthood became established in Northampton.

CCS ministers also did a fair amount of public speaking about the abortion issue. They were joined in these events by social workers and mental health counselors from UMass, by women who had received illegal abortions, and by members of local women's rights organizations. Public forums on abortion were held in such places as the UMass business school and the Amherst Rotary Club.

Moving Toward Legal Abortion

While it is impossible to know for sure the exact number of women in the Pioneer Valley who had unplanned and/or unwanted pregnancies each year during this period, it is obvious that the numbers were significant. Two to three hundred students each year came through the UCF's CCS chapter alone. Another few hundred women, both students and community members went through the Western Massachusetts chapter. And these are only the women who thought of contacting a clergy person. Others went through women's groups, networks of family and friends, or sought out back-alley abortions or tried to cause abortion themselves through a variety of means.[30]

When legal abortion on demand went into effect in New York State on July 1, 1970, both the climate and methods of the Massachusetts CCS chapters changed radically.[31] The clergy counselors now had a list of legal abortion providers to whom they could refer women without having to sneak around or conduct extensive background checks. In the pre-Roe days, UCF had sent a few referrals to illegal providers in New York, but according to Fraser "that was really chancy—those sites could change all the time." The majority of referrals, therefore, were made to providers in England, where the practice was legal, or in Canada or Puerto Rico, where the practice was technically illegal but prosecutions were rare. Legalized abortion on demand in New York meant that domestic abortions were finally available, and that the costs would be far less than that of a foreign abortion. It also meant that the national, political, and social climate was at last changing and perhaps their work had made an impact. This galvanized the CCS groups to work even more out in the open and to join forces with clinics and other social organizations with similar aims.[32]

By mid-1972, the Western Massachusetts CCS chapter was seeing very few women and by September 1972, CCS Task Force minutes reveal state that "no calls whatsoever have been coming in over the past few weeks."[33] There are several possible explanations for this change. The most likely is that women were finding their own way to New York—only a four hour drive away—for legal abortions. Another explanation is that the local family planning clinics that had recently been set up throughout Western Massachusetts with the help of Title X funding were also doing their own abortion referrals.[34] Yet a third possibility is that more and more women were going for options counseling and abortion referrals to a drop-in feminist cooperative, the Valley Women's Center in Northampton, or to other area counselors affiliated with the women's movement.

While legalized abortion in New York meant a different set of rules and referrals, the counseling work at CCS continued, albeit in reduced numbers, until *Roe. v. Wade* went into effect on July 1, 1973. At that point, a clinic in Springfield, Hampden Gynecological Associates, quickly mobilized and opened its doors, followed soon thereafter by abortion services at Amherst Medical in Amherst. Both clinics provided counseling along with the abortion services. In fact, many of them hired women who had been doing such work as feminist volunteer counselors for years. The CCS chapter at UMass continued its counseling services through the first few months of legal abortion in Massachusetts. Available statistics indicate that CCS referrals resulted in 53 local abortions during April, May, and June 1973. In July 1973, Elaine Fraser was hired as a counselor in the Mental Health division of the University Health Services and left the United Christian Foundation. Problem pregnancy counseling literally moved across campus. After Elaine was gone, and abortion was legalized, UCF made a proposal to the university to collaborate on a new problem pregnancy service. When this was not approved, UCF soon stopped doing counseling altogether. However, Elaine Fraser, in her new position at Health Services, continued to provide problem pregnancy counseling and make abortion referrals. In the coming years, she would train other Mental Health staff, including counselors, nurses, and nurse practitioners, to help her in this work. And at the abortion facilities in Springfield and Amherst, counseling was made an integral part of the abortion procedure. While this kind of counseling had never really been hidden, now it had truly gone public, standard practice in the new world of legal abortion services.

THIRTEEN

Reverend Richard Unsworth

Reverend Richard Unsworth holds a B.D. from Yale Divinity School and a Th.M. from Harvard Divinity School. He was Professor of Religion and Chaplain of Smith College in Northampton from 1954 to 1963 and again from 1967 to 1980. He has also served as Dean of the William Jewett Tucker Foundation, Professor of Religion at Dartmouth College, President and Headmaster of Northfield Mount Hermon School, trustee of Mount Holyoke College, and as a member of the Overseers Committee to Visit the Divinity School at Harvard University. Currently living in Virginia in retirement, he is also a senior fellow at the Kahn Liberal Arts Institute at Smith College.

Reverend Richard Unsworth was interviewed by David Cline on April 5, 2002.

Encountering the Pregnant College Student

I first came to the Pioneer Valley in 1954. I came to Smith College as a member of the Religion Department and as a college chaplain. I was there until 1963, and then went up to Dartmouth. I came back to Smith again in 1967 and was there until in 1980, when I went off to be Headmaster at the Northfield-Mount Hermon School.

I had run into this issue of unwanted pregnancies a little bit at Dartmouth but much more at Smith later. Well, actually, I would say that the path into this started a lot earlier. And it has to do with the stories of a few individuals. There was a student, a freshman student, Deborah, in 1956, maybe '57 at the latest, at Smith. She had come to me for counseling several times over a period of a couple of weeks and was obviously very upset. I tried to work things through with her but I wasn't satisfied that I could untangle what it was really all about. I rang in the help of the psychiatric social worker at Smith who also interviewed her. And we couldn't, either of us, dope it out. And then I got a call one morning—she had hung herself. She had gone down to the local hardware store, bought a hank of rope, walked out in the woods behind the infirmary, and hung herself.

We were thunderstruck, as you can imagine. And still had no idea what it was that was so troubling her. Well, they did an autopsy and found she was pregnant. She was a little Catholic girl from Chicago and so conflicted internally that she couldn't even talk in confidence to a social worker, psychiatrically trained, or to me as a minister who had counseling training. And I thought, that's got to be a terrible impasse. I laid it up to a Catholic background and the high level of moral repugnance, well, not of the pregnancy, but of any thought of terminating the pregnancy. Although she hadn't, of course. We didn't know she was pregnant, nor did she talk about terminating the pregnancy. At that point I don't know how I could have helped her if she did. In any case, that student just stuck in my mind.

As time went along, you know, one or two other people came to me for counseling about being pregnant. Another one that I remember at Smith was also a freshman, from New York. She had already made up her mind that she was going back to New York to have an abortion. I think she really wanted to make contact with me before she went so she'd have someone to talk to when she got back. And indeed she did come back and talk for a while. I think with her it wasn't a matter of deciding—and it was all strictly illegal—it was a matter of a commitment she'd made to herself. She really had a lot to thrash through. Then at Dartmouth, in maybe 1965, the daughter of one of my colleagues on the faculty, who was a grown woman, maybe in her late thirties, came in to talk. She too was going to have an abortion but she was very much conflicted by it and wanted to talk it all through.

And when I came back to Smith in '67, another case just hit me square between the eyes. I had been in Africa in 1961, and I had taken a special interest in getting African students to Smith. One of the students that came as a result of this Foreign Student Committee effort was a girl from Ghana whose parents were both members of the faculty of the University of Ghana in Lagon outside of Akra. "Nancy" was a very bright, very able girl. And she had a boyfriend at MIT (Massachusetts Institute of Technology). I got the news one day that she had died. It was a case of her getting pregnant, under circumstances that would be so understandable, and Nancy and her boyfriend thought they had no options. They sought out an abortion in Cambridge or Boston and got in the hands of somebody who was not antiseptic. She was hospitalized and she died. I had to conduct her funeral. Then when I was in Africa next time I went to see her parents. Her parents had the news by then, of course, but I went to visit them. And you know that just tears you up. Why should that happen? So anyway, that had softened me up for a period of time before there was anything like the Clergy Consultation Service.

How I Approached the Notion of Abortion

I was trying to think back, by way of context, what the sequence was here. The sequence is uncanny when you think about it now. Abortion had been accepted by the AMA (American Medical Association) way back in 1937. The FDA (Food and Drug of Administration) approved the marketing of birth control pills for the first time in 1960, and they went on sale in 1961. That opened the gate on the whole issue. It really was a movement, that's the only way you would describe it, where the indignation and stress of a great many women in their years of fertility came to a head. This included married people well into their years who were just so incensed. I think this was a fair part of the feminist movement actually. There was an awareness that birth control for men was easily available, just walk into a drugstore and buy a set of condoms. But for women to even be fitted for a diaphragm at that point was chancy at best. It was a rare doctor who would be willing to do that in those days. Who could miss the fact that there was terrible imbalance in this? Particularly when the woman had to bear the consequences physically.

When my wife and I first came to Smith, I remember when one of my colleague's wives started the pill and that had to be in the 60s or the very late 50s. It wasn't available in Massachusetts. But she started using the pill. And that was just a brand new revolutionary idea. You think about it now, it's kind of incredible to me, but there it was.

Speaking about abortion during counseling wouldn't have been a problem for me. Most of us clergy knew about Margaret Sanger who had been at this since the 1920s. And many of us, I think, had some notion that there were circumstances under which an abortion might very well be the appropriate thing to do, but it was unavailable because ruled illegal. I actually sat on a National Commission of the Presbyterian Church, of which I'm a member, on sexuality issues, and we dealt pretty forthrightly with abortion issues. We tried to get some "pro-choice" legislation across in the general assembly of the Church—that was kind of an adventure, as you can imagine. But it did get across! I was always pleased that we managed to get the legislation in. There were some very good people on that commission who were very active, including a doctor, Mary Calderone, who was speaking about these issues around the country all the time.[1] She was a very well-known person. Other people like her were on this commission, including a number of theologians. So the issue had really been worked through quite thoroughly and fairly early in the game. Also quite early, I was on a committee with another group of people working on these issues, including Allan Guttmacher and Millicent MacIntosh, and we put on a week-end seminar at Princeton that was published in press within the next several months.

Let me put it this way: the notion of abortion was not a casual notion. I don't think it should be and I don't think it ever was. It wasn't up to me to *recommend* one in any case. In my interviews with people who came through the Clergy Consultation Service, I always rehearsed the range of possibilities. With people who were 16 or under, I tired to get their parents involved, or have them get their parents involved, although I didn't make that a condition. Or get the boyfriend involved if there was a boyfriend. People, at least the very young, were in most part responding in panic to their circumstance. To seek an abortion was a desperate thing to do in the atmosphere of illegality and threat and moral condemnation.

One obligation I think we all had was to make sure that they got past their panic and could take a little bit more of an arm's length view of what the options really were and try to imagine themselves inside the process of these various options. It wasn't a way of talking somebody out of an abortion, just saying before you decide, you really need to consider these various options that have been historic courses for people. Try to walk yourself through, in your own imagination, not in panic, and say just exactly what would I be likely to do, or to feel, or to choose? And then, if they elected abortion, which 90 percent of them did, I think then we had the option to do what we could to facilitate it. The business wasn't one of making it easy, it was one of making it safe. The haunting of Deborah hanging herself and Nancy being butchered is something you could never shake. For me, the biggest crime was that those things had to happen.

Developing the Clergy Consultation Service of Western Massachusetts

Initially I did not know where to turn to find a doctor who performed abortions. I did talk it over with the college physician, who was very understanding of the issue, but she felt very much constrained by the law, and rightly so. She would have been charged with a felony if she had been a party to recommending an abortionist, so I didn't expect to get an answer from her—not because she was hard-shelled about it, just because she was in a very, very deep bind about the law.

So I didn't have any resources that I could recommend. And I was hesitant to look deeper for them. That one girl who went off to New York, when she came back and came in to see me, she was in pretty good shape. She had only been away for a couple of nights, one full day. So it must have been a fairly early pregnancy and the process, not a whole lot different from a D&C. But I couldn't imagine asking her to divulge the name of the doctor, even if she would do it, which she probably wouldn't. And then, without knowing that doctor's credentials, how responsible would I feel recommending that doctor to anybody? So, it took the Clergy Consultation Service to provide some resources.

There was a network of clergy that grew in the civil rights movement, and a lot of us stayed in touch with each other. I'd gone down to St. Augustine and to Selma and to Mississippi, and so on over three or four years. There was a network of us clergy in Massachusetts and around New England who were involved and did things together. We were all Protestant clergy; the Catholics who were most involved in some of the things that I was involved with were the nuns. They were really marvelously involved, but not in the abortion issue.

I can see now, in retrospect, a track that moves from the civil rights movement to the anti-Vietnam War issue to women's sexuality issues and feminism. I wouldn't put the abortion issue in a simple way in a bucket with feminism in general, but there was the same quality of people being constrained irrationally and against their will by powers outside themselves. I guess that's the way I'd put it. So we tended to respond the same way. And I'd heard about Howard Moody, the founder of CCS. I didn't know him, but I just heard about him in the jungle telegraph among us in the profession. And I thought, boy, there's a guy with a lot of balls, to step up to an issue of this sort and be pretty out front about it too. As far as I know, it was his idea to get a group of clergy willing to undertake counseling and set up a responsible network for doing so and some criteria about how you conduct all this.[2] He managed to get his church, Judson Church in Manhattan, very much involved. But that was the sort of church that could get involved; it had a kind of clientele that took such issues very seriously. He had some problems with his congregation about it, but not a lot. Though he was under a lot of legal pressure, there was a tremendous backing for him. Then the next thing I remember about this was being in touch with one of my Yale Divinity School classmates, Harvey Cox, who was on the faculty at Harvard Divinity School. Harvey and I did various things together over the years, and so it was very easy and very natural to be talking through these issues. He was trying to round up interest in the Boston area in doing something more systematic relating to pregnancy counseling, and I said I would pick up the threads out in our area to do something more systematic too. So our chapters were related to each other, but were both really spin-offs of Howard Moody's effort.

It would have been 1968 when I started, a year before the United Christian Foundation at UMass started doing their counseling. It was a pretty preselected group that you contact about these things. I had a bunch of connections at the University of Massachusetts. A lot of the university clergy had been involved in civil rights issues and in anti-Vietnam issues, and we were all, in one way or another, identified both publicly and to each other as sharing a lot of convictions that some people in this society would have called left-wing. We got together with one another fairly often, and I remember that we had a couple of meetings to discuss CCS so that everybody was clear about the legal exposure. It was something we undertook rather soberly. We were pretty open-eyed about it. I wish I had a closer, more detailed memory of individual members of the clergy in the area with whom I talked, because I'm sure that there were people who elected not to do this, but there's only one that I can remember now. He took it very seriously and he wasn't scolding us, but just said he didn't feel in good conscience that he could do abortion referrals, and that arose from his own feelings about the abortion issue.

I think Howard put on one or two get-together seminars that I couldn't attend. But that didn't mean I wasn't in touch with him and the National CCS headquarters at Judson. We were on the phone back and forth, we exchanged letters when that was appropriate. So it wasn't as if we weren't in touch, but CCS was much more of a movement than it was a bureaucracy.

The names of abortion providers came from Howard Moody, but there were very, very few. At first we only had just one physician, in Washington D.C. He was the only one on the East Coast who was openly willing to undertake abortions. He was fighting cases in the federal district court in Washington. He said, here's a real issue, I do know what I'm doing, and I think it's the right thing to do. I'm going to do it and I'm gonna pay the penalty if I have to. He wasn't making a crusade out of this, he was just saying this is something I have to do, and I'll face the courts on the question. So that was it for the East Coast that I knew about.[3]

We did refer people abroad to both Japan and England for abortions. There were people in Latin American countries; Puerto Rico was one, but South America also. But I didn't know anything about them really. It was a very uncomfortable kind of thing to be doing, too, because you realized that you didn't have any more credentials than the good word of a friend who was probably getting the good word about three levels removed from other friends. Credentialing all had to be done by word of mouth and by investigating what anybody knew about them and what their standing was in the practice of medicine. We tried to get as thorough a read as we could on the people, and were inclined, therefore, to keep the list of doctors very narrow, in order to be sure that we were on secure ground in terms of safety.

Leslie Laurie and Planned Parenthood had our names and phone numbers. They made recommendations not just to some named organization, because we weren't in the phone book or anything, but she knew each of us, and I think she just gave out our names. They also informally put out the word a lot in our immediate area, because they were getting the traffic that would come in. They were a natural magnet in their little office on Center Street. At first, we were very leery about actually giving out a recommendation, a name and a phone number, to their clients, because it would have made Planned Parenthood publicly liable. I mean, all of us would have been, but their organization and everybody in it would have been severely compromised. For others of us, it would only be an individual who was liable; it wouldn't bring a whole apparatus down.[4]

We had made an arrangement among ourselves that if a call came and we weren't around, one way or another we would cover so that the person who called wouldn't be left hanging. I wouldn't say we were flooded, but I had people in every week. Once this was widely known, and I think when Leslie Laurie began circulating the information, most of us had somebody come in about every week. It was a rare week when I didn't have somebody.

My congregation was Smith students and faculty and staff members for the most part. There was an occasional community member, not a lot of them. But for the pregnancy counseling I saw many more community members than Smith students, many more, because we were now part of a public network and you'd just try to respond to whoever came in the door. And when I say community people, I include students at colleges other than Smith. We were seeing young women and a lot of the young women in the area were at those colleges, so the majority of women we saw were students. I don't know how many people I saw altogether. I'm sure it was in excess of a hundred a year but I would say that 80 or 85 percent of them were community people.

At first we were getting the UMass traffic, so the United Christian Federation clergy there got together and they worked out how they were going to handle. I'm sure they probably had heard about CCS from Howard Moody, but my recollection is that I was asked on a handful of occasions to go share some experience about problem pregnancy counseling and give them a little bit more palpable understanding of what it all involved. Because they too, like all of us, knew that they were walking on thin ice. And they needed to be careful, because they didn't have only their own personal ministry as a congregational parson, they had an apparatus called the UCF that didn't have the standing with the university that a college chaplain would have had. They were more vulnerable because they were there at the tolerance of the university. I think they were aware that they were more vulnerable and needed to be pretty deliberate and careful about how they worked out their process.

We were in pretty close touch. We got together a few times to talk and share what was going on. The meetings would move around, sometimes we'd go over to Amherst to meet with the UCF people. And as new referral sources became available, we were quick to share those with each other. People were very cooperative with one another. There wasn't ever any territoriality about it, not that I remember.

And when the abortion laws changed in New York State that really opened up our process a lot.[5] A lot of us felt a lot of relief because we'd been working under so many constraints with so few places to refer to for what seemed like a long time. I think it was only a couple of years, but it seemed like a long time.

Answerable to a Higher Power

As you might imagine, I thought a lot about how I would defend myself if arrested. I would feel, periodically, that somebody was going to take us to the cleaners. And that was very troubling so I tried to not just willy-nilly say, "Sure, you want a phone number?" But having been on that Presbyterian commission and having written about these issues, I had a pretty well-thought through position on this. I had worked it through ethically and theologically. Ethics was my field. There's a whole history of biblical concern about the practice of contraception. It's pretty easy to find, even though a lot of people wanted to pretend it wasn't there. Abortion has a shorter recorded history but there was plenty of recorded material about abortion practices in the nineteenth century.

The dialogue about the ethics of abortion was pretty clear to me. I argued ethically that in first trimester abortion, fetal life was not yet "quickened."[6] The period of quickening is actually a biblical distinction. After the period of quickening it becomes more perilous and more debatable. I think the Catholic Church is standing itself on its left ear by trying to say that when that active sperm squirms into the egg that all of a sudden there is a human spirit—that's a lot of baloney. I've always felt that it's got no real biblical basis. It's just trying to put an agricultural image on a human condition, and it doesn't work ethically or theologically.

So if I were arrested, I would have said: "I do this in good conscience. I know it's against the law and if you have to put me in jail, put me in jail, but I'm going to hold this position because I think it's right and proper and I think the law is wrong." I would have made that kind of defense as a matter of conscience. And I don't mean by that that your conscience is the same as being right, but there are some occasions where conscientious and discerning attempts to deal with an issue of conscience have to be undertaken. You're never casual about that, but if you're absolutely persuaded that a huge injustice is being done to somebody and being done legally, you say, "Sorry. The law doesn't make it right, it only makes it enforceable." There are points, lots of them in life in a democracy, where conscience and law get into headlong conflict.

I remember there were a couple of psychiatrists that I worked with who were very sympathetic to us and on occasion would be called on to certify that the person in question should be offered an abortion because it was a medical necessity. It went in sort of predictable gradations: rape case, incest case. It seemed kind of self-evident and everybody could get their minds around that sort of thing ethically more easily than they could about other occasions for abortion. And then there were other cases. I'll give you one case of an Amherst couple. They'd done their graduate work and I think one of them maybe was on the faculty. Anyway, the wife in this case had a medical condition where her life would have been threatened by becoming pregnant. She had been pregnant once before and had aborted spontaneously, and in the course of getting her medical treatment was told that she should not get pregnant again.

They had been very meticulous, trying to make sure that they took every proper contraceptive precaution against pregnancy. But every once in a while those things fail, and she had become pregnant. They were really desperate because if the pregnancy advanced she had a high probability of dying. And that's the kind of case I would talk about to a lawyer if I were being prosecuted. I would say, now how would the law make the distinction that I have to make between conditions and motives? I think I'm in a peculiar position to make those distinctions. I try to make them conscientiously and I try to make them against a sound ethical backdrop.

Reflections

I sure do remember when *Roe v. Wade* was passed! Thank heavens, because of what it meant for people like me. It wasn't just that we were legally exposed; we weren't very competent to make many of these judgments medically. I remember the college physician asking to talk with me about all this. She was very concerned, chiefly with the quality of the abortion service that was being offered; that is, what doctor was going to do this and where. And she went through the risks with me, the physical risks and infection risks and so on, not by way of trying to scare me off but just by way of saying, look, this is a very, very serious undertaking. Yes, you're dealing with a matter of conscience but to really ensure the quality of the medical care is very necessary and very, very difficult under these circumstances. And she was right. I already knew that, but all I could really do was to do my best to see to it that any referral was as well guaranteed as it could be under the circumstances, and then make sure that the people who were taking these recommendations were doing so in a mature, realistic, and informed fashion. That's the best I could do.

So when *Roe v. Wade* came along and it was no longer a question of a guy like me having to be the source of this information, I was frankly relieved. I was on sound ethical ground but that was only half the battle. After Roe, CCS was then not needed. We still had plenty of people who were coming in to talk, but not the people who had been referred from Planned Parenthood or elsewhere. They would have been more likely my own students coming to talk about issues, just as humans in search of some guidance and a chance to work things through, out loud with somebody who had some experience.

FOURTEEN

Reverend Samuel M. Johnson

Reverend Samuel M. Johnson received his B.A. from DePauw University and his Master's in Divinity from Harvard Divinity School. An internship at the United Christian Foundation in Amherst turned into a several-year job, which involved Johnson in draft counseling, abortion counseling, teaching, and other activities. He spent 27 years as a church pastor before joining the Boston University School of Theology as Director of Professional Development, where he also directs the school's Continuing Education Program.

Reverend Samuel M. Johnson was interviewed by David Cline on January 14, 2004.

Origins: Joining the United Christian Foundation

I came to the United Christian Foundation as an intern. I was a student at Harvard Divinity School. I had completed two years when I came to UCF full-time for a year, which then ended up being three years.

UCF is an ecumenical venture supported by [United Ministers in Higher Education] and a bunch of the mainline Protestant groups. Before UCF existed, each of those had their own campus minister that they supported. So this was an effort to work together. Though we kept some connection to individual churches in the area, it also gave us a lot more independence. I was provided housing and was paid, so in one sense I was in a training position, but I functioned pretty much as staff. There was some supervision, but a lot of it was an opportunity to learn what I wanted to learn and do what had to be done.

Initially, I was hired to work with the antiwar movement and to be in touch with students in a variety of ways: to find out what was going on, to just be available, to run alternative worship services, and help do some training of [mental health and health education] counselors in the dorms for the university. But soon after I was there, one of my colleagues, Ron Hardy, told me about the Clergy Consultation Service on Abortion (CCS) that he was involved in. Also Frank Dorman, a congregational minister in the area and president of UCF, was also involved and asked if I would like to become involved. In fact, there was another intern beside myself who was also asked if he wanted to join CCS. He turned it down. But I was interested and agreed to become a part of it. I went to some of the meetings that Dick Unsworth chaired and became part of the group. At first I was trained by Ron by sitting in on a couple of his sessions before doing it myself. That was in 1969. I was there from 1969 to 1972.

One of the things that happened and that impacted my involvement in CCS was that Ron Hardy committed suicide in 1970. So instead of there being two of us doing abortion counseling, there was just one of us. And then we decided that it would be better for there to be a woman to do counseling, so I trained Elaine Fraser, who at the point was actually the secretary for UCF. She then became part of the professional staff, and one of her major responsibilities was doing the counseling. We also had connections to the health facilities at the University of Massachusetts [UMass]. Elaine, I would say, expanded that, but I was also involved. My involvement in counseling decreased as hers increased.

Radical Times, Radical Measures

The year 1969 was at the heart of the era of "movements," and it was a fascinating time to be a campus minister. The antiwar movement was at its height. I remember one of my duties was to organize the Five College area antiwar demonstration at the time of the U.S. invasion of Cambodia. We had it on the Amherst Common and all five of the local colleges and universities were involved.[1] I was also involved in the women's movement, as well as the civil rights movement. I taught a class in alternative lifestyles in which we went out and looked at communes, looked at alternative lifestyles, a couple that was living in a homemade log cabin using horses, and so forth—looking at alternative ways of life. And within UCF I really was trying to look at a different way of worshipping.

There were two groups of students involved with UCF. One was the more radical—the Students for a Democratic Society [SDS] group and they were very much involved with Ron. They stayed involved after Ron's death. I knew them and had contact with them. All of them, but the women in particular, were supportive of the whole women's movement. And then there was another group that was not as radical politically but was still very involved in UCF and supportive of CCS. I think, partly because of the need for confidentiality, the students' support, at least as I experienced it, was not direct. It was just as support for a program that was an important thing for us to be doing. The other part of what we did at UCF, and this goes back to training counselors at the campus, was that we had a lot of interaction with Mental Health at Health Services. And so there was an informal network as well as a formal network that helped with those cases. This would be another way that students would hear and would know [about CCS and our services]. And out in the community, the Everywomen's Center and other people would be aware, but that was more iffy.[2]

Our values at UCF were really counter to the values of the mainline society. One of my colleagues, Tom Lindemann, was very involved in working with faculty and really trying to critique undergraduate education in particular—making sure teachers were really valuing the education and not just using it to do their own research and so forth. So there was a critiquing in everything that we were doing. CCS fit into that, in that we were critical of women being controlled by men as well as by society as a whole.

Before joining UCF I had been involved in, and I think very aware of, the women's movement, but not of abortion itself. I had given it some thought but had not either been personally involved or ever studied a course on it. So the context for me was the women's movement not the abortion rights movement.

CCS was a justice issue as well. I would use the term "pastoral concern," but you could also say CCS was done out of a humane concern for individual women who found themselves pregnant and had no options. So this was to help them by providing options for them, for them as individuals. But we also were very aware of how that fit into the larger issue of women's rights.

The Ethics of Abortion

One of my roles [at UCF] was not just the CCS part, but I was on a lot of panels about abortion. I remember going to Springfield, Holyoke, Amherst, and particularly

UMass. But I also remember going to the Rotary Club to talk about that issue. There were usually three or four people on the panels. I don't who the other people were, but there was often a medical person and someone who was strictly a women's rights advocate. I would be speaking on behalf of abortion rights, which was particularly important in terms of my being clergy. I could speak about Christian ethics and why Christian ethics could support abortion. I remember laying out the ethical analysis of it, as well as being able to talk from experience of having talked to a lot of women who were faced with that situation.

There are basically two kinds of religious ethics. One of them is called *obligatory* ethics. You take something that comes out of the Bible, and either you can do it or you can't do it based upon that. The other, *teleological* or *situational* ethics, is based upon what is most caring, or what is in line with the vision of the world that you want. The easiest [ethical rationale for abortion] comes out of the situational ethics. You say, in this situation, what is most caring and is best for everyone concerned— particularly those who are immediately concerned—is to go forth with an abortion. And I think that in the scriptures, Jesus always comes out of a compassionate per- spective and out of caring for the people involved. I think my own position would have been that it is too bad that an abortion has to happen. Why does this person find themselves pregnant? Why does this person find themselves in a situation where they cannot be glad to be pregnant? Or where it is counterproductive or not good to allow the pregnancy to continue? And so it's out of that larger understanding that it seems ethical to allow abortion, and often, in some situations, to *mandate* it. It is often the best choice, the best action. The way I would now state it is that abortion itself is not "a good," but it is the *right* decision. It is the ethical decision. And I would say that particularly most women who've had abortions would really agree with that. And I think there are a lot of things in life that fit that category: the act itself isn't a *good*, it isn't what we would *want*, but it is what *needs* to happen.

To say exactly when human life begins can become absurd. Is it this moment? Or is it exactly the next moment? It is a continuum that takes place from the time of conception to the time of birth. It does take place some place in there. And there is also a whole mystery about when there is a soul. I think we are on awfully slippery ground at that point. I have never pushed myself to say, okay, at what point would I say you should not allow an abortion? I would not base my ethics about abortion on making that decision, because I think it's too slippery. I would say that the older the fetus, the less a good it is to do, but that doesn't mean that it isn't necessary.

Later, my wife became pregnant, and at five months the fetus stopped growing for no particular reason. And I thought about it. There are some abortions that take place at that time. I had a lot invested in this fetus, and this fetus was in fact, I would say, my daughter. And it was very interesting for me to see what I would call ambiguity. I think life is full of those ambiguities. And I am willing to live with that ambiguity. But there is always regret—and I don't want to deny the pain or the regret about abor- tion, or that we are dealing with values and with life. But at the same time, I wouldn't want to say that the fetus of my daughter was a human life. It was some place in that in-between place.

Another part in terms of context is that my grandmother died in childbirth because she refused to have an abortion. She had heart problems and they knew it was dangerous but she refused to abort. Consequently, neither the child nor she lived. And the consequences that I saw happen upon my father were pretty disastrous. Very painful. And I know that that shaped how I understood and how I entered into CCS, and my feelings and beliefs about abortion.

Problem Pregnancy and Abortion Counseling

I joined CCS in the first month after I'd arrived at UCF. I'm sure it was then, because Ron Hardy took a sabbatical and they needed somebody to replace him. So it was within the first month. If for some reason I couldn't see a person, we had people that we could refer her to. There was that collegiality. [The president of CCS, Frank Dorman, helped out but] basically I was doing it solo. And I wasn't doing it just for people at UMass, just for students, I was also doing it for the Five-College area. I saw students from Smith and Mt. Holyoke and Amherst, as well as women in the community. I would say probably at least three-fourths were students from UMass, but it was by no means only UMass.

I also think that the health counselors at the university knew of us and would refer women to us. The Everywoman's Center too. The referral would not be to have an abortion, but for "problem pregnancy counseling." It would be if you are not sure that you want to have this child and wanted to look at the various options, which *might include* abortion.

We had a close working relationship with University Health Services. We never used their facilities, but we would have conversations with them.[3] I remember going over there just to talk with them. From the top, the doctor in charge and also the nurses, they had a particular staff that would talk to women before they would do the referral to us and I would say I was very struck, not just about the openness to us, but how compassionate they were toward students about any situation. I thought they were really excellent that way. I had a lot of respect for who they were as people and what they were doing. Our relationship to the Health Services was unique. I think at first we felt very isolated and then the University Health Services, and that relationship, brought us more into the institution. I would say that most of the stuff we were doing was pretty radical—outside institutions or anti-institution—and suddenly we were becoming part of the institution. So that was really interesting. And then, the final thing, was when the law was overturned, immediately, suddenly, we were very much part of the establishment, so to speak.

I think the effect of Ron Hardy's suicide was, in a strange kind of way, helpful. Why that was had nothing to do with Ron, but had to do with the fact that before his death two males were doing the counseling. When one was no longer involved, it opened the door more for Elaine and then Ruth to come in—to have women involved and be there. I think that was a very important move, both so that women were talking to women, but also at that point in the history of the women's movement, that women were having power over themselves and each other. I think that the collegiality of women was key, important.

There was a Valley CCS group. I don't remember how often we met, but somewhat frequently. Dick Unsworth had really been kind of the grandfather and overall leader of it. But at UCF we were doing so much more than anyone else was. I don't think anyone else was doing CCS counseling as often and as much. So we were off the scale. And it was unique in having Elaine and Ruth becoming a part of it and taking over. So our connections sometime were more direct to the national and to the state [than to the local organizations]. And that kind of kept growing. When I first got there it was smaller but it developed and grew.

CCS had been worked through collectively at UCF before I got there. It was helpful that the president of UCF was also involved. At no time was there anybody questioning whether we should be doing this or not, or what the legal ramifications were. It was not necessarily a litigious time back then in terms of being sued. I think it would be more problematic now because of that basis.

We were also doing a lot of other "radical" things—draft counseling, sanctuaries for people who were AWOL from the war, the civil rights movement, civil disobedience. I had had a lot of training and discussion in civil disobedience. One had to be willing in a sense to pay the price, always hoping that price would not be expected. That was where the abortion work differed from civil disobedience. In civil disobedience it really is confronting the authorities to force you to pay the price, to see if they're willing to do that to you. And this was definitely not that. But I think coming out of that milieu and that thinking, to enter into this abortion counseling one had to already be resolved and willing to do it. I mean I turned in my draft card two years before that. I had also taken back my draft card because of ramifications on my family. So I had thought through those things and it really seemed that no one was pushing that issue [legally].[4] I would say [doing the abortion referrals] seemed to us relatively safe, though I think we were trying to keep it under the radar. At no time did I ever feel threatened or insecure about maybe being in legal jeopardy. I was also in my early to mid-twenties and it's easy to feel that way then! Also—I think it was more so back then than now—the legal authorities would not want to arrest a minister. So there was that kind of protection.

But Elaine and Ruth, who were not ministers, also did counseling. That concerned me, I don't want to say it worried me, but it concerned me that we ministers felt more protected. And I would say both of them would say they were following a higher law also. But it is not as easily or readily apparent. And the law wouldn't recognize it at all. Well, I don't think they recognized it for us either. I think that it would just help explain why we were making that choice. There was also the cover of working within UMass in that we had a close relationship with the medical facility and they were referring people to us. I think there were two kinds of protection about that. I think there was some actual protection, but also we felt a sense of authority about it—this must be okay, this must be right, nobody is going to come after us because of that status within the university, a state university. So that also made it feel legal, even though it may or may not have been. We really don't know—never will, because it never got pushed.

The conversation with the woman was also protected. I would say now that it probably wasn't, but at least at that point our hope and thought was that it was protected. I suppose going back to the term, we were *not* doing "abortion counseling." And we really believed that. We were doing "problem pregnancy counseling," helping a woman make the right decision and then providing the means if she needed it. So that also provided protection. And we also made sure that we kept some boundaries— we did not take the woman to the place of abortion, we did not provide money. She would have to raise the money for that. We did not want to abet somebody for whom this was not the right decision. I don't know of anybody who was not able to raise it, but how they raised it, I don't know.[5] They had to do those things themselves. What we did was provide the necessary information.

The sessions usually lasted around an hour. The first part was just helping the person relax. Sometimes it would be a woman and sometimes the couple would come, the partner would be there. Then it would be time to ask them to talk about the situation, what had happened and help them explore it, ask them how they were feeling about it. What were they thinking about what to do about the pregnancy and look at the various options: keeping the baby, keeping the pregnancy to full term and giving the baby up for adoption, and looking at abortion as an alternative. And then going into how they felt about it and basically trying to help them figure out their own ethics in regards to it. And part of that too was in some ways protection. We did not want one of them regretting [the decision] and then placing charges or suing [us]. I can remember very few who carried to term. We're talking about a handful.

One of the issues that would almost always come up was how the student's parents would feel. Another part was how this fit into their being a student and the ramifications it would have upon what they were doing. It also had to do with the relationship. There were some cases where the pregnancy was not by the person that they were involved with. One case was a person who had gotten stoned and was not even aware of having had sex. That really was the exception. But there were a lot of different reasons for looking at those relationships and how abortion fit into all of that.

If they chose an abortion, then we had a doctor in Puerto Rico and we had a doctor in Montreal that we could refer them to. I also think there was one in London. I think London was the one where it might have been legal, but the cost of it was prohibitive to most. And then there was a whole process that they had to follow to get the abortion, which was, I would say, hideous to have to go through: secrecy, using different names, and the like. So part of the counseling was making sure that they understood that, trying to figure out if they had support, and looking at their support base. Who could go with them? How would they get there? How would they get back? And then wanting them to come back and talk to us about what had happened—which sometimes they did and often they did not. I think that often the *last* person they wanted to see was the person involved in that situation. I think there's a lot of denial and a lot of other things going on.

One of the issues we had to talk about with students is what happens if there is some bleeding afterwards or there are some complications afterwards. The Health Services would have been open to caring for that. They could go there. I'm trying to remember if there were some doctors in the community to whom they could go if for some reason they couldn't go to the Health Services, if they were not a student. But I think we had some doctors who would be open to treating them if that was the case. [Another issue was] keeping things private, which is kind of obvious but needs to be stated.

There were also financial concerns, particularly for Puerto Rico. There'd be a transportation issue because they'd have to fly. I think I remember it was $350 for an abortion, which comes to like a $1,000 now. So it was not inexpensive.

But I want to say that after talking to hundreds of women, not one of them took it lightly. There was not one of them who didn't really try to think it through and feel it through. The degree of regret, of remorse, I think varied a lot from one to another. One would have to do a follow-up study to know what the repercussions were later. And we'd have to know what the repercussions were later about the pregnancy as well as about the abortion, because you can't separate those two things. I'd be willing to bet that all of them had regret about the pregnancy and abortion, but how many had regret about having chosen abortion rather than one of the other options, that I don't know. I think that's a point where life gets pretty complicated and partly depends on what happened to their lives afterwards. But I don't regret having been a part of it. I'm glad that I was. That comes from sensing that for most of these women, for 99.9 percent of them, abortion was the right decision.

I remember at one point trying to figure out what proportion of the women at UMass had been pregnant. As I looked at it, it was close to a fourth. Somebody else would need to do the statistics to see whether this was true—I cannot prove that, but it was pretty high. The numbers that we were seeing were pretty high.

There were also various stories of the women coming in, individual twists and turns—hearing them, and hearing their pain, as well as hearing how these things take place. For example, I would say the primary means of birth control for these women [who got pregnant] was "the pill in the hand." That means that they had the pill but they hadn't started taking it yet. That happened again and again and again.

There are a couple of particular stories that I have thought about since. There was a UMass football captain who came with his girlfriend and really supported her and was really concerned for her, but also concerned about his situation. I thought that was really interesting. Another woman who was actually from Smith came back two or three times. Now part of the reason why that's interesting, is that it stands out in my memory. It means there were very few repeats. That was very rare. But other individual stories, they've kind of all melded together.

Looking Back: Life After Roe

When I first heard about the Roe decision my reaction was disbelief! I could not really believe that it had happened. It felt like it was out of the blue. I didn't see it coming. And when it happened there was a real question about how is this going to impact us. What did it mean to us? And how quickly it did change everything! Suddenly things were possible, overnight. But I also had some concern. I thought that the service we provided was a very important service and I had some concern that it was really not going to be used any more after Roe. The concern was that when the clinics began taking over, it wasn't at all clear that they would do the same level of counseling that we were doing, with the same intensity or degree. As well as the fact that if a woman knows she can have an abortion, she may be able to avoid looking at all the issues more easily than when she knows that what she's going to be doing is a rough ordeal. So I by no means had regret about the change in the law, but I did regret that women were not going to receive the same service that they had received before.

I think what happened was—and obviously this was a good thing—legalizing abortion allowed Planned Parenthood and lot of other clinics to become involved. The downside of that is, and one of the ways that I see that our society corrupts movements, is the money issue—it becomes a consumer-based market and loses its humanity in the process. I think that happened. But legalizing abortion also did have some good things and helped, in terms of the movement, [others] pick it up after we let it go. The church historically has started things that hospitals, educators, movements, and others then pick up. I think this is just another one of those [issues] that got started, nurtured in the church, and then was taken over by others.

Since Roe, I've been supportive of women's health issues, reproductive and all that, but it has not been a major part of my ministry. I went from UCF to being a pastor until about 1995 when I came to Boston University. I think where the CCS work had an impact upon my life has been in terms of greater sensitivity to women. I've been much more individually supportive and supportive of issues in parishes through being able to hear about the messiness of life—that life seldom goes as planned, that things happen. A person doesn't understand quite how it happened, but there they are in a situation. So I think it really increased my sensitivity. And I think it helped me be able to listen better. It was a good training, and coming out of that I was probably a better counselor.

The abortion counseling was a major part of my ministry and yet it was one that I could not talk a lot about. I could talk about abortion rights, could talk about all those issues, but could not say: "I've seen this many people and I've seen this person and that person" and all that. So that part in itself was interesting. And it was interesting being a male involved in it. I actually feel a sense of pride about all that—about my involvement as a whole, but also about being a male who was able to promote women's power and rights and be a part of that movement.

I was trained by the generation of clergy that came out of World War II, that really got radicalized by it. Not just liberalized, but radicalized. And I think they helped form my generation that grew up in the civil rights movement, and Vietnam, and the women's rights movement and all of that. And the question is what happened to that? There seems to be something about being a liberal that prevents good organization! For some reason, I think we could organize around issues better than we can just organize generally. There needs to be an issue to bring us together. I think partly it has to do with an anti-institution distrust of power, distrust of order. If you distrust order you're going to be in disorder!

Today, I'm really disappointed by where we are as a society with our attitude toward people, particularly toward those people without power—in our attitudes toward women, our attitudes toward people of color, our attitudes toward poor, attitudes toward people in trouble, whatever that problem might be. At that point in time, particularly right at *Roe v. Wade*, I was much more hopeful that we as a country would be much further along than we are now. There has been much more regression, meanness, that I see. I really regret that. In terms of specifically the abortion issue, no, I'm not surprised about where we are today. I think that if the wider context had been different, that we'd be in a healthier and a better place, particularly for women.

FIFTEEN

Reverend Franklin A. Dorman

Franklin A. Dorman was born in New York City on April 29, 1927. He was raised and attended schools in Englewood, New Jersey. He graduate from Phillips Exeter Academy in 1944 and enlisted in the U.S. Navy that same year. He was discharged from the Navy in 1946, graduated from Princeton University in 1949 with a major in Spanish and received a Master's in Spanish from Middlebury College in 1956. He taught at Tabor Academy in Marion, Massachusetts from 1951 to 1955 and the Pingry School in Elizabeth, New Jersey, from 1956 to 1963 before enrolling at Drew Theological School where he received his Master's of Divinity in 1966. He was ordained as a Congregational United Church of Christ minister and began a pastorate in 1966 at North Congregational Church in Amherst. He became Director of the United Christian Foundation (UCF), where he did problem pregnancy counseling and other activities. He became involved in Clergy and Laity United Against the War and worked with them from 1972 to 1975, before entering the wilds of dormitory life to become a Head of Residence at University of Massachusetts (UMass) for four years. He moved to Cambridge, Massachusetts in 1979, and has been employed by the Harvard University Divinity School, the State Conference of the United Church of Christ, and Witness for Peace in Nicaragua. Associated with many antiwar, antinuclear, and prochoice organizations, Dorman was arrested 19 times for nonviolent civil disobedience from 1973 to 1991. He is the author of two books on genealogy. He is married and has five children, two step-children, and ten grandchildren.

Reverend Franklin Dorman was interviewed by David Cline on February 3, 2004.

Origins

I grew up in a family that was not religious. I didn't have any religious training as a kid. I didn't go to Sunday school, any of that stuff, though my mother insisted I be confirmed. I was raised in New Jersey, but I went to Phillips Exeter Academy up in New Hampshire. And then went in the service for a couple of years, in the Navy. Then I went into teaching. I taught at a couple of prep schools, including the Pingry School in Elizabeth, New Jersey. Then I decided to go to seminary. I graduated from Drew University in New Jersey and got ordained in Chatham, New Jersey, in 1966. Afterwards, I got a job up in Amherst with the North Amherst Congregational Church.

I had become involved in the civil rights movement when I was in seminary. I went down to Selma with four divinity school professors, and I picketed some barbershops in Madison, New Jersey—that kind of thing, kind of low key. But Selma was an eye-opener. This was 1965, 1964, something like that. It was still fairly early in the civil rights movement for a lot of people, up North anyhow.

My ministry at North Church lasted four-and-a-half years. Initially I did a lot of civil rights stuff. I took a busload of kids down to see the encampment on the Mall and the Poor People's March on Washington. That was just a month after the burning of Washington after Martin Luther King's assassination. That was an eye-opener for the kids. We traveled all around the burnt down areas, and were given a tour of the encampment on the Mall.

When the Black Power movement came along it seemed that whites were not as effective—or let's say, *welcome*—in the civil rights movement as they had been up to that point. So I got involved with Clergy and Laity Concerned with the War. I had become aware of the Vietnam War while I was in seminary but didn't pay much attention to it. But when I got up to Amherst, things were really starting to go to the devil over there. I think Dick Unsworth flew me down to Washington three times for demonstrations and marches with Clergy and Laity Concerned. I've known Dick for a long time. He was actually a classmate of mine at Princeton.

The Clergy Consultation Service on Abortion

As far as the Clergy Consultation Service [CCS], I was not recruited by Dick, but by a doctor in my congregation named Carl Brandfass. [He] had come to UMass Health Services and worked with Dr. Gage. He came down to North Congregational and liked what I was saying about Vietnam I guess, and he became a member of the church—he and his family. I left that particular church after five years, because the congregation just couldn't take me anymore. And when I left, he left too.

I remember Carl came into my office at the church one day and he said, "What do you think about abortion?" I said, "Well, frankly, Carl, I hadn't thought much about it at all." So he proceeded to tell me about the Clergy Consultation Service on Abortion. He probably knew about it through Gage. He wasn't part of CCS himself—I don't think there were many doctors involved in the counseling part of it. But there were doctors in the actual, medical work of it. I think that there was a doctor at Cooley Dickinson Hospital who did abortions disguised as D&Cs. He finally decided he couldn't continue with that. He was getting pressure from the hospital, asking why are you doing all of these? How come there are so many of these D&Cs?

So Carl knew about CCS and I don't know that he talked me into it, but he got me interested in it. So I pursued it. I guess I probably got in touch with Dick Unsworth and some of the others, such as Jim Clark, the minister at the Episcopal Church in town. I think it was a little bit later that I became president of the United Christian Foundation and I hired Sam Johnson and Ron Hardy and others. I was at UCF while still at North Congregational Church—that overlapped a bit. The Clergy Consultation Service mainly worked through the United Christian Foundation because they couldn't exactly work through the infirmary. But later, when Elaine moved over to the infirmary, to the Health Services, she and her colleagues continued to do this sort of counseling and abortion referrals.

Further Radicalized: Abortion Counseling and Other Work

Ron Hardy's death happened when I was president of UCF. We had a small group of UCF staff: Ron Hardy, Sam Johnson, Tom Lindemann, myself, Elaine. We had a support group, into touchy-feely, Esalen kind of stuff. And it became fairly obvious that Ron Hardy was . . . disturbed. And he felt deeply about the war. So he immolated himself. His wife called me; I was one of the first people on the scene. I led the service at his funeral.[1]

His death was a major factor in my radicalization. He was the "token" radical in Amherst at that point. He was a college chaplain and could get away with all sorts of stuff! But I think Ron and his death convinced me that I should not continue to expend energy in the local church, fundraising bakers and that sort of thing. I preached against the war, frequently, but his death made me say, okay, somebody needs to pick up the standard and run with it. So I did. I resigned from North Church and got heavily involved in activism.

After Ron's death I got more involved in CCS. Again, part of my motivation was really to take up where Ron left off. I can remember, it seems to me, doing two or three counseling sessions a day for UMass students. And I always felt pretty positive about how those sessions turned out. I tried to present the options without trying to talk them into doing one thing or another. There were some guidelines, obviously. I think there were initial questions about the partner, the other person involved— whether he knew, whether he was supportive. But there was never a time when a partner accompanied one of these young women to the counseling session. And I'd ask about family, did family know? And if not, how did she imagine they were going to react? And the various options: about where she could go for an abortion, the option of adoption, and about raising the child herself. They seemed to listen and I usually felt pretty good about how the sessions turned out.

When *Roe v. Wade* came down it was probably a relief because then I didn't have to do any of these things any more. It had been a strain on me. I was glad to do it, but I was glad to be relieved of it at the same time. Also, my wife was not happy about this—my first wife. We had adopted two Korean mixed-race kids when they were infants, and something about that turned her against abortions. I remember her argument was, you know, these kids never would have been born. I'm not sure that's true, because I don't think they were doing many abortions in Korea. So, I did the counseling up until *Roe v. Wade*, but it probably didn't help my marital relations.

My mother had an abortion. So to me, abortion wasn't something that was so horrible and who would ever think of that? It existed. And I saw it as necessary to have that kind of service and advice and counseling. My mother, my conservative Republican mother, was a power in Planned Parenthood in New Jersey. And my sisters have told me that they are convinced that she was pretty heavily involved in abortion then and would take some of the women to their appointments and so on. I never discussed that with her, but according to my sisters that's true.

Still a Radical

I do see my involvement in social issues as a progression, but it's not vertical, it's horizontal. It's a natural consequence. You toss a rock in the water and the ripples go in all directions. Yeah, no question about that. I see it as part of the social problems that we have. It's an attempt at a solution to some of these problems. I was a radical, definitely. I was involved in the strikes at UMass and the nonviolent training for students and faculty. When I left North Church, I went to work full-time for Clergy and Laity Concerned and organized antiwar groups in Pittsfield, Springfield, Amherst, Deerfield, Greenfield, and Williamstown. There were probably 30 or 40 people in each one of those groups. They were mostly church-connected, and they became branches or local groups of Clergy and Laity Concerned. They each did different kinds of work. The Williamstown group did fundraisers and raised a lot of money and bought medical equipment and got a chartered plane to fly from Canada to Vietnam to deliver this medical equipment, incubators and stuff like that. It was wonderful. And when Nixon was elected for the second time, we had what was called a Counter-Inauguration in Amherst. But the big thing in the Valley in those days was protesting at Westover Air Force Base.

About 1,400 people were arrested over a period of 2 or 3 months. I went to jail for a couple of weeks in Springfield with four of the other organizers because we were the first ones arrested, and we got the first court appearance and refused to pay a $10 fine and this cost us ten days in the slammer, which was okay. That was the only time I made the *New York Times*. And it was about an inch, you know, because I was a minister. That was where my mother saw it. She didn't hear it from me. Some friend of hers saw it and read it to her. She was fit to be tied. I come from a long line of conservative Republicans; I don't know where I got going.

I got arrested four times. After the third time, I thought I don't have to do this anymore; I'm getting too old for this. But my daughter decided she wanted to do it, and I figured I really wanted to be with her. I had taken my two oldest children down to Washington for an anti-war demonstration and we succeeded in getting ourselves teargassed so, you know, we had a good relationship along those lines.

Nothing has changed as far as my attitude toward abortion is concerned. I went down to Washington D.C. with a group of women, including my wife, her sister, my sister, and a bunch of other women from church for some anniversary of *Roe v. Wade*. There was a huge crowd on the Mall. I'm proud to have feminist daughters. And my present wife is very into that stuff, no question. She had two daughters when I married her, who are my daughters also now, and they are both strong along that line. I remember I went to a pro-choice rally with one of them at City Hall in Boston. Now she's a doctor. She started a pro-choice group in her first or second year at Columbia Medical School, brought in speakers and so forth. I thought that was great.

I'm now worried that if they can get one more conservative appointee to the Supreme Court they might just well overturn Roe, but I think there's still enough life in the women's movement to prevent that kind of thing from happening. I hope! But we may have to go back to doing the Clergy Consultation Service again if they do. That will be a hardship for a while, but in our system, hopefully, it can be reversed again at a later date. I'm taking the long view. I'm not sure how qualified I should be at my age to take the long view, but it kind of puts it beyond my responsibility, you know. I don't have to worry about these things if I know in the end that justice will prevail—at least for a while.

SIXTEEN

Rabbi Yechiael Lander

Rabbi Yechiael Lander was raised in Winnipeg, Canada and following high school and agricultural college, moved to a kibbutz in Israel for five years. He worked as an educational director at synagogues in Winnipeg and Los Angeles before entering Hebrew Union Seminary, where he was ordained as a Rabbi. He spent several years working for the seminary, before becoming the Jewish chaplain for Smith College and Amherst College in 1967. He held this position nearly 30 years. He still lives in Northampton with his wife Rose, a violin teacher. He has two children, a son Jeremy who is a woodworker, and a daughter Shira, also a rabbi.

Rabbi Yechiael Lander was interviewed by David Cline on February 16, 2004.

Family Background

I grew up in an Orthodox Jewish family in Winnipeg in Manitoba. My father was a farmer. My name, Lander, means farmer in Yiddish. He came to Western Canada from Lithuania in the 1890s to settle on the land. Actually some other families related to us had come as the earliest Jewish families in Manitoba in the 1850s and had established themselves on the land. And so my father had some relatives nearby upon whom he could depend. My mother came a little bit later.

I grew up in a family of five siblings. My oldest brother was 20 years older than I was. I was a child of old age, what's called in Yiddish a *mezinik*. I went to a Jewish parochial school run by the Zionist Socialist movement in Canada. It was called a *folkshule*, I don't think there are any left. When I came home from that school I had [instruction by] a *malamud*, an Orthodox rabbi. The only condition upon which my family would send me to a non-Orthodox school was if I would have that supplemental education at the end of the day. But that was good. I almost never felt overburdened. I loved it and fell in love with the tradition very early.

At about nine years of age I joined a Zionist youth movement and that became the center of my life. We were dealing with issues of the growing Nazi phenomenon in Germany and what was happening to the Jewish people. My early beliefs as an Orthodox Jewish child were highly challenged—how could God let such a thing as the Holocaust happen—and I abandoned belief, but not without struggle and pain. This Zionist youth movement and its dream of a Jewish homeland became essentially my religion and occupied me almost totally.

After I went to public high school, I got a certificate degree from a school of agriculture in Manitoba, hoping to go to live on the land in Israel, on a *kibbutz*. I eventually did. I went to Israel in 1947, helped to establish a *kibbutz*, and lived there until 1952 when I returned to Canada. I was the only unmarried child and felt a responsibility to aging parents to return. I also wanted to go back to school to get a liberal arts degree, which I subsequently did—a Bachelor's degree in psychology. I also worked for a friend, *olev ha'shalom*, who established the first Conservative synagogue in Winnipeg. I became the Executive Director and Educational Director of this growing synagogue.[1]

When I felt that I had somehow prepared my parents for aging, I went to graduate school in Los Angeles, California. I worked for a very large synagogue to support myself there—a synagogue called Temple Isaiah that's on Pico Boulevard, right across from the golf course. It was very symbolic, for California! Again I was Executive Director and Educational Director. There were eleven hundred families when I came to them, a huge institution. I went to school whenever I could—I was able to get morning classes and evening classes and somehow do the degree. It wasn't the best way to do it, but I hadn't an alternative. I really had to support myself. I reached the Master's level and was working for a Ph.D. in clinical psychology when I changed course. That began to happen in the late Fifties.

Faith: A Crisis and a Resolution

I had not been able to resolve this issue of my belief, which somehow eluded me from about 11 years of age until my twenties. I just couldn't find a way out of my dilemma: What was God doing during the Holocaust? A critical point was a meeting with the rabbi Abraham Joshua Heschel, *olev ha'shalom*, who was a great rabbi and Jewish philosopher and theologian.[2] I had great respect for his writing and for what he did. I heard he was coming to Los Angeles to raise money for the Jewish Theological Seminary so I wrote him a letter. I just poured out my heart and said that for 20 years I'd been trying to resolve this [issue of faith] and I couldn't. Would he find some time for me? And he did. He was very gracious. It was a turning point in my life. I didn't suddenly begin to believe, but he helped me through the process of rethinking my beliefs in perhaps a more mature, more adult, more rational way: a new way. That was an important corner for me. Once that happened, I began to think about the rabbinate. My grandfather was a rabbi. My wife and I talked for a long time about the possibility of doing this because we were planning a family, and we both had incomes and lived quite well. And we decided together: if it's important, we will do it together. I applied for rabbinic school and was turned down the first time for being too old— I was in my thirties. I knew a lot of influential Jews in California and I decided for the first time in my life to use a connection. I asked them would they call and they called. Of course the next day I was accepted.

I began my studies in California and I continued to work part-time for a couple of new synagogues. I finished whatever Los Angeles could offer me in the way of study, and then went off to Cincinnati to the Reform seminary to complete my studies. I was there from 1962 to 1965 and was ordained a rabbi. I was hired to become the Assistant to the President of the seminary; it was probably the biggest mistake of my life. I had illusions that I could change things, but that evaporated very, very quickly; old institutions don't change easily or readily and not because of a single person. But I didn't want to walk out on what I had committed myself to, so I stayed.

A New Opportunity (and New Challenges)

At one point, I was traveling on behalf of the seminary—raising money, recruiting people, visiting alumni—and I was talking at Harvard. The rabbi at Harvard then was a model for me in the rabbinate, Maurice Zigmund. Ziggy said, "I loved your talk but you looked so unhappy when you talked about the seminary." Yes, I said, I think I've got to get out. I could remain in that position, but then I'd have to become part of that culture, and I didn't want to do that. And so he said, "What's the problem? I have just the place for you. There are a couple of colleges in Western Massachusetts, Smith and Amherst, that are looking for a rabbi and a chaplain. I think you would like it, I think you would like the students. Why don't we drive down?" It was April. We got in the car, and when we got off the Massachusetts Turnpike and went through the Holyoke Range, I thought I had entered Paradise. The trees were blooming, the dogwoods, all of them were in bloom. It looked idyllic.

I was interviewed and it was clear that I could have the job if I wanted to. And I had a nice Jewish incident. When the Smith president interviewed me over lunch at the faculty club, he had asked somebody in the Religion Department what can the rabbi eat? I observed *kashrut*, the dietary laws. Could he eat fish? Yes, he could eat fish. Could he eat scallops? Yes, he could eat scallops, those are fish. This was a scholar at Smith. So I arrived and there's a plate of scallops sitting there with kasha, buckwheat groats—a favorite Jewish dish. What a combination sitting on the same plate together! I decided I'd just play it cool; after all, I am applying for a job. I'll eat the kasha and I'll just leave the scallops on the plate. But President Thomas Mendenhall asked me, "Is the fish not good?" And I tried to *fumpkh* around and evade the question. At first I said, well, you know it's a rather large meal for me at lunchtime, and then I told him [that scallops are shellfish and therefore not kosher]. In any case, that should have given me some insight into the school's culture. At Amherst, we didn't have lunch, so, it was fine—coffee with George Plimpton who was then the president.

In any case, my wife Rose, who is a violin teacher and a violinist, flew out here and she felt the same way as I did about it. I had an offer from a university in Washington D.C., which wanted to establish a Judaica program, the first Catholic school in the country to do that, I believe. I was very excited about the possibility of going to Washington. But I had two children. My wife said we can't think only of ourselves, we have to look for the place that would be the best to raise our children. And she was right. And so we did come here. We came just after the Six Day War in 1967, and stayed 37 years. I spent 29 years working for Smith and Amherst and I loved most of it. I feel somehow I was *bashert* to come here, despite the difficulties that we faced.[3]

After we got here I realized that their vision of a Jewish chaplain and rabbi, at least at Smith, was very different from my own. I'm an activist. I quickly became involved in all kinds of issues, Jewish and non-Jewish social issues that interested me, and I moved quickly to enrich the Jewish life on the campuses. I had a colleague who had been here for 20-some odd years before he moved to Boston. He had been content to be the scholar/rabbi-in-residence in a sense: students would come to him with issues and he would provide certain kinds of basic Jewish services. That wasn't enough for me. I had come late to the rabbinate. I was a person in a hurry and I wanted to do some things. So I became very active.

I learned very quickly that Smith saw it as a good public relations move to appoint a rabbi as chaplain, but it really didn't understand the full implications of having a rabbi who would then speak for the Jewish community and other minority and religious communities. Those were difficult years of struggle for me and the struggle went on almost throughout the course of my time here, although it was most intense in the beginning. But I was determined to stay and change the culture here.

For a long time the rabbi did not appear at public events where the chaplains were to appear. [The rabbi] never got up and made an invocation at graduation or sat on the kinds of committees that chaplains must be involved in on campus. I changed that, but not so easily. It was very hard. My successors who have come after me have come into a different kind of climate. There's still some lingering of the old culture of the Protestant community as being the dominant one and the privileged one. There's a lot to be said about the nature of what Smith was, and maybe is still a little bit. But I determined to stay, and I stayed, and I think I had very productive years. There were very few rabbis in Western Massachusetts when I first came. That has changed, thank God.

Getting Involved in the Clergy Consultation Service on Abortion

I think Dick Unsworth told me about CCS very early and about how it had been started by Howard Moody, a wonderful, wonderful, Baptist minister in New York who I then came to know in later years. Dick told me that young women who were pregnant and decided on abortion couldn't get a safe procedure in this country because it was illegal, and that a group of clergy had, in a sense, contracted with each other to provide counsel and help for such women. There was a little risk involved in that it was not legal, and you had to be aware of that when you signed on. I was concerned because I was a Canadian living in the United States, so there was an extra dimension to my anxiety, because I thought if I got in trouble I might be deported. But I felt my understanding of Judaism permitted me to help—in fact, called on me to help—and I decided I must do it. The CCS provided me with some basic materials as to what were some of the questions that might be raised. I had a background in psychology so I knew something of the human dimensions in such a situation for a young woman. I had both sympathy and understanding and some way of relating to these young women in a difficult time.

I didn't see that many people. I cannot really tell you numbers any more. I would say it was evenly split or maybe a little bit more Smith students than women from the community. I don't mean only Northampton women, but referrals from other places in Massachusetts or Vermont. I don't remember where the next clergy "cell" was, but we seemed to get a fair number of people from other places. We tried to keep the people private to guarantee them as much privacy as we could. We tried to arrange and make appointments ourselves rather than through our administrative staff. I remember writing some of my letters by hand when I identified names or talked about people. I didn't feel I should do that through my secretary.

It was a very important thing to do, as I look back upon it now. I haven't thought about it for many years. I think it was a critical thing to do. I think it did address my commitment to *pikuach hannefesh*, to the saving of a soul, to the saving of a human being. And I feel good about having served in that way. I was torn, though, in my feelings about abortion, because my orthodox background was still very present in me although I am a liberal rabbi. You know, I observe the *mitzvoht*, the commandments. I live essentially a traditional life, although my theology is far away from what my Orthodox colleagues believe. And I was torn by that—but not for long. When I began to study some of the sources, I understood that the mainstream of rabbinic Judaism permitted me, *commanded* me, to respond to people in need, whose lives were being radically changed or challenged by their pregnancies. It also taught me that the child in our tradition is not viable until a month after birth. That made it easier for me. I guess I believe very much in *pikuach hannefesh*, a central belief in Judaism about the preciousness of life, about preserving life, and that drove me to be involved. I felt that this was such an occasion when I could help make a contribution. But it didn't come easily—I didn't say: here's another cause, let's jump in and do it. Because every time I face those questions, my grandfather the rabbi appears in my dreams. So the decision wasn't made easily. But once it was made, I decided to proceed even with the difficulty and some slight danger to me that I could get deported. My name was put on a list, a referral list, and I was ready for people to come. I did that work until *Roe v. Wade*.

The counseling did not consciously push a person in the direction of abortion. We felt our first responsibility was to explore with the individual what she wanted, what she needed at that point, to help her clarify in her own mind the options that were available to her. But once that judgment was made to seek an abortion, I must tell you, I had some anxiety in sending people off. Howard [Moody] or somebody, of course, checked out the places we were sending people to, but I had not seen them myself. I had not interviewed the doctors [performing the abortions]. I could not make my own personal judgment as to their adequacy for these young women. If I remember the list, it was quite widespread. There were some people in this country, but mostly abroad—Sweden, England, and I think in the Islands. That was a mixed part of the experience, not really being able to validate those places for myself.

I'm sure the college administrators must have been generally aware, although I don't remember sharing any of this with the presidents of the institutions. I didn't feel the need. Again, these were people, as I discovered very quickly, from very different cultural backgrounds than I was. So, no, I don't remember discussing it. I may have discussed it with some of my clergy friends, the few rabbis that I had contact with.

The counseling sessions were different from each other depending on the personality, the age, the character of the woman, the circumstances, and how she was addressing this new situation in her life. I remember some people being very upset, very anxious, very teary. And others who, at least on the surface, approached the decision quite stoically. But essentially I think the parts of a session were: getting acquainted; learning much more about the individual and her situation; helping her to learn as much as I could about me in a short time so that we could develop some level of trust with each other—because I wouldn't proceed unless I felt that; and then talking about what the alternatives might be. We were not necessarily resolving it at that time, if I remember correctly, but at least raising the alternatives for her decision. It may have happened a couple of times in that first session, but sometimes the young woman would come back and we would talk a little bit further and deal with some of the questions, some of the issues that existed there. Again, we were not pushing the young person toward any kinds of conclusion because we happened to be part of this network, but rather helping the young person do that.

There were some who chose adoption. I remember a young Jewish woman facing this dilemma and she felt she couldn't abort, it was not morally, ethically possible for her to do that. I suggested being in touch with a Jewish Family Service where she lived because the Jewish Family Services around the country were often the main avenue for Jewish adoptions. I don't know what happened afterwards. I remember some others which were not resolved, at least not resolved in my presence. Usually that was the woman, after maybe one or two sessions, saying simply, I can't, I'm in conflict, I think I have to resolve this for myself. There were some of those people and I don't know what happened to them. I know some young people who took our referrals to particular medical centers, or doctors who would perform abortions. I don't ever remember anybody coming back to me after the procedure. I don't know what the experiences of other [clergy members] were, but I can't think even of an instance where that happened to me. That's okay—I think that people have to find their own way.

An Activist at Work

This CCS work was a continuum, absolutely [from my earlier social justice work]. The synagogue I worked for in Los Angeles was a pioneer in social action and social justice starting from, probably, the early 1950s. They were at the forefront of civil rights actions in Los Angeles, the antiwar movement, of everything progressive. It was a wonderful place for me to be; I learned so very much. Because, you know, my vision of religious Judaism had been the vision of myself and my family and my *shul* [synagogue] at Winnipeg. It was an Orthodox *shul*. It had wonderful things about it, but there was not too much concern about things outside the Jewish community. And so what had been my commitment to social justice through my understanding of the prophets and the Bible was now enlarged in a living way that I had seldom experienced before in the Jewish community.

In the Sixties I became a very early voice on behalf of Soviet Jews and their right to either live their own lives there or to emigrate to Israel or wherever else they chose to go. I was an early anti-Vietnam person, one of a small minority in my seminary. Rabbinic students have to conduct services and preach for their colleagues and their teachers once a year at that seminary. And my preaching, for which I actually won a prize in 1965, was against the war in Vietnam. Afterwards, the president got up, walked over to me, and he had obviously been crying. He said to me, "You know,

Yechiael, I don't agree with you, but you articulated your position so beautifully." So, I was an early, early civil rights advocate.

The women's movement began to crystallize in a political way in the Fifties and Sixties. Betty Friedan's book [*The Feminine Mystique*] was one of the first expressions of that. She was a graduate of Smith. So I was very much aware of such issues cooking in the community. The synagogue in Los Angeles was an egalitarian community and that was a great lesson for me. Women could come up to the pulpit or be officers of the synagogue or be engaged fully. I had never seen that before, except of course on the *kibbutz*. My *haverot*, my buddies, my female buddies, on the *kibbutz* taught me a lot of lessons about the equality of women! I feel good about that, though the immediate experience was not such a pleasant one sometimes. But, yes, I did become aware of those movements for equality. There was no woman student at the seminary when I was there. Part of my responsibilities as the Assistant to the President was being the Dean of Admissions of that seminary and I helped recruit the first woman who completed her studies. I was very much aware then. And of course my wife taught me a lot as far as equality, as far as how I viewed those issues. It's always been truly an equal marriage. And then my daughter growing up, that was an important experience for me. Shira is a deeply committed feminist. She taught me a great deal. And then the students at Smith.

There were points when I thought I was way ahead of them—maybe that's an unfair thing to say—in the sense of their consciousness as women. Too many of them brought those early learnings of women as being subjected, quiet, secondhand citizens, into the classroom. I hated that. When I first came here, I found a lot of the women were very passive human beings. And I found many of my colleagues wanted that and liked that—my male colleagues, but some of my female colleagues as well. They liked being the voice of wisdom, with women listening and writing down quickly what they were saying, but not engaging with them. I think it has changed, but not completely. The institution itself lagged behind in terms of the feminist movement.

The Roe Decision: Looking Back, Looking Ahead

When the Roe decision came down it was a relief. We didn't have to do this as an underground network, as an illegal act any longer. I can't remember the specific feelings, but yes, I was obviously very supportive of it when it happened.

I did have some reservations about abortion. What still troubles me is abortion for convenience sake. I can't make judgments, I can't offer percentages, but I do know that the presence of abortion was part of a larger movement of things opening up in terms of men and women and the whole sexual revolution. I know that there are some women who choose it relatively easily. But it's sort of—how shall I say it—social abortion. But listen, I have no intention, desire, or ambition to rule the world. We have one ruler, that's enough.

Roe could be overturned. I'm not sanguine enough to believe that it's established—it could be overturned; although, you cannot always predict what happens with those judges. Some have conversions to liberal positions on the Court. The Court itself is a powerful and dynamic instrument. But it could go, it could go.

Elaine Fraser

Elaine Rae Fraser was raised in Detroit and received her B.A. in Economics from Connecticut College and her Master's in Education from the University of Massachusetts at Amherst (UMass). She and her husband Duncan Fraser owned and published The Niantic News *in Niantic, Connecticut, between 1954 and 1967. She first joined the United Christian Foundation (UCF) in Amherst as a secretary in 1968 and was soon trained as that organization's first female problem pregnancy counselor. She worked with UCF's Clergy Consultation Service on Abortion (CCS) until 1973, when she became a clinical social worker at the UMass Health Services. She retired from the Health Services in 1993 and from then on volunteered as a patient ombudswoman at Cooley Dickinson Hospital in Northampton. She passed away in August 2001 at the age of 73. She had a daughter and two grandchildren.*

Elaine Rae Fraser was interviewed by Judi Fonsh on October 17, 1999.

Origins and Identifying as a Feminist

I'm Elaine Fraser. I'm retired from the University of Massachusetts. I worked for 20 years as a medical and clinical social worker. As part of that job, I did problem pregnancy counseling.

I grew up in the city of Detroit, and went to high school there, and then came east to college. I went to Connecticut College where I was, believe it or not, an economics major. I was very interested in economics, but all the social work courses were in the Economics Department too.

I first identified as a feminist after reading Betty Friedan's book [*The Feminine Mystique*]. That really was the beginning. Before then, I just thought, "Well, I'm funny. I feel different." I was married and had youngsters, and so forth, and at the time, you know, African violets were a woman's excitement. But it just wasn't for me. I worked all those years when women did not work. I was helping my husband for a good part of them, and so that was okay. I also did the volunteer stuff. I was very active in the Girl Scouts and then I was a volunteer church secretary. So that was okay, too. But nobody else was working.

But when I read Betty Friedan's book I felt that marriage and motherhood was not all there was, and I thought, "Why did I spend all that time in college, to . . ." That was also a part of it—of asserting yourself as a woman and knowing who you are, and all the skills that you have. You might as well use them! I didn't hate house-work. I loved it. And I did all the domestic things, but I just needed something more. And the something more started out as helping my husband with publishing his newspapers. He had first one paper, *The Nyantic News* in Nyantic, Connecticut, and then he and two others owned a chain of papers in Connecticut, ranging from Deep River to Mystic. I did just about everything there, all the darkroom work, and the bookkeeping and the circulation—you name it—and also some writing and covering of events. I still enjoyed being a mother, and I enjoyed my daughter, and I still do, very, very much. But it was just nice to have a purpose to living. And I learned there was nothing wrong with me! There weren't a lot of professional or working mothers at that time, but there was one other woman in Nyantic who was reading *The Feminine Mystique*. Then I told a friend of mine who was very active in the Girl Scouts, and very much of an independent soul, and she got very interested too. She got so interested that she went back to college and ended up doing cancer research. It just opened everything up for her, too.

The Clergy Consultation Service on Abortion

My husband and I moved to Amherst where he edited the *Amherst Bulletin* newspaper. I started working as a secretary and receptionist at United Christian Foundation at the University of Massachusetts in February of 1968. At that time the Clergy

Consultation Service was just beginning to evolve. For the first few months, I didn't work with them; I was just indirectly involved because of being in the office. Not too long after I started there, it suddenly dawned on somebody that there weren't any women involved in this process and that it might be nice for a woman to talk to a woman. That's when we started the rearrangement. I began doing the counseling, and also education—information about what to expect [during an abortion procedure] and so forth.

Clergy Consultation [in Massachusetts] started around 1968. The central meeting point was a Unitarian Church in Newton, near Boston. All the denominations, other than Roman Catholic, were involved. In our area, I don't think the local Lutheran pastor was involved in it, but I know certainly all the Congregational and Episcopal and Methodist ministers were. I'm not sure about the Baptist, but there were Baptist ministers in other parts of the state.

There was a great deal of pulling away from the Catholic Church at that time because of their stances on contraception and abortion and unwed pregnancy. It was a no-win position for the Catholic Church, really. So a lot of women were disillusioned, but I always checked out the religious affiliation [of the women I counseled], because you may leave the Catholic Church, but the Catholic Church does not leave you. It's a part of who you are, and your whole background and training, and you need to work through that. If women were having problems afterwards with it, we had priests that we could refer to. I don't think I should say who.

Problem Pregnancy Counseling

The counseling was mainly to help women decide how they wanted to resolve this particular issue [of being pregnant]. All the options were open to them, and we discussed them all: how they could keep the child, if they wanted to, as a single parent; adoption; as well as abortion. And we would help people with all of them. We didn't want them to feel that they made the decision without a complete knowledge of other resources. We'd also discuss what it would mean if they got married, and was that a viable option, or would it be better to wait and have the child and marry afterwards, so that there wouldn't be that constant pressure of a "had-to" marriage.

And we discussed birth control, absolutely! It was semi-legal. For married people, it was legal. But the [University] Health Services was beginning to sort of edge into that, as some of the doctors were prescribing for unmarried women. Very quietly, mind you, since it was supposedly strictly for married couples.[1]

Women came in with friends, partners, and by themselves. Maybe 15 or 20 percent brought their partners with them. But when they came with a partner or friend, we'd ask them, "Do you want to talk to me alone?" And that was very important because sometimes if the partner would come in, he was exerting undue influence on the woman, one way or another. I mean, she might want to keep the child, and he'd say,

"You gotta have an abortion." So it was important [to be able to speak to the woman alone]. And then, we'd say, during the interview, "Would you like your partner to come in?" Many of the partners did not even know about the pregnancy because it was a casual thing or, basically, a date rape. A lot didn't know about it or said: "It's not mine." Very often, alcohol had been involved—an inexperienced drinker and fraternity parties. Some of them were pretty wild!

I think the cost was $375 for an early termination, plus the cost of travel and, if they had to stay overnight, there was that too. It was a lot of money. The later procedures, well, I guess they were very expensive, because that was in England or Japan. So they were probably a $1,000–$1,500. Late abortions took really, really big bucks.

We never lost anybody. We had some serious infections, but we tried to instruct the women to guard against that, and they were always put on antibiotics prophylactically. We'd tell them all the signs and symptoms [of infection] and tell them to get right to the Health Services, no matter what.

It was sort of learn-as-you-go. I had all kinds of medical resources if I wanted— I'd just call the nurses at the Health Services and ask technical questions, incredible questions. That's how I've learned everything, all the medical social work. Now I'm a pretty good diagnostician simply because I've asked so many questions. I also took a graduate program in education and counseling, so that gave me some skills. And though I didn't belong to women's groups, I also just sort of absorbed a lot of my counseling skills by osmosis [from them too]. I sort of naturally had the counseling skills, and I learned from observation of the clergy who were doing the actual counseling. And then [the book] *Our Bodies, Ourselves*, that was the Bible.

As far as the referrals were concerned, the clergy gave the woman a phone number to call. It was a Boston phone number which would give her the address of where to go. That kept all the information clustered, because a clergyman here might make a referral today, and the woman goes, but the central location knows that place has been closed, so then they would divert and redirect her.

Operating Outside the Law

Clergy Consultation was completely illegal at that time. It was a conspiracy—that's the way they planned it. If there was any prosecution, every clergyman in Massachusetts would stand up and come forward. And we thought that that was a great protection. Every now and again, you'd think, "Well, I hope this really works, this conspiracy thing!" But I was doing nothing since I never made a referral. I would talk with someone, and explain all about the procedure. I'd explain *everything*—what to expect with the procedure, what to expect afterwards, medical concerns, lab tests that they would probably need, and I'd explain about their options. *Then*, at that point, I'd call one of the clergymen in and I would leave the room for that time. We worked in tandem. The clergy did the actual referral, which consisted of giving them a name, an address, and a phone number. We never gave a woman a written referral. It was oral only.[2]

They [the abortion providers] were mainly in Canada, Puerto Rico, and Mexico, but we didn't use Mexico very much. It was harder to monitor. All the sites and the clinics were monitored by certain people in Clergy Consultation, and then we'd get feedback from the women. If there had been inappropriate treatment in any way, emotionally or otherwise, we'd send it on to the main information source, and very often, we would abandon those particular sites. We did a few in New York, before it was legal, but that was really chancy. Those sites could change all the time. I think that everybody did it out of concern for the women because otherwise, why would they take that risk, really?

One of the excitements was when there was a change in the referral location, because there'd been a shutdown. We then had to reach the women who we were trying to keep as anonymous as possible. God, I can remember one time, I was absolutely panicked about a woman that was going off to Puerto Rico, and the location had been closed down. I had no way of contacting her. And by golly, if I didn't meet her on the street! Talk about relief! I caught her just the day before she was going.

One day a state police officer came in to the office with this woman, and we thought, "Oh, dear. What do we do now?" She had an appointment, so we spoke with her. We were just waiting for the ax to fall—but actually it was his daughter, and he had brought her in. We were quite surprised that he had come in uniform, but I think he didn't have time to go home and change! As a father he was very supportive and very crushed, and very concerned and worried. I think he wanted to check us out to make sure that we were using good resources, not that he knew what the resources were.

Almost all of the women came back for a follow-up interview.[3] Very seldom did we not hear from them. [If we didn't], we'd do an outreach just to call and check, and say, "If you don't want to talk further that's understandable. We just want an evaluation of your experience, because that helps us." We'd always explain beforehand that "Your evaluation and feedback is going to be helpful to other women." It also gave us a contact point so that if things weren't going well, we could pick up on it, and make another referral if necessary, or see them on an ongoing basis. And all the clergy, whether they were involved in pregnancy counseling or not, were available to talk with women if they had some problems afterwards. We also tried to do some postabortion support groups, but they were not terribly successful because the women didn't feel the need of it. They wanted to get on with their lives, and getting together that way was just a reminder; it pulled them back to the event.

Most women felt comfortable with their decision. The ones that didn't worked it out by very shortly becoming pregnant again. And then they would go through another decision-making process. We had some regular repeats. I think that ran about 5 percent, 5–7 per cent. There were also some extremely fertile women, who were conscientious about birth control, but it didn't help.

Getting a Legal Abortion in Massachusetts

There were also legal abortions [in Massachusetts]. That was quite a scene. We would have to refer the woman to a psychiatrist and two physicians.[4] The two physicians were not a problem. It was the psychiatric referrals—they could be pretty difficult. We had a couple that were pretty good, but some of the psychiatrists were really very unfeeling and some were absolutely outrageous! Some really did an interview, and for others it was just—MONEY. I remember one woman who walked in and the psychiatrist said, "Okay, put the hundred dollars right there on the desk if you want me to sign." There was no psychiatric consultation; it was a fee gathering thing for the most part. It was available to anybody that could afford it. And they were very expensive. By the time everything got together, even if it was an early one, it was about $800. And there were no guarantees. They had to get to the right doctors and the right psychiatrists. And the right psychiatrists were not the most desirable ones. But we were always trying to improve upon it.

After New York State Legalized Abortion

Abortion became legal in New York in 1970. That was exciting. I was in New York at a conference on women's health and contraception and counseling. And New York legalized while we were at the conference right in New York City. It was exciting. We were watching the television way into the late hours, and it was a grand celebration at the conference. I was there with two UMass nurse practitioners when the announcement came through that it had passed in the New York legislature. That was a pretty exciting time, I'll tell you! It really was wonderful!

It was a tremendous relief when New York legalized abortion. Then everything was out in the open, and we ourselves could check out our referral resources. We [then] had very close liaison with them, and I think there was much better quality control. We would go down and visit the clinics, and so we were dealing with people we knew instead of just addresses. And [once it was legal], then the University Health Services could be much more directly involved.

Once it became legal in New York, the clergy were pretty much out of it.[5] But then there was a new question—is it legal to send women across state lines? I guess we dealt with that by ignoring it. We didn't want to know! But I was always a little anxious. Not anxious, but it was always there.

Counseling at the University of Massachusetts Health Services

Well, when it became legal in Massachusetts, it certainly was a great deal more comfortable. And that, of course, changed the whole complexion of the problem pregnancy counseling. It was shortly after that that the UMass Health Center assumed responsibility as a part of women's health care. I moved to the Health Center from United Christian Foundation in 1973. I had been the only specific [problem pregnancy] counselor at Clergy Consultation, and it was that way at the UMass Health Services, too. I was the only [female problem pregnancy] counselor there until 1980. I was the only one doing it for the entire university. That was truly over-whelming. I mean, I just could *not* get sick! My work record is incredible, because I didn't *dare* stay home. These women were on a tight timetable, and you couldn't disappoint them by not showing up. I had to be there for those appointments, and it wasn't like you could refer them to somebody else. My grandson was born in 1980, and there wasn't anybody to take over, and I finally said, "Whoa. Something's gotta give here." So then we began to diversify it some, and some of the nurse practitioners began to be involved. It was a great, great relief to me when the University Health Services diversified it, because sometimes I'd see a couple hundred women a year, sometimes more.

At that point I was not only doing the problem pregnancy work, I was also doing other mental health counseling stuff. I was working one-on-one with all our severely disturbed mental health patients. In those days, I think they just shot them out the first of September from every institution in Massachusetts and enrolled them at the university. The first week of school was absolute mayhem. It was just full, because people came that no way could handle the university. And then, more and more, I moved out of problem pregnancy counseling, and did training for the counselors. I had trained Ruth Fessenden [at UCF] and I trained all the nurse practitioners that were involved [at the Health Services]. And I was still training a few just before I left the university. I worked very closely together with Lorna Peterson and Robin Dizard, who did the Abortion and Birth Control group of Amherst Women's Liberation. They have an awful lot of skills too, but yes, I taught them the nitty-gritty.[6]

I have a wonderful knack of compartmentalizing, and I never would take it home with me. It could have been just an incredible week, with everything sort of up in the air when I left on Friday, and I would not think of it. I wouldn't even remember the women's names over the weekend. Monday morning it was front and center, and then I was back on again. Each night, I left my work at the office—which is the only survival technique. Only if you take care of yourself can you do the best for the client. Otherwise, you've got nothing to give.

I would have liked to have had a little help a little sooner! That's the main thing. And there's no one to blame for that but myself, because it was only when I said, "I can *not* do it all anymore" that I got some help. It was supposedly to come from the Mental Health division, but that was kind of a halfhearted involvement, what with people on call, and so forth. And so, the support really came from the nurses, and the nursing staff. They were wonderful. I think I needed to have *demanded* earlier. And asserting my own needs in a work setting is not [what I do ordinarily]. I can be assertive any place else, but I just figure, well, if I'm doing a good job, somebody's going to notice. Well, forget that! You've got to say, "You know, I'm really doing a good job and I should be paid more," or, "I've got to have some help here."

The Abortion Loan Fund

The "Medical Emergency Loan Fund" started out just as a grassroots thing. There was a group of about five of us, Ann Gross, who was a nurse at the Health Services, and Ruth [Fessenden], and Michael Booker, a student whose father was an obstetrician in Springfield, and Sam Johnson, who was one of the clergy. There might have been a couple of other students there too, nursing students, and one or two of the women at UCF that were involved. Because of the expense [of an abortion], we established the fund by a collection at the Student Union. I think at first we did a small, minor collection among students, then we managed to keep it revolving. It was very basic, and we had very, very little money. It grew and was added to through contributions over the years, and people were good about paying it back.

Then it got to seem that it was not appropriate for the ones that were doing the counseling to be the ones saying yes or no about granting the money. Also, the person who was counseling didn't seem to be the appropriate person to go and collect the money if it was overdue. So when things became legal, then it was administered by a woman at Student Affairs, who took over the responsibility for handling the actual loan procedure itself. So, it was separated. I think we had some pretty influential students in Student Activities, and the students had a great deal of say to what went on there. And so, they lobbied to get it there. And the woman that handled it was also very sympathetic to the cause. So she did it very graciously [since] it was an addendum to her job and not part of her job description. But we did some initial evaluation and assessment and we would give some advice. We kept close liaison, and we would write a referral letter to her. We felt that was appropriate, since we did not have the final say.

And then when we started using clinics regularly in New York, and particularly when we used Hampden [Gynecological Associates] in Springfield [which did the majority of terminations in the Valley after Roe], a certain amount of the fee was rebated; in other words, for every so many abortions, there would be one free. So that was another way of building the loan fund. We told them very clearly that unless they paid it back, there wouldn't be anything there for other women. We also helped them look at all other resources that they might have. The loan fund was the choice of last resort, in order to conserve it for women that really, really needed it so desperately.

Someone to Lean On

It wasn't formal, but we had a kind of "catch-as-catch-can" support group. Somebody would say, "Have you got a minute?" If somebody was feeling stuck or concerned about something, we would share things like that. You really need somebody to talk it through. You maintain confidentiality, but just in generalities. We had a board at UCF—Leslie Laurie, Ellen Story, Ann Gross, and Ruth Fessenden were part of it. That was my support group. I met Leslie Laurie about the first week that she came here. And then, not too long thereafter, I met Ellen Story, who was Leslie's assistant. So, that's been a long association with the two of them. Plus, at UCF, the clergy were my support. But it was just mainly Ruth. I tell you, it was a very, very close relationship.

I did supervision for a bit when people were first trained, until they were feeling really comfortable. When I joined the University Health Services, they put me in the Mental Health division. Then I was part of a clinical group and there was support there too. If I had difficulties, I could present cases there. As others got trained, I was doing less and less problem pregnancy counseling, but would take a share of it along with the others. In the meantime my inpatient responsibilities were increasing because I worked with all the psychiatrists. At one point, we had five psychiatrists, and we had a lot of severely disturbed patients. They would keep them on the floor for evaluation until they could be placed. I was very, very much involved with them, and also, with the regular inpatients in helping them work out practical problems, or spotting people that were having emotional problems.

I used to go to meetings of the Western New England Counselors Cooperative. It was a very loose association. And that was helpful as far as support and information and in keeping on top of latest developments. And it was a good communication and support. But we didn't meet all that often, nor, I don't think, for that long. I think it sort of dwindled a little bit.

Looking Back

I counseled probably a couple of hundred a year, in the early years. In the later years, maybe a hundred a year. My math isn't the greatest, but probably about thirty-five hundred women, all told. There were some years that the stats were up . . . three hundred, two hundred. They were dropping toward the end, but then AIDS came on the scene and I think that that pushed people to do birth control better. And more women were willing to take the pill too—there was a time there that nobody wanted the pill. When women got to be more willing to take the pill again, that dropped the statistics, although the pill is not foolproof. There were quite a few condom failures and a few IUD failures too, but diaphragm failures were the greatest.

I *loved* my work. I loved every part of it. When the opportunity first presented itself with the clergy counseling, it wasn't something that I consciously thought, "Wow, this will be my career." But I could see the incredible need, and I could see that women needed to talk to a woman at a time like that. Believe me, the clergy were sensitive, warm, kind—they were wonderful. But they were men. And that drew me into it. I felt it was important not only for the women, but for the potential children. It was my belief that the worst thing in the world is to be an unwanted and abused child. That made it more comfortable for me, in that I knew that, when someone came to me, the child was basically unwanted at that point. It's no "birthright" for a child to have that history. I just think that being an unwanted child would be the most awful fate in the world. And I think the cruelest thing that can happen to a child is child abuse, and there is [often] abuse—whether it's physical or mental abuse—when parents are saddled with unwanted children. Certainly, it would have been better not to be pregnant in the first place, but why ruin three lives—the child, the woman, the partner—to say nothing of parents, grandparents? I just thought, it is the greatest good for the most people. But I was equally willing to help women set up counseling and placement of a child. And sometimes there were marriages, and that was kind of fun and exciting, too—if it seemed right. I mean it was really not my decision to make, but you could tell sometimes if [a marriage] was headed for disaster. But many of them have lasted very, very well.

I was concerned about retiring, but I always said, "When you need the job more than it needs you, that's the time to go." I just really enjoyed the women, and in so many ways, I got as much out of it as I gave. It just felt like it was a mission, that it was my thing to do in life, and I loved it. You know, over the years, seeing the women around on campus and so forth, it was just really great. It used to be that when we went out for dinner, wherever we went, we'd sit down at the table and everybody would say "Hi, Elaine!" "Hi, Elaine!" They always came over. I can remember seeing one woman when I went to a choral concert about a year [after I had counseled her]. She had a perfectly gorgeous voice, and she sang a solo. She came over afterwards and she said, "That was for you." That was very touching.

EIGHTEEN

Ruth Fessenden

Ruth Fessenden was born in Pittsfield, Massachusetts, where she attended public schools. Ruth was a first generation college student, graduating from the University of Massachusetts, Amherst (UMass), in 1969. From 1970 through 2002, Ruth worked at UMass, first with the United Christian Foundation (UCF) from 1970 through 1976. These years included work with Clergy Consultation Service (CCS) and with the Western New England Counselors' Cooperative (WNECC). In 1976, Ruth was hired as Coordinator of Programs against Violence against Women at Everywoman's Center and worked with a dedicated group of community and university volunteers to found a 24-hour rape crisis hotline and initiate education and advocacy efforts for the Franklin/Hampshire County area. Subsequently at EWC Ruth worked as Coordinator of the Resource/Referral Program with a talented staff of students and community volunteers who responded to as many as 16,000 walk-ins and call-ins per year. In the 1980s Ruth moved to an administrative role at EWC, serving as Associate Director with a highly competent student staff, until taking early retirement in 2002. Ruth has served on the Board of Directors of Tapestry Health (formerly the Family Planning Council of Western Massachusetts) since its inception in 1972, and is currently Chair of Tapestry's Board. Ruth lives in Montague, Massachusetts with her partner, John Findley, and their son, Cooper Findley.

Ruth Fessenden was interviewed by David Cline on March 12, 2002.

"An Amazing Web"

I graduated from the University of Massachusetts in May of 1969. By the fall of 1970 I was looking for employment and was hired by the United Christian Foundation to work as an administrative assistant. I had been away from the campus for a year-and-a-half or so and I hadn't even heard of the Clergy Consultation Service on Abortion and didn't know what UCF was up to on the campus. I just needed bread money! And the job couldn't have been more absolutely a surprise, more different than a typical administrative assistant's position, nor more interesting to me at the time.

I came to the table with a strong involvement in women's issues. I had been involved in early women's consciousness-raising groups, and had connections in that way in the Valley—some early fledgling support groups where we were just talking to one another, making connections, comparing notes. The group that I met with was a group of probably fifteen to twenty women. We met in Northampton. And we were community women, you know, and a variety of ages. Really a fantastic group of women.

Reproductive rights was a compelling issue for the women that I knew as an undergraduate here at the university. We're talking about a time when contraception for women who were single wasn't legal in Massachusetts. So the underground information market was lively and thriving around all kinds of reproductive rights issues. I think that people talked about abortion, but it was such a leap to access services at that time—1965–1969—that it was still a rare actual experience for women at that age to have. I had a vague sense that you could be talking about very far away places—Puerto Rico, England, Japan. But this was not particularly a part of my universe.

The Clergy Consultation Service on Abortion

I started at UCF in the fall of 1970 and was there until 1977. For obvious reasons, my thoughts on abortion were explored in my job interview. At that point UCF was involved in a lot of left activities, so problem pregnancy counseling was just a piece of what was going on there, but clearly a busy piece. When I entered UCF, the staff was Elaine Fraser, Sam Johnson (he was an active counselor as part of CCS), Ron Hardy, and Tom Lindemann. That was the cast of characters. And there was also a sizeable group of student activists that were very attached to UCF and a regular part of the landscape too.

In those times when lots of political things were happening on the campus, UCF was one more gadfly for the university. But because it was funded from off-campus by United Ministries in Higher Education (UMHE), it was really quite independent. I suppose that the administration could have leaned on the organization because they gave it office space. But since these were clergy, that would seem so mean spirited. How could they do that?

I don't know whether or not we received university funding directly, though clearly UCF received in-kind support such as space. The bulk of UCF's budget came through UMHE, and we received individual donations. And we were connected [to the university] in ways that were fascinating to me in retrospect. We were housed on the top floor of Hampshire House and on the other half of the floor was the fledgling National Public Radio station, WFCR, which at that point was beginning the Black Mass Communications project. The individuals who were breaking into public radio through that vehicle were also connected to UCF around social activism. So it was a potboiler of a floor between one thing and the other.

The person I worked with most closely was Elaine Fraser. I was in an office adjacent to hers and quickly became involved in CCS. Elaine was really the lynchpin for problem pregnancy counseling at UCF. Even though the connection was through clergy and she was not a clergyperson, she was really "the woman on the job" in terms of delivery of services. The clergy were an interesting group, pretty varied, very committed. I wasn't familiar with a lot of Protestant clergy before I encountered them, so it was interesting to me. Frank Dorman [the president of UCF], was a person with an intriguing perspective in terms of politics and how one needed to proceed in relation to what was happening in the world. He was an activist, but in quite alternative ways—into civil disobedience or that strain of thinking about how you make things happen. He was deeply involved in organizing against the Vietnam War through Clergy and Laity Concerned. And others there worked through very traditional channels in terms of working with faculty to value undergraduate education. My own religious background was Roman Catholic, so I wasn't there as a person working within my religious tradition.

I worked closely with Elaine and over time she revealed to me more and more of what was happening procedurally, and then I was trained to talk with the women, to do the actual problem pregnancy counseling. I had some training and experience as an undergraduate peer educator and counselor, so that was helpful.

My recollection is that there was a phone number for Western Mass Clergy Consultation Services that was covered in a rotating way by the clergy who were involved—and this includes ministers and rabbis. The Western Mass CCS group did also meet occasionally, so these were warm bodies that I saw. Occasionally people would walk in, but most of the women would have gone through this step of the phone contact. Obviously the service was not advertised, so women were unlikely to drop in unless they knew from a friend where the office was. UCF was doing the lion's share of the referrals, as near as I could tell. We were based in this age-appropriate setting where lots and lots of the referrals were coming from. The university was a big catchment area.

Beginning in 1973, community women [nonstudents] were probably going to Family Planning Council of Western Massachusetts, which began that year. The Council, at that point, would have absorbed community requests. The Valley Women's Center, which later evolved into the Valley Women's Union, also had an

"A and BC" group, the Abortion and Birth Control group that was a real feeder into the counseling services in the area. There were individuals who were in that who were part of Western New England Counselor's Cooperative of which Clergy Consultation Service was a member.[1] The community networks always overlapped. You can name any two groups and there was probably overlapping membership.

Ann Hardy was the chair of the board of UCF at the time and the board was very involved, and committed to the work of the organization—to the whole spectrum of what was going on. This was definitely an in-for-a-penny-in-for-a-pound group. The death of Ron Hardy, Ann Hardy's husband, was just a profound tragedy. It shook the organization and everyone in it. He was someone whom I had met briefly at the time I was being interviewed for the job and perhaps had seen once or twice more before his death. It was just staggering. In some ways it was also a measure of how unsettling the state of the world was at that point—if someone had the ability to take that all in, really, they wouldn't be able to withstand what it was all about.

Problem Pregnancy Counseling: Steady Traffic at an "Options Super Market"

Counseling sessions were scheduled throughout the week and typically the appointment book would include anywhere from two to six women per day. And this was very steady traffic. We're talking about hundreds of women in the course of the year, not thousands, but not dozens either. The volume was really substantial. Counseling sessions were one-on-one with the exception of women who brought their partner, friend, or parent. Based on the assessment of that relationship with the individual woman, some portion of the counseling session might include that other person.

The counseling sessions were variable in length, and sometimes women were seen more than once. In some cases, women came to a counseling session at the beginning of a process of thinking about what their options and their decision might be. In other instances, women had made their decisions already and were looking for referral information. Even in the instances when a woman had already made a decision, the options counseling piece was covered again—just to see if there was more that she wanted to talk about and to give her another opportunity to work through what was happening. So it felt to me like it was a very affirmative model in terms of both the ability and right of women to choose. CCS, at least as I saw it operating at UCF, was very involved in options counseling and had equally strong referrals for any option that an individual would elect.

Our focus was really on the women who needed services as distinct from a particular position. UCF worked closely with groups in the area that were in fact anti-choice—groups that would provide strong support for single mothers, such as a place to live, clothing, baby furniture, sort of a start-up. (We still have a house on South Pleasant Street here in Amherst that's run by Birthright and is considered to be a fine option if somebody wants to continue a pregnancy and is looking for support.) It felt really important to involve the full spectrum of people who were concerned about these issues from a variety of angles. Similarly, for adoptions, we had connections in the area if that was an option that a woman wanted to explore. And happily, since it was a clergy setting, if what people really wanted to do was get married, then that process could be facilitated as well. So this was definitely a supermarket!

I think at that point they were called "problem pregnancies"—that was the term of the day. I talked to people about how the situation had evolved and what might happen next time around. Clearly the majority of individuals who came through thought that their option was abortion, but there were certain people who were interested in adoption, carrying pregnancies to term, and also people who came back repeatedly as they continued their pregnancies and got support throughout that time. However, you often didn't know how things turned out because women left with the referral information and you didn't always know the end of the story. Follow-up appointments were suggested, particularly for those individuals who elected abortion services, but women didn't always keep those appointments.

Abortion referrals were made directly to the facilities providing services and the conversation included planning around transportation, around finances, all of the practical logistics that people needed to grapple with in order to get themselves to wherever they needed to go.

There were some individuals whom we saw more than once, even over the short time that I was doing this work. There were lots of reasons why that was true—contraception wasn't very available, clearly there are differences; in fertility rates, contraception failures did happen. But I think the literature was very wobbly at that point in terms of what repeat abortions meant for a woman's reproductive future. So there was concern when we saw individuals more than once.

Problem pregnancy counseling in itself was demanding because you saw individual women really caught in their life circumstances without appropriate support from the society as a whole. And they were dealing with secrecy around an issue which clearly wasn't theirs alone. It was difficult to see that repeatedly over time. There were certainly individual situations that were just very, very painful—individuals who were very young or had family situations where this was just a tragedy.

Breaking the Law

[When it came time to the do the referral, Elaine or I was supposed to leave the room and a clergy person would come in to do that part]. That may have been the protocol, but I don't remember that last part happening every time. I know that in some instances, [referral] sessions happened directly and there wasn't a clergy person involved.[2] But I would say I felt, perhaps naïvely, that the blanket of coverage [protecting the clergy] would have included Elaine and me too.

At the time it was illegal to provide information to anyone in Massachusetts about abortion services. So, as a mechanism to go around that, information was always transmitted orally from the counselor to the individual who'd come in for counseling [so there would be no incriminating written record]. I think it worked in two ways: specifics of referrals weren't written down because there was real concern about the legality, and, secondly, because people working around these issues trusted their connections and were accustomed to being able to do business using their word. It was a part of the culture.

I was aware, and probably more aware as time went on, of how risky the work was. If you transmitted written information to an individual about abortion services it was illegal and the penalties in terms of the Massachusetts law were clear. I think UCF did a good job in orienting me about the legalities of the situation. But I could also see that in day-to-day practice these issues were, of course, being dealt with a bit differently. So there were kind of two realities, as there often are. I assume that day-to-day practices at UCF were evolving in response to the changing legal situation and that clergy alone may have provided the referral information at an earlier point. My recollection is that the way things actually happened was that referral information was provided to women by Elaine and me. We read the information and provided pen and paper if need be. The women wrote down and read back the information. No written referral information was to change hands and that rule was adhered to scrupulously.

After New York Legalized

Abortion was legalized in New York shortly after I started at UCF, and things shifted dramatically. After New York legalized, it was just a mad scramble because facilities needed to be set up very rapidly. CCS wanted to make sure that the services were high quality and included a counseling component on site in New York. At that point, Clergy Consultation Service also negotiated with providers so that some slots were "discounted." This was a financial subsidy for women who were really in need.

Once things shifted in New York, it felt like things were going to go pretty rapidly in Massachusetts. We did our own evaluations of providers once abortion was legal in Massachusetts. By 1971 Leslie Laurie had organized a consortium called the Western New England Counselor's Cooperative (WNEEC) and that group then did evaluations of its providers in Massachusetts, Southern Vermont, and New Hampshire. The group included CCS of Western Massachusetts, CCS at UCF, the Valley Women's Center, Planned Parenthood Leagues in Massachusetts and Vermont, and individual referral agencies in North Adams, Pittsfield, Greenfield, Worthington, and Springfield. WNECC defined quality abortion services, did evaluations of providers, and established a credit system so that abortions could be subsidized. The Western New England Counselor's Cooperative was an organizing vehicle for negotiations with providers, rather than different sites negotiating individually. We had much more clout, basically, as a large entity, making thousands of referrals. We met regularly—this was a very diligent group with a very fine organizer! I'm happy to say we dealt rigorously with issues of medical standards, counseling practices, responsiveness to clients, aftercare. There was also a legislative piece to WNECC's work.

Abortion Loans

Dr. David Booker was one of the original abortion providers in Springfield after Roe. His son Michael was an undergraduate student here at the university and worked to create MELF, the Medical Emergency Loan Fund. The fund was a resource for women who were going to an abortion provider. It was run out of the Student Activities office in the Student Union. The staff person there understood both its purpose and how it should appear in Student Activities. It was administered as a revolving loan fund theoretically for medical emergencies, but it was understood that "medical emergencies" meant abortions. It provided a wonderful resource for under-graduate students, many of whom diligently paid back loans at the rate of $5 or $10 a week, or came back later and paid in full, understanding that it would create access for another woman. I thought it was an inspired arrangement. At UCF we would refer people to the woman who administered it at Student Activities. There was just an amazing web of people involved in providing pieces of this service.

The UMass Health Services: Responding to the Need

There were some physicians in the Valley who were willing to provide contraception, but the University Health Services was generally not an option for undergraduates in the late Sixties. I can testify to that! As a student, I saw a physician at University Health Services and said that I was interested in contraception. He explained that if I would sign a statement that said I would be married within a short period of time that he would prescribe something, but otherwise that wasn't possible. In a sense the physician was accurate; it was still illegal in Massachusetts to prescribe contraception to someone who wasn't married. But it was archaic.[3]

UMass Health Services began to provide problem pregnancy counseling only when Elaine began to work there. There was a literal, physical transition when Elaine moved to the Health Services. Health Services [regarded her as a] presentable soul who could render services responsibly. That transition was a delicate negotiation that took months. University Health Services seemed very uneasy with being that close to a controversial service. But it certainly made sense to do it there since problem pregnancy and family-planning counseling are part of comprehensive health care. After legalization, University Health Services was the correct place for it to be situated on campus, and it freed up UCF to deal with other issues.

What was interesting though was that over all of the decades that Elaine provided that service at UCF and then at University Health Services, the peaks and valleys of demand over the course of the year remained constant. That was fascinating to see. At UCF, we could plan for what would be predictable peaks in demand every year. We had our theories about what caused these. Holiday vacations, spring break, major blackouts—these all contributed.

I think that there was not an expectation that Health Services would have provided [abortion] referral services before the law changed in Massachusetts. The Health Services here was cautious on the issue [of abortion]. They wanted to know not only that the law had changed in Massachusetts but that it was well changed— that it was going to stick, that their peers were going to see the service as part of comprehensive health care. I believe Bob Gage, the physician who directed University Health Services, was good on this issue. My sense was that he was solidly rooted in the reality of people's lives—not people's lives as he wished they were when they came to see him, but solidly rooted in what the real public health issues are for people.

Life and Work After CCS

After Elaine left UCF, I was running a series of colloquia for undergraduates on violence against women, working with UCF's board, doing fiscal management, working with individual students, continuing to work on women's health-care issues—a smorgasbord. The work on women's health care included continuing with WNECC, serving as a founding Board member for The Family Planning Council of Western Massachusetts [now Tapestry Health], and focusing on violence against women. I convened a group of community and campus women beginning to look at issues of sexual violence—which were pretty untouched in Hampshire County at that time. In turn, Everywoman's Center at UMass decided to fund a part-time position to create a 24-hour hotline and educational services. In 1976, I was hired by Everywoman's Center, and left UCF. Since Everywoman's Center in those days was deeply involved in social action, this move was definitely "out of the frying pan and into the fire!"

When I moved from UCF to Everywoman's Center the notion of working with a new service was an intriguing one. Everywoman's Center provided an opportunity to develop a service for Hampshire County around issues of violence against women. That was new and, like the CCS service, predated there being "solid" services in hospitals, medical facilities, and police stations. It was interesting to see how parallel the work was in some ways.

Looking Back

What I remember most from that time is how remarkable individual women's stories were. At one level you would think that after you've talked to the hundredth or the two hundredth about a situation, which in a broad sense was the same, that it would feel a bit the same. But it really never did. I remember one woman who came in whose father was in the Mafia. I mean, he was *in* the Mafia. And although her concern was about the situation that she was in, her real concern was about her man friend not being executed if her father learned about the pregnancy. I remember another woman who was Jewish and deeply concerned about whether or not this fetus that she was carrying might be the Messiah. That was a look into another whole world and set of considerations! The prism of any individual person's perspective on this issue is amazing.

What also intrigues me is that there was an understanding of the collective power of many people taking a moral position, as we saw conscientious objectors [doing] during the Vietnam War. In UCF terms, this was "speaking the truth to power." It felt, at least in this area, like there was a strong, committed community of people who were working from a variety of angles on a host of issues that were related: issues of war, issues of civil rights, women's issues, choice, access to services, sexual orientation, class, all of that. And they felt intertwined—not only in a rhetorical sense, but I think truly felt intertwined. It was a moment of awakening and understanding.

PART FOUR

The Feminists

Feminist Lay Abortion Counselors

In 1970, when a young college student died after an attempted abortion, it was not only members of the local medical and religious communities who responded, but also members of the Amherst Women's Liberation "consciousness-raising" (CR) group. The very next day, the women met to discuss how they could tackle the abortion issue. They immediately formed the Abortion and Birth Control (ABC) group whose tasks would include both public education and counseling of individuals with a "problem pregnancy." Down the Valley in Springfield, women in another CR group were already well involved in problem pregnancy counseling. The Springfield Women's Health Counseling Service collective had developed from a CR group into an education and referral center. The women of this collective, some of whom also lived with each other communally and shared interests in the larger women's movement and in the civil rights and antiwar movements, ran their referral clinic from 1970 to 1973. This group not only made referrals, but also provided transportation to clinics in New York and often helped to arrange for payments in the case of indigent women.[1] Though both groups worked in the same geographic area, and relatively openly given the illegal nature of their activities, they remained unaware of each other's existence for some 30 years.

These groups were community based and expressly feminist. They viewed their abortion referral work as building upon the work of the clergy and health professionals, although they had a different set of motivating ideologies. They believed that a woman should have the power to make decisions over her own body and that other women should be the ones that helped inform her of her options. There was also some concern that those women who viewed religion as "not necessarily a positive life force" would shy away from the Clergy Consultation Service on Abortion (CCS); the feminist groups hoped to fill the counseling gap. But even though approaching the work differently, these activists recognized the expertise held by the clergy and public health workers. The Amherst ABC group's first training session was conducted by Elaine Fraser of CCS. They also received their first lists of abortion providers from CCS, and shared the stage with a clergyman and a UMass social worker at a public forum on abortion. Amherst ABC recognized that they were able to hold public forums, speak-outs, and outreach programs in the UMass residence halls because "Dr. Gage [of the University Health Services] paved the way."[2]

Though they sometimes worked in concert with clergy and the medical profession, the women's groups in the Pioneer Valley should be considered in the context of the development of the women's rights movement and second wave feminism throughout the United States. As members of the Valley groups recall in their oral histories, Betty Friedan's *The Feminine Mystique* was for many women the spark that lit the fire of a desire for change. In fact, one young wife of an Amherst College professor was so inspired by the book that she reportedly went door to door along the street where most of the faculty lived, asking the other wives, in a paraphrase of Freidan's catch phrase, "Do you ever cry in your kitchen sink?"[3]

Amherst Women's Liberation and the Springfield Women's Health Counseling Service were part of a wave of consciousness-raising groups that began to form in communities nationwide beginning in the late 1960s. Some historians point to the CR groups as a dividing line between two branches of the women's liberation movement—the old school organizational feminists from groups like the National Organization of Women, and younger, more radical feminists who focused on personal change. Indeed, it was a member of one of the more radical groups, Carol Hanisch of New York's Redstockings, who is credited with coining the phrase, "the personal *is* political."[4] Eventually, NOW recognized the usefulness of "rap groups," and local chapters of NOW began to form CR-type groups.[5]

A CR group was a gathering of women that met to talk about issues in their lives that usually went unmentioned; sex and reproduction were always near the top of that list. Not only was talking about these topics in public a revolutionary act, it was a revelatory act as well—many women simply did not know, until they began sharing in these groups, that other women had the same experiences and concerns. Abortion was one experience that many of these women had in common and about which they had not spoken before. The members of CR groups, including those in Springfield and Amherst, began to believe that "controlling their reproductive lives was central to the liberation they were beginning to envision."[6] The March 1969 "Abortion Speakout" held by the Redstockings helped to push the issue further out into the public.[7] This speakout model—women publically recounting the stories of their illegal abortions—would be used by the Amherst ABC group, and similar speakouts were held annually at Amherst's Hampshire College beginning in 1986.

The women of the Amherst and Springfield collectives did not have the backing of a major organization in the way that Elaine Fraser and Ruth Fessenden at Clergy

Consultation Services (CCS) did, nor did they have the clergy's putative legal defense of answering to a higher law. By providing abortion referrals they knowingly broke the law; a choice they felt they had to make in order to change society according to their understanding of the personal as political, but which brought with it stress and sometimes paranoia. Members of the groups relate incidents in which they believed an FBI infiltrator had been sent into their midst, although no proof ever materialized, and others recall the rush of being involved in an illicit activity, comparing it to the Underground Railroad.[8]

Amherst Women's Liberation's Abortion and Birth Control Group

In the town of Amherst, a group of women in their twenties and thirties, most of them the wives of young faculty at Amherst College, formed Amherst Women's Liberation, a feminist discussion group known in the parlance of the times as a consciousness-raising or CR group. After the death of a local student from an attempted abortion in the summer of 1970, their Abortion and Birth Control Group set to work organizing public forums, speaking out in the UMass dorms, and counseling women out of their homes. While some of the women involved in the ABC work were trained nurses or social workers, most were not. They had in common that they were feminists and committed to making, as one of them later recalled, "abortion no longer a secret." Robin Dizard was one member of the group who had personally had an illegal abortion—she had undergone one in Chicago in 1964—and her revelations about this experience drove the group toward the issue.

Robin Dizard and her husband Jan and their five-year-old son moved to Amherst from Berkeley, California in 1969 so that Jan could take a position teaching in the Sociology Department at Amherst College. Robin, who would later complete a Ph.D. in American literature and become a professor as well, had just finished five years of elementary school teaching in California and was taking time off to have a second child. She was, as a faculty wife, expected to join the Ladies of Amherst, the loose but very traditional organization of faculty wives.

A friend recommended that Robin look up the writer Tillie Olsen, then a visiting professor at Amherst College. Olsen and her husband became good friends of the Dizards, and as their friendship progressed, Tillie Olsen was determined to get Robin involved in the women's movement. Dizard remembers she had previously rejected the women's movement: "I said I had no interest in it because I was happily married. You can make of that logic whatever you want to. Anyhow, Tillie began loaning me booklets, including *The Myth of the Vaginal Orgasm*. Tillie began to urge me to take these booklets and what they said seriously."

The Ladies of Amherst were being confronted with a changing culture. At first Dizard and other young wives tried to fit in, going on Ladies field trips to Broadway and collecting recipes. But they soon found they had little in common with the old guard. These young women of the Vietnam generation, although some were still primarily homemakers, were feeling the early stirrings of the new women's movement, and within a few years cooking classes and evenings at the theater had segued into consciousness-raising rap groups, abortion rights speak outs, and vaginal self-examinations.

The CR group that met at Mel Heath's house in 1970 began, according to Dizard, with the basics: "We began talking about whether we could understand that there would be a special women's interpretation to events. We certainly wondered whether there was a special way to define women's oppression. We had a lot of vocabulary from Marxist sources and we later debated such subjects as "Is Mrs. Rockefeller my sister?" We wondered whether class would ever trump gender." The group that would become known as Amherst Women's Liberation included not only Amherst faculty spouses but also some women married to Smith professors and a few young women who were themselves professors at UMass and Smith. Dizard remembers that some of the husbands were a little nervous knowing that their wives were off talking about their sex lives: "There were a number of the Amherst College professors who were very anxious about what their wives might be getting around to discussing!"

As the women in the group were exploring various issues, someone suggested that Robin, since she had had an illegal abortion while her husband was in graduate school in Chicago, start working on this issue. She got in contact with Elaine Fraser at the CCS chapter at UMass, and Fraser helped guide her through the basics of problem pregnancy counseling. Dizard realized that many women might prefer to talk to another feminist woman rather than to a minister or rabbi. Besides, Dizard said, "All of us understood that it might not be the first thing that somebody in trouble would think about, that Protestant clergy would have been organized to help her, although that had been the case for ten years." There were also some women who did not trust the CCS groups on two counts: they were clergy and they were men. These women in Amherst Women's Liberation felt that women should handle a women's issue and should do so without the moralizing framework that religion implied to many. Dizard later said diplomatically in a public speech: "We reasoned that the Clergy Consultation Service, though active in this area, was not well enough known. [Besides,] we could assume some risks they could not."[9] So Dizard and a few other women formed the Abortion and Birth Control Group and began holding educational sessions and counseling pregnant women.

Amherst Women's Liberation gained in popularity and membership and it was soon hard to hold meetings in people's homes any longer. Joining forces with the Smith [College] Women's Liberation Group and the University of Massachusetts Women's Liberation Group, they searched for a new location, and in January of 1971 opened the Valley Women's Center (VWC) in three rooms on the second floor of a Main Street building in Northampton. The Center provided a drop-in location and library, organized consciousness-raising groups, taught courses in carpentry, plumbing, and mechanics, organized a speaker's bureau, helped women apply for welfare, and continued to do problem pregnancy counseling. Over the next few years additional counselors would volunteer and the name of the group evolved from the Abortion and Birth Control Group into the Abortion and Birth Control Committee and then into the Pregnancy Counseling Service of the Valley Women's Center.

Even after abortion became legal in New York State, simply providing referral information remained illegal in Massachusetts according to that state's Comstock laws. Despite this, the VWC openly publicized their counseling efforts. One of the ways the Amherst ABC Group spread the word was through printed stickers which bore the words Problem Pregnancy followed by a question mark and the VWC telephone number. They posted these stickers throughout the area—stalls in public restrooms were a favorite target site. They counseled women both from the Valley Women's Center's office on Main Street and from their homes. From 1970 to 1973 they counseled about 800 pregnant women.[10]

Despite the illegality of transferring written information about abortion, the Valley Women's Center openly listed their counseling services in the local phone book and newspaper. In the *Holyoke Transcript*, the newspaper serving the town of Holyoke, which is about halfway between Springfield and Northampton, an article appeared on April 20, 1971, announcing the availability of free problem pregnancy counseling at the VWC. If a woman opted for abortion, she would be referred to New York. The article quoted Robin Dizard as one of two counselors at the VWC: "The clinics in New York are very generous in accepting non-paying patients because they charge enough for one abortion to pay for two or three."[11] Another short article in the same issue, quotes excerpts from a letter Dizard wrote to State Representative John Olver of Amherst: "The present laws, after all, do not even prevent abortions. But consider what horrors the present law does foster. Privacy is invaded. Poor people are denied medical aid that the rich can easily buy. Quacks and sadists prey on desperate women. Children are born unwanted and abused. And women die. In the name of [Nancy Kierzek], who died during an abortion her boyfriend tried to perform in the Connecticut Valley, help."[12]

Just as they had done after Kierzek's death, members of the pregnancy counseling service at the Valley Women's Center responded to another local case that made major news. A pregnant welfare recipient in Holyoke, whose doctor had told her she would undergo "serious physical and mental problems" if she did not have an abortion, sued the Massachusetts Welfare Department for refusing to pay for a therapeutic abortion. The three judge federal court in Boston ruled on November 18, 1971 that the woman did not require an illegal abortion, thus side-stepping the hot button issue of whether Welfare should cover the costs of terminations.

Reached for comment by the *Holyoke Transcript-Telegram* that same day, Britt Guttman of the Valley Women's Center claimed that the judges' decision could condemn certain women to death. "Three men have effectively decided a medical matter and decided it against the woman despite the testimony of her doctor and psychiatrist that it was essential for her health. Because of the court's decision, a woman who could not scrape up the money for an abortion could be condemned to death."[13] Guttman further announced that the VWC was beginning a fund drive to help the woman and solicited contributions. This fund successfully gathered enough money to pay for the woman's trip to New York to procure an abortion. This is likely the origins of "The Lucy Fund" discussed in the interviews. The VWC would continue to raise money over the next few years in order to help women pay for the costs of abortion.

At the beginning of February 1972, Britt Guttman sat down at the old typewriter in the VWC office and typed up a review of her experience counseling pregnant women at the center over the past year. She recorded her views of the problems faced by pregnant women and counselors at a time when abortion was still illegal: "We have met, in this work, many women who are our neighbors, our sisters, our doubles. There is no line between 'them' and 'us.' Any woman is liable to the disaster of unwanted pregnancy; to the violence of rape; to sterility from undiagnosed gonorrhea; to blood clots from the pill; to perforation of the uterus by an IUD." She closed by noting that, "We see the lucky ones. Most of the women who get legal abortions in New York (or in Massachusetts) are well-to-do. It is the people who are already down and out who carry the additional burden of many unwanted pregnancies, and who risk home remedies or some quack with a catheter and lye. The women who really need counseling and information are also the women who never hear of the availability of these services."[14]

Guttman noted that from January 1971 to January 1972, the pregnancy counselors had seen 110 women ranging in age from 15 to 53, with 53 percent of them over age 21. Fifty-four were students, 28 were married, 13 were on welfare. Twenty-nine of them had been using some method of birth control which failed. Of the 110 women, 14 had had previous abortions.[15]

The Springfield Women's Health Counseling Service

Meanwhile, 20 minutes down Interstate 91, women in Springfield were organizing around the same issues. A group of women, several of whom lived together along with their husbands and families in a collective housing arrangement, had formed a CR group in the late 1960s. Radical left organizations at the time were notorious for not including women in leadership positions and the women in Springfield reacted to this by forming their own women's group.[16] They were also interested in action rather than rhetoric—they wanted to get out into the streets and affect visible social change. Within this CR group, a smaller group of women—Alice Zaft, Betty Wright, Ann Meeropol, Sherri Oake, Ann Bell, Eve Spangler, and a seventh woman, an attorney who now wishes to remain anonymous about her abortion counseling work—felt at a certain point that they had "processed just about everything there was to process about being a woman in those days. We all kind of came to the sense that we needed to *do* something. We didn't want to just talk, we wanted to do." What they wanted to do, initially, was explore issues that pertained specifically to women and help women to learn more about themselves, their health, and their bodies. They did vaginal self-exams. They spoke about their sex lives. And they talked about abortion. It soon became clear to them that helping other women get access to pregnancy options counseling and safe abortions was one way that they could translate their talk into deed.

They named themselves the Springfield Women's Health Counseling Service, because, as Alice Zaft recalls, they wanted a subtle, professional sounding name, something more generic than "Women Who Take Women for Abortions." Feeling that women should be counseled in a neutral, professional environment, they established an office on Main Street in Springfield.

Two of the women in the group were nurses. They spent a fair amount of time educating one another, meeting with area obstetricians who agreed to do postabortion checkups, and traveling to New York to observe abortions in clinics there. While some of their work involved guiding women through the therapeutic abortion process, including putting them in touch with sympathetic gynecologists and psychiatrists in the Springfield area, some of the women also operated what one member termed an "underground railroad" ferrying patients to the New York clinics. There they would hold the women's hands and wait with them through the recovery period before driving them home. These kinds of services—counseling, handholding, a woman to talk to—would become standard practice in clinics after Roe, largely because of the pressure of women's groups to include counseling as part of general abortion practice.

As with the Amherst Women's Liberation ABC Group, secrecy was necessary and preserving the clients' anonymity was key. The Health Collective members kept records of their counseling, but the clients were identified only by their first names and last initials.

The membership of Women's Health Counseling changed over time as the women became involved in other issues.[17] By 1973, most of the original members of the pregnancy counseling group were no longer directly involved with the day-to-day operations. In late 1971, a very active feminist named Liza Solomon moved to the area and began volunteering with the group. She was one of the women who was most involved with reviewing New York clinics and in establishing relationships with Springfield obstetricians and gynecologists to do aftercare for the women returning from New York. The main clinic she worked with was Hampden Gynecological Associates (HGA) in Springfield, headed by Dr. Joel Bettigol. (Dr. David Booker, whose son Michael was one of the founders of the Emergency Abortion Loan Fund at UMass, was a also a partner in this practice.) After the Roe decision went into effect, HGA immediately started abortion services and became the first large-scale clinic in the Valley to offer legal terminations. The doctors of HGA decided that pre- and postabortion counseling, until that point done "illegally" by members of the women's groups, should be an integral part of legal abortion practice. HGA hired Liza Solomon to put together the abortion counseling program for them. She in turn hired Sherri Oake from Springfield Women's Health Counseling and Jeannie Jones and Pat Green from the Amherst Women's Liberation and Valley Women's Center's ABC groups; Jones and Green also provided counseling at Amherst Medical Group, which began performing terminations soon after HGA.[18]

Sherri Oake recalls that the practitioners were at first reluctant to add the counseling component but relented under pressure from the women's groups. And Leslie Laurie, who convened the Western New England Counselor's Cooperative (WNECC) and later directed the Family Planning Council of Western Massachusetts, recalled bringing these organizations' clout to bear on the doctors: "We had a model in our heads as to what good abortion service would look like and Amherst Medical Associates and Springfield HGA were willing to deal with our insisting that we wouldn't refer someone if there weren't women counselors."[19]

The WNECC distributed lists of available counselors to potential abortion providers in the area. In this way, the "radical" feminist counselors were able to both bring pressure to bear on medical practice and, as they were hired as counselors, to actually become a part of it. This happened not just in the Pioneer Valley, but across the country, as counseling became an integral part of early legalized abortion practices. One patient recalled both group and personal counseling sessions prior to her abortion in New York in 1971: "The counselor, with the help of a plastic diagram, described the female organs during pregnancy and what would occur during the operation. She went into the drugs that would be administered and their effects. The possible pain we would encounter and why it occurred. It was a real good thing to understand what was going to happen and the reasons behind it. The whole time she had her hand on my shoulder and for me it was reassuring." After the procedure, "they brought me juice and my counselor, who knew I was hungry, bought me a half a sandwich, which was real cool."[20]

The Transcripts

The two oral histories that follow differ from the others in this volume in both the manner in which they were gathered and the style in which they are presented. Each is a group interview. The Springfield interview took place in one sitting and the Amherst Women's Liberation transcript contains elements from four seperate interview sessions. The women's collectives were by definition non-hierarchical groups in which all meetings and all decisions were made by consensus. To preserve and replicate this essential construction of the group dynamic, it was necessary to interview collective members as a group. Since they share memories and references in common, the way in which they collectively tell a story can be very different from an individual oral history. As in the solo interviews, I have removed the questions and edited the transcripts; however, for these group interviews, I retained the names of individual narrators so readers could identify who is talking. Very little research has yet been done on the methodology and presentation of group oral history interviews, and it is my hope that these two examples will contribute to discussion in this area.

NINETEEN

Amherst Women's Liberation's Abortion and Birth Control Group

The Amherst Women's Liberation consciousness-raising group was formed in the fall of 1970. Initially composed mostly of the young wives of Amherst College professors, the group provided a feminist respite from the old-school Ladies of Amherst, a more traditional tea-taking group of faculty spouses. Inspired by Betty Friedan's The Feminine Mystique, *the group began meeting to discuss the burgeoning women's movement, their roles within the community and their families, and issues in which they might take an active role. Robin Dizard, one of the group's members, had been the survivor of an illegal abortion, and when the death by abortion of a local young woman made the news, she and others were prompted into action. Together they formed Amherst Women's Liberation's Abortion and Birth Control Group. They spoke at public gatherings, demonstrated contraceptives, and undertook problem pregnancy options counseling and abortion referrals. Early on they did this work from their own homes; in January 1970 they opened the Valley Women's Center in Northampton, and continued the work there until the Roe v. Wade decision legalized abortion on demand in 1973.*

Susan Tracy interviewed Pat Green, Lorna Peterson, Robin Dizard, Jeannie Jones, and Judi Fonsh on June 29, 1999. Judi Fonsh interviewed Pat Green and Jeannie Jones on February 12, 2000. Marilyn Smith interviewed Robin Dizard on May 5, 2001 and May 11, 2001.

Beginnings

PAT GREEN: I'm Pat Green. I'm a nurse and I do a couple of different types of nursing.

ROBIN DIZARD: I'm Robin Dizard. I teach English literature at a college in New Hampshire.

LORNA PETERSON: I'm Lorna Peterson. I'm a college administrator. When I started with the Abortion and Birth Control committee, I was a new mother and I'm about to be a new *grand*mother.

JEANNIE JONES: I'm Jeannie Jones. I'm a librarian at Mt. Holyoke College.

JUDI FONSH: I'm Judi Fonsh. I'm a social worker and a psychiatric nurse.

ROBIN: I can tell you this part of our origins. Amherst Women's Liberation began meeting at Mel Heath's house in 1970.[1] Like every woman, I can tell what year that was because that's when my son was born. Within a short time we had somebody come from Boston who asked why weren't we doing support groups. We asked what they were, and then we formed two. In my support group's discussions, one of the things that I told about was having had an abortion. Very soon thereafter Mel Heath said, "You know, you should work on that issue." She arranged for me to meet Elaine Fraser over at the United Christian Foundation. I'm sure other people must have begun working on the issue just about the same month. My memory says it must have been around February 1970. What do you think?

LORNA: I think so, and I think when the people came from Boston—it was Ellen Cantero and Pam Lowry—and talked about forming support groups, they also talked about action committees. And one of the groups that we formed was the Abortion and Birth Control Group. But prior to that, or maybe as the first activity of the ABC Group, was a public forum on abortion that we held at the Junior High School. And Robin spoke.

ROBIN: But we couldn't hold it at the Junior High School! They called us "the Women's Liberation Front!" We had originally applied to the Junior High School for space to hold this forum, because that's one of the best large public meeting rooms in Amherst. But we were refused because we were the so-called Women's Liberation Front. We were not democratic, we did not permit men to be members. And of course the riposte that we made up was "Well, the Boy Scouts can meet in the school, and they don't permit girls!" In any case, that gives you an idea of the widespread anger toward "uppity" women—and the confusion, because Women's Liberation "Front" obviously bled over from discourse on the Vietnam War. So we were seen as threats to the State. I think some of us really liked the idea of being threats to the State, but that was because it was a joke. So we held the forum at one of those freestanding auditoriums at the UMass business school.

LORNA: Right. Because I made the phone call, and Paul Healy [at the school] said, "No, you cannot in fact hold an activity sponsored by the Amherst Women's Liberation Front." And I said we weren't a "front."

ROBIN: Anyway, we had a beautiful advertising poster showing a woman holding a globe, holding up the world, and we were able to recruit five or six people to talk. I talked about having an illegal abortion and somebody who used to live on Sunset Street talked about having a legal abortion on the grounds that she had been diagnosed as having measles during pregnancy. Dick Unsworth talked from the point of the view of the Clergy Consultation Service, and I think Dr. Gage was there. One of the things which occurred that really gave a spur to a lot of our actions was that a university student had tried to perform an abortion on his girlfriend. It wound up that he perforated her and she was taken to Cooley-Dickinson Hospital in Northampton where she died. He was arraigned, I think, for double murder.[2] When people questioned the morality of what we were doing, that's the story that some of us told. And that was one reason, I believe, that Dr. Gage was so insistent that the University Health Services should take a proactive stance on abortion counseling and making sure that in all the residence halls, that the RA [Resident Assistant] counselors understood about counseling college kids. The Clergy Consultation Service did the actual abortion counseling then.

JUDI: That university student comes up in this story over and over.

JEANNIE: Did many people come to that forum that you held?

ROBIN: Yes, it was jammed.

LORNA: We had protestors. We knew we were going to get people in the audience who would protest. It wasn't untoward; it was just people questioning the idea of abortion. We did advertise it and I believe we had a poster. We certainly had fliers.

ROBIN: And as for the name, Abortion and Birth Control Group, let it be noted, that it was Lorna who said ". . . and birth control should be part of it."

LORNA: Because Dr. Gage paved the way, we started going to the university and talking in dormitories. Eventually we even got as far as the doors of Smith College and spoke to students at Smith College, about both women's liberation and abortion. I and a few other people also went to a training session at Planned Parenthood in Springfield.

ROBIN: Elaine Fraser also set up a day of role playing and training for us to learn some of the counseling techniques so that we wouldn't be in the position of always saying, "Oh well, no matter what your problem is, you need an abortion." We were well aware, early, that we didn't want to have unitary outcomes.

Amherst Women's Liberation and the Valley Women's Center

LORNA: We moved in to the Valley Women's Center in Northampton around 1971.

ROBIN: I think it was 1971 because I had Seth on my back when I was helping to paint the wall purple. So it certainly wasn't 1970.

JEANNIE: Before that, we met in people's houses. I remember going to Brit Guttman's house.

LORNA: The support groups met in her house, but I think the ABC committee also met in people's houses. Probably most frequently in the beginning at Brit's because she could accommodate us.

ROBIN: One of the things that Brit could especially do for us, since she had been trained as a secretary, was that she was very good at getting copies, and making sure that all kinds of things were kept in order. So it was thanks to her that we had the first lists of telephone numbers and addresses of the clinics in New York State where we could take people who needed abortions. We went and inspected them.

I don't know how people got in touch with us at first. Once there was the Women's Center, they could call there, leave a message, and then get information as to who was on duty and taking telephone calls that day.[3] [They probably knew about us] because there were those wonderful little stickers. You see, it had been established by Bill Baird and his activities that you were breaking the laws of Massachusetts if you gave somebody information—that is, if you *handed* printed information to someone else. But there was the guarantee of free speech, as had been explained to us at one of these training sessions. And so we decided we were going to use the guarantee of free speech. We knew a woman who was the spouse of a printer and may herself have been a printer. She had gotten pregnant after 40 and did not want to carry that pregnancy to term, so she understood abortion as a personal issue. She made us the stickers that said: "Problem Pregnancy?" and gave a telephone number. We gave them out at the big meetings and [we put them up in bathroom stalls in public restrooms all over the area]. Wherever people went and used the toilets, they put these stickers up. But that didn't pre-date the Women's Center.

LORNA: Also I think our own phone numbers must have been out there by word of mouth, because we were doing counseling before Valley Women's Center.

ROBIN: I'll never forget the time somebody came to my house virtually in disguise! You know, she was wearing big dark glasses and a wig, and she was simply terrified of me and whatever I represented. Anyway, I'm sure she arrived by simply having my phone number.

LORNA: The other thing is that there was a regional network as these women's groups were springing up all over the Northeast and were establishing something like our ABC committee. Maybe they were called something else and maybe they were connected with other organizations. So people knew about us—they knew to send people to us. And we knew to send people to closer groups if we got phone calls from a long distance. I remember when Ann Kiddleberger, who was was part of the ABC committee, moved to Rochester, we already could establish contacts for her with the groups there. This is pre-*Roe v. Wade*.

JUDI: Well, I certainly remember, in the beginning, using Clergy Consultation as a huge backup to make [access to abortion services] go in a way that seemed more reasonable. They felt like they had really protected themselves, or tried to, because they were clergy.

LORNA: And we had doctor's lists. We went and interviewed all the physicians in the area—the OB-GYNs and the Family Practice people. I interviewed them and asked questions.

ROBIN: I will never forget going to interview a psychiatrist in Northampton, because in some cases we wanted to be able to use that avenue. He was an old-fashioned psychiatrist, a guy who had a couch. He wanted me to sit, or *lie*, on the couch and tell him why I wanted to do this, and why I was interested in his opinions.

LORNA: I went and interviewed one of the few women doctors in the area, a Southern woman, and really had a bad time with her. When I went back and reported to Brit, who was from the South, she said it was just the wrong accent meeting the wrong accent. And Brit went and we got her to sign on.

This was all done secretly in that we assigned a number to every physician who saw a woman when she returned from her abortion. This system was all done by numbers so that we could keep track of who the docs were without identifying them on paper by name and jeopardizing their positions. These records were then kept in two different places.

JEANNIE: It's funny. I don't remember any of this assigning numbers to doctors. That must have been in the very beginning. The big change in the summer of 1970 was that they changed the laws in New York State.

JUDI: I think that I probably got actively involved in the fall of '70. I don't remember numbers either, so it must have been the way you set it up [at the beginning].

ROBIN: We had, in some ways, a quite lighthearted, giddy attitude toward what we were doing. At the same time we understood that it was very damn serious. When the Abortion and Birth Control Group got organized, we were way ahead of the ball in terms of anticipating our opposition, which didn't get organized until years later. But we were worried about whether the Women's Center would be attacked. We were worried about whether our houses would be robbed and people would be looking for information as to who the doctors were who helped and cooperated and who the women we saw were. So, we made up a protocol. As soon as someone who had been informed about her options had come back from having her pregnancy terminated—having had an abortion—we would tear her name off of our interview forms and put the records in another ABC member's house. And we felt sure that the houses were messy enough so nobody was going to find a whole bunch of little slips of paper with names on them. Meanwhile, we had the beginnings of statistics so that we could tell approximately how many people were asking for abortion referals. We could begin to formulate a profile which said that not all the people who were seeking abortions were unmarried, young women. Not at all. At least 50 percent of the people who came were married, and did not want another child for any number of reasons.

From my point of view, the experience of going to inspect a clinic was also totally weird. I felt like a fraud, of course. I'm not a nurse and I don't know what I'm seeing. I couldn't tell if something was really clean beyond shiny linoleum. But it seemed to me that my presence mattered, and so I did that.

LORNA: I don't think we should forget the role that Pam Lowry and MORAL played in all this. That was the Massachusetts Organization to Repeal Abortion Laws, which ultimately became Mass NARAL. They were large and very active and they were a resource for us. We were able to contact them for the names of clinics and they were directly connected to Bill Baird.

JEANNIE: Did you do your inspections once these clinics were up and running legally? That's how I remember it.

ROBIN: Yeah, but the difference between legal and illegal, I think, was probably [only] a matter of papers and lawyers, because they were certainly already [operating] in hospitals or freestanding clinics.

JEANNIE: I don't think that was true until the law changed in New York. I think they just sprouted right up [after the law changed].

ROBIN: I remember going to the Beacon Health Center, but I'm pretty sure that was after the laws changed. It had to keep a very low profile because a community of extremely pious, old-fashioned Jews opposed it. They opposed abortion completely and would have been picketing. This place had an awful lot of examination rooms and a way of putting people through so that they had time to recover, and talk to somebody and so on. I don't know what the community nearby must have made of all this activity. That was probably 1970.

JUDI: Clergy Consultation was going on when we started so they had their own people to send people to.

LORNA: There were lists of names. There was a whole network nationwide.

Learning by Doing

ROBIN: We had meetings to go over things that had happened. As I recall, decisions were informally consensual. I don't remember any votes. I usually remember votes that I lose pretty well, and I don't remember any.

LORNA: All of our meetings and decisions were based on more and more information and self-education. And so the decisions had a kind of logic to them, in that we learned more and we agreed to adopt what we learned to what we were doing.

ROBIN: There was a woman who was very, very overweight. I didn't understand that as a difficulty until I had taken her to New York—I think to Eastern Women's—and then came back to get her. I found no procedure had been performed because they weren't sure how pregnant she was. It would have to be a late term abortion after all, and that would have been a whole different thing. The first thing I did was to turn around [to the group] and say, "we have to keep track of something like that."

JUDI: It seems like in the beginning, I remember going to monthly meetings [of the ABC group], and then people just kept doing the work. I was trained by the [other women in the group]. They knew what they were doing by the time that I came.

LORNA: Robin was really the most knowledgeable about the physiology and about all kinds of things.

JUDI: Well, the other thing that I think is really important was the decision to use the *Our Bodies, Ourselves* book to run courses for young women. I certainly remember doing that at Valley Women's Center. And teaching myself all that stuff—that book made it easy to do.

PAT: I also remember doing some anatomy stuff for a men's group. I don't know if it was one or two times. I remember I had to really brush up on male anatomy.

ROBIN: I well remember when I first saw a copy of *Our Bodies, Ourselves* and learned that it was printed in Roxbury, Massachusetts. And so we began ordering it. Sometimes, if somebody was going to Boston, she would buy a bunch and bring them back. The other important publication, at least for me, was called something like *Radical Healthcare*. I don't remember its name exactly, but it was there that I got a lot of the material that I used in my rabble-rousing speeches.

LORNA: Also [there were] these shorter pamphlets, also done on newsprint the way *Our Bodies, Ourselves* originally was: *Birth Control, VD*, and so on. We were getting them in cartons so that we could give them out every time we either went to speak or were doing any counseling.

ROBIN: I had some very funny experiences as it got known that I did *Our Bodies, Ourselves* courses. One time, a well-known man in the community, just at a counter at a store, seemed to think that I was going to be able to give him counseling on his sexual impotence. I didn't! I just wanted to get out of there. And there were people who were afraid of me and people who would not talk to me. And of course, I would be belligerent right back. Somebody who met me in those years says that when I introduced myself, I didn't say "Hi, I'm from Amherst," I'd say "Hi, I'm from the Women's Movement." That was my address!

LORNA: Let me add that Robin and I did a number of stints together—public talks. It takes a lot to embarrass me, and Robin embarrassed me. But she was terrific about actually taking all the forms of contraception with her—she had foam, and she had a diaphragm and by God, she'd let them know what you did with it. And it was just really terrific.

ROBIN: I'm sure I would be embarrassed now by me then.

LORNA: But it worked, because what we were doing was making it not a secret.

ROBIN: When I was working on the Abortion and Birth Control Committee our emphasis was inform, inform, inform. A lot of our public speaking was assisted by these booklets. And we always operated in teams because we understood that that was part of the message—that women do too get along, and women aren't all catty to each other. We support each other. So we went in teams and we gave speeches. In particular I figured out that I'm the kind of personality that will do almost anything if somebody is standing behind me. I would explain why abortion was so spottily available. We explained that abortion was one of the few medical procedures that was subjected to anything like this degree of scrutiny. A man could be sterilized without going through a board and public humiliation. Our analysis was that the reason that the doctors who did perform abortions were so secretive about it was that that increased their power. If it was a matter of going, as I had done, to a doctor in his off-hours at his house, blindfolded so that I didn't know where the place was—that was a way of keeping it scarce and scary and expensive, and, in a far extension, keeping you scared and barefoot and pregnant.

Vulnerabilities

ROBIN: It seems to me we were very unsuspicious that somebody might turn out to really do a lot of damage to clients. We didn't even think about it. None of those considerations occurred to me. I remember talking a lot with my husband, whose parents are labor organizers, about problems having to do with popular movements. I would complain sometimes after a meeting and say, "It seems as if every loose flake is coming in!" And he'd say, "Oh, that's always the way it happens!" And so I'd remember to be patient and wait for things to sift out and [eventually] the people who really had no business being there would leave. I also had an idea—and this is completely based on faith—that if somebody had tried to infiltrate and hurt us, they would wind up being convinced that we were right.

LORNA: But we did have one person we were very suspicious of and it was not just paranoia. About a year after the Valley Women's Center was established, someone appeared on the VWC doorstep and she had a lot of time. We just were suspicious. At the least she was a troubled person and at the worst she may indeed have been a plant. I think she was a very troubled person but the way it was manifested made us very suspicious.

ROBIN: There were persistent rumors that our women's movement had been worrisome enough to the FBI for them to have sent an agent or somebody to check us out. This person came in and knew a whole lot about organizations, had lots of free time, and had to make periodic trips to Boston. She said they were for chemotherapy, but she never looked very sick. I remember her saying something like, "Of course I have children, but I left them." So if this person was our FBI infiltrator, she did a bad job! But she did a lot of really good things for the Women's Center because she wanted to organize it. [For example] she said, "You know, if we say that we are thinking of buying certain kinds of equipment, we could have it on approval for a month." And so she would get this equipment, and suddenly we had a good mimeograph machine for a month—that sort of thing.

Counseling Sessions: No "Typical" Client

LORNA: What was extraordinary to me is that there wasn't any "typical" client. We got amazing responses from all over the region. Two that I worked with stand out in my mind. A woman from Belchertown came with a fifteen- or sixteen-year-old daughter who had had whatever with a twenty-one-year-old who was described as "an older man." When I insisted on talking about birth control—which was one of the things we always said we would do—the mother said, "I don't think that she should be talking about birth control." I said, "Well, considering her condition, don't you think we should talk about birth control?" And the mother said, "She won't do this again." I responded, "Well, some day, she probably will."

JUDI: Well, the worst thing about that story is it's still true.

LORNA: The other one was a woman in her late thirties who came with her husband. I'll never forget this—it was so poignant. They had four children, they lived in a small town up in New Hampshire. They had just bought a grocery store that they were running as a "Mom and Pop" business. And she said, "A fifth child would not make it possible for us to realize our dream of this store really working." And so they came together. She was no kid. She was a shopkeeper, and I would say middle class, lower middle class.

ROBIN: I agree with Lorna that there was hardly a typical case. One time I was talking to someone and lightening struck our house! While we were talking!

JEANNIE: Did it make you feel like there was some symbolism?

ROBIN: Yes, it certainly did! And so I rushed upstairs to make sure that the baby was still asleep. He was. Then I noticed that there was steam coming up from the roof and indeed the barn was on fire! I had to call the fire department. But we finished the talk! Another one I remember was the high school girl who was *very* unwilling to follow my advice to let her mother know. I think she was fourteen or fifteen. I said, "You don't have any real choice. She has to know. And furthermore, she's going to know later, so you might as well do it now." And I got a happy call from her saying, "My mother has agreed to help me, and I'm going to have the baby and she's going to raise it." It was the outcome that made sense to both of them.

Another time I remember a mother and daughter pair. It was difficult to keep the mother from dominating the conversation. Because what *she* wanted to tell about was the time that a doctor somewhere near here said, "Oh, yes, I do abortions, but I'm going to rape you first. It won't make any difference." I didn't get his name, I didn't want to know it. And then there was the time a couple came and the man reacted as if I was such poison that he only would talk to me through the half rolled-up glass of the car. He was only willing to drive her. And I remember the woman who came who was staying in a campground near Amherst while her husband was here taking courses in the summer. They had come east from, I think, Ohio, and she had to get an abortion performed. She was the mother of 11 children, and was *not* going to have a twelfth. He didn't support her, which made me very angry, but I tried to keep from interfering. Since she was from far away, I had to countersign her check so that she could take the cash she needed to New York. I'd venture to say that groups like Amherst Medical, which began doing lots and lots of procedures, might tell you about their typical clients. But I estimate—maybe this is wrong—that we might have talked to around 800 people and I don't think that we found that we were getting a "typical person."

PAT: I remember one woman telling me that her father had raped her and that was why she was having an abortion, and that this had been an ongoing thing with him since she had been a little girl. I remember another woman who came in with her husband. They were from India. She had had an ultrasound, and knew that the fetus was a girl. The husband was really pushing for the abortion on the basis of the sex of the baby. This was a cultural thing, and I recall there being some difficulty with English. In those kinds of situations, we always tried our best to make sure it was the *woman's* decision and not some other person pushing her into that decision.

JEANNIE: Most clinics are pretty unhappy to be doing abortion procedures for that reason, aren't they?

PAT: We were all very unhappy, but if she wanted it, we weren't about to say, "No, you can't do this." We weren't in the position of evaluating people's reasons to have abortions. I remember another case that one of us had. There was a woman who was from a Middle Eastern country, I don't remember which one, and she said that if she had the baby and her family found out, they would kill her. Even if her family found out she was having an abortion, perhaps she would be killed. And she *was* killed. I remember Sherri had to go to court. That actually happened.

And the ten-year-old stands out in my mind. I remember there being a big discussion about whether she had been raped. It was her mother's boyfriend, I think, who got her pregnant. It sounds like she was a little bit precocious, but a ten-year-old and a twenty-five- or thirty-year-old? Then there was another woman who was thirty-five who came in and she was too far along to have an abortion, so she must have been twenty-eight weeks. She had just found out she was pregnant the day before. How she could not have known is beyond me, but she just had not been watching the signs. Those are the kinds of stories that stand out.

LORNA: We thought that we would essentially be helping the young student population that's so prominent in the area. And I think what we found out is that that wasn't necessarily the only, or even primary, group that we were helping. In part, I think a lot of the young women [from the colleges] probably went home for that.

JEANNIE: And there was Elaine Fraser at UMass Health Services.

JUDI: And UCF.

ROBIN: So maybe it's no surprise that we didn't see the students. We saw many who were in their early thirties. I remember when Amherst Medical was beginning to set up their own service they asked us to come and tell what we had found out. They were surprised that we were saying that about half the people we see are around 30—women from the community.

JEANNIE: Because they got the UMass referrals, it turned out that what Amherst Medical actually saw was much more of a student population. Amherst Medical worked out a deal with this group of obstetricians and gynecologists from Springfield [Hampden Gynecological Associates (HGA)], who would provide these services. They only rotated in the doctors who were willing, however reluctantly, however ineptly, to do abortions. We were just grateful to have doctors perform abortions. Bettigole was the first one, but he stopped going to Amherst.

PAT: Certainly if there were doctors at Amherst Medical who didn't approve of abortion, I don't think we knew about it. But in terms of the HGA group in Springfield, there were clearly a few who didn't approve.

JEANNIE: And didn't do them.

ROBIN: When I was working for a local health insurer I heard from a young African-American woman that there had been a concerted effort among the African-American students in the area to talk any women who were pregnant out of ever considering abortion. It was part of the ideology of "they are trying to kill off our race."

JEANNIE: [Once we started working at the clinics], there wasn't a typical client [there either]. After all, everybody's experience and circumstances, their reasons for having an abortion, and their reasons for why they were pregnant, was very different. I would say the average age was much lower than mid-twenties—it was closer to eighteen, maybe, or nineteen. But there were people who were married and had kids, and the size of their family at that point in their lives was the size they needed. There were people who had been very faithful users of contraception and it had failed. And there were lots of people who weren't using any sort of birth control; obviously, that was the bulk of the people who were there. It seems to me there were a *thousand* reasons.

PAT: The pill had too many side effects, the diaphragm was too much of a nuisance, the IUD caused too much bleeding. What else was there? Condoms were too much of a nuisance. You know . . . .

JEANNIE: And, yes, they *had* been using something, and then there was just this one slip-up, or there was a contraceptive failure, or they weren't using it right.

PAT: It's hard to come up with any one thing. Certainly many of them were not using anything. Especially many younger people, who had not been sexually active for that long, weren't using anything.

JEANNIE: I would say that the bulk of the people that we saw in Amherst—and again, it may be because of the age skew, with the five colleges—were unmarried. In Amherst, they were 95 percent European-American.

PAT: That wasn't true in the Springfield [clinic]. We certainly saw a number of Blacks and Hispanics, and even a few Asians. Not too many, but a few. I think there were more mid-twenties in general. We saw a lot of older people as well, especially the mothers who were on welfare and didn't want another child. We definitely saw a fair number of those.

The Lucy Fund, Networks, and Spin-offs

LORNA: I remember the Lucy Fund. The way it got established, and this is maybe apocryphal, is that there was a young woman who needed an abortion and there wasn't sufficient money. Her name was Lucy. We collected money in order to send her to New York, so it means it was *after* the New York law changed. We realized that we really needed to have a fund to help poorer and indigent women, and somebody donated the money. We all donated some, but somebody gave more to it so that it actually could be a fund.

JUDI: And then we got Eastern Women's Clinic to give us credit for every woman we sent to them.[4]

LORNA: Yes, yes right. That was the big one we were sending to. Then it was HGA and Amherst Medical, but that's after '73.

JUDI: The Western New England Counselors Cooperative then kept the statistics and made sure they were in the position of continuing to negotiate with the providers to keep the free abortions going. That concept just kind of got moved over to the Counselors Cooperative.

JEANNIE: So that's an answer to whether there were any spin-offs from our group. I would say that that is clearly a direct link. In theory people would try and repay the money that was given to them. It was a loan. There was definitely a book-keeping element.

JEANNIE: Wasn't there some connection between [us and] Family Planning?[5] Were Ellen Story or Leslie Laurie at all involved in the Abortion Counseling group? Was there any sort of spin-off?

JUDI: Well, if you want spin-offs, *there* was a spin-off. What happened was Leslie got a group of people together—which was a broad group of people—to talk about creating Family Planning. I remember going to that meeting and I was over-whelmed by the prospect that anybody could pull this off. Some people got involved in working on the project. I didn't because I thought it was too over-whelming!

JUDI: It was '73, I think, because it was the 25-year anniversary last year. And cer-tainly some of the people involved in the Valley Women's Center were a part of the original board [at Family Planning].

From Volunteers to Professional Counselors

JEANNIE: In 1973 it was so exciting to think that this service was going to be pro-vided [legally] in Amherst. I had been doing abortion counseling through the Valley Women's Center, and was very committed to what I'd been doing. Also I was not working at any other paying job at the time. So, it seemed like a great oppor-tunity to continue to provide counseling for women who were considering an abortion.

PAT: Well, our backgrounds in this are a little similar. Because we both were doing abor-tion and birth control counseling at the Valley Women's Center, we sort of fell into these jobs. I had small children—yours were a little bigger—and I had not been work-ing. I also was very committed to choice, and it was just wonderful to get *paid* for doing something that I was so committed to. I had been working as a volunteer for what seemed like a long time. I worked as a paid counselor at Amherst Medical from

1973 until probably '76 or '77. And then, in '75 I also began working in Springfield at Hampden Gynecological Associates. I worked there until 1985. So, for a couple of years, I overlapped with both clinics. Hampden Gynecological Associates contracted with Amherst Medical to be OB-GYN doctors for the Amherst Medical practice, and to provide abortion services. And when they first set this all up, the head counselor who had been working in Springfield, Liza Solomon, hired Jeannie and me to work at Amherst.

JEANNIE: Liza had talked both to people in Family Planning and people involved with the Valley Women's Center about suggesting names.

PAT: Liza and the counselors who worked in Springfield had also been active in the abortion and birth control group at the Springfield Women's Center and we knew each other in that respect.[6] My memory is that Liza felt, "Well, there's no such thing as real training for abortion counselors, so why not get people who have already been doing it through other means?" I also remember that Amherst Medical did not realize that she had been given permission or the go-ahead to hire us. They thought they were hiring their own counselors, and suddenly we were there! But they were gracious, and kept us on and paid our salaries. We met with everyone who was having an abortion, prior to the procedure. Sometimes they would be having the procedure that day, sometimes they would be having just the counseling and coming back another day.

JEANNIE: Right. In Amherst, *most* of the clients had already been to some sort of Family Planning clinic or came from University Health Services. They'd already talked about what they wanted to do and discussed their options, and had basically gone through a counseling session. They were usually fairly committed about their decisions. But it wasn't true of everybody. If somebody hadn't had counseling somewhere else, usually they weren't there the same day for the procedure. Often, they were just coming for counseling to talk about what they wanted to do. But Springfield was different.

PAT: Well, in Springfield we did it both ways. We would see some people in the morning and they'd be done that afternoon. But we would put it off if someone came in and we didn't feel they were ready, or they felt they weren't ready. Later abortions—after twelve weeks—almost always took two visits. In Amherst, we only did them to twelve or twelve-ish weeks. We also went [along for] the procedures. We were sort of the support system—the person supporting the patient, or the client, while she actually had that procedure done. We were in the room with her.

JEANNIE: We went into this work with very strong philosophical beliefs about women's right to choose, and about what women should know about their bodies and about birth control. We had enough time in the counseling session to really show them pictures of their uterus, and what the procedure would involve, and talk at some length about birth control methods. I think that that was part of what we brought from the Valley Women's Center and the counseling that we'd been doing.

We brought that to the clinic setting, and I think it's stayed on. I think that in some ways, the [doctors] accepted *grudgingly* the idea of having counselors in the first place. That wasn't a natural part of an OB-GYN practice. And it wasn't true for most other—*any* other—procedures.

PAT: Although there wasn't any formal training, I do think that some of the doctors were eager to teach and explain what they were doing, and were open to questions. I think we got "on the job training" and did learn a lot as time went on. My memory is that we used *Our Bodies, Ourselves*. That book was like a bible [to us] and it explained procedures and how they were done. Then, of course, as technology changed, you would learn on the job what was different about your clinic versus that book.

JEANNIE: Or one doctor from another.

PAT: That's true!

JEANNIE: One of the things that always seemed sad was that there wasn't that much opportunity for follow-up with people. Even when they came back to the group of gynecologists for their follow-up, often it would be not the day that we were working, or there wouldn't be an opportunity to really see them. And so there was sort of a disconnect.

Referral Agencies

JUDI: How did you work with referral agencies?

PAT: The Family Planning agencies, UMass, the Western New England Counseling Cooperative, the Health Care Project in Florence [Massachusetts]—those were, for the most part, the referring agencies to both clinics. And the Western New England Co-op negotiated with both Amherst Medical and Hampden GYN Associates to offer a credit system to make it easier for poor women to have abortions if they didn't have the money. I think the Co-op met on Saturday mornings, I don't remember how often, just to kind of network and talk about what was going on and talk about how much credit there was available for poor women. The system of one free abortion for every ten had already been set up by the time Amherst opened, and perhaps it was a given that that would go on.

JEANNIE: I think our relationships were very good with those referral agencies. It was very supportive and we all worked together very well. If there were any problems, people could talk about it. I think there was mutual respect.

JUDI: So you as the counselors from those for-profit agencies, so to speak, were the people that established the relationships, helped them to grow, and to keep them even.

PAT: Oh, I would certainly say that we nurtured those relationships. But I think we counselors all had the same basic philosophy, which made it easier to negotiate. I think if the doctors had been trying to negotiate it, there would have been a lot more tension.

JEANNIE: But certainly in Amherst, the built-in assumptions didn't even need to be nurtured. I mean, Family Planning and University Health Services—they wanted these services to be an option for people, so they provided in advance the kind of counseling that women needed.

JUDI: Can you remember what the cost of an abortion was?

PAT: Yeah: $150 for the longest time, and then it went up to $175. In Springfield it went up, but then it went up even more if you were over 12 weeks. I can't remember all the prices.

JUDI: And were some women not able to get abortions because they couldn't afford it?

PAT: There may have been some women who couldn't get a late-term abortion in the hospital without money. I don't know that we ever offered a free abortion, but I don't remember ever turning somebody away from Amherst Medical for lack of money. Usually we could easily do anybody affiliated with the Co-op, even if there was no credit. And if we had an unusual case in Springfield, we would often make that decision ourselves [to go ahead with the procedure and find the money later]. We had to be careful, but we could do that. And very often, we made a decision to reduce the price. Although, if you had a late-term abortion by saline, it was much more expensive. I don't remember the price of that, but it was more in the range of $400 or $500, and most of that was the hospital fee. We had no control over the hospital. We couldn't get them to reduce their fees, as I recall.

JEANNIE: Amherst was really different because so many people came from a referral agency. The financial end of it had been worked out in advance. I don't believe we turned people away ever.

The Silence Continues

JEANNIE: I became convinced within a year or two of doing abortion counseling to great numbers at Amherst Medical that this whole thing—society's condemnatory attitude toward abortion—was going to change so dramatically because there were all these women of all ages who had abortions and members of their families who knew about it. They had this experience of making this tough decision. I thought that was going to change the political landscape and I can't believe [the resistance to legal abortion] is still going on. There's this enormous number of women having abortions still, but it's like you had one and you don't have any sympathy or concern for anyone else. Where is this enormous population of people who've personally had this experience? Where are their families?

ROBIN: They're still keeping it a secret.

LORNA: Well, it also has to do with power. Power is still mostly in the hands of men. I think—I really do, I have not changed my mind—that men are very afraid of women being solely responsible for making these decisions. I think that if you look around at where the violence against abortion clinics is coming from, it's coming mostly from men. Very few women are being violent about it. The opposition is led largely by men. Not that there aren't women who agree with them and women who stand on these lines [outside abortion clinics].

JUDI: I think that what was said about our work bringing it out of the closet was accurate, but unfortunately it still is secret to some degree.

JEANNIE: I think that's good to point out, that yes the secrecy has changed, but in many ways it hasn't.

ROBIN: A campaign could be done about that secrecy.

JEANNIE: But it's a very personal decision. I don't think it's something you want to necessarily just talk about.

ROBIN: I know. But it's something that has been used very effectively in outing [of gay people], for example. I'm not in favor of it, but look what it does. And look what happens when the hypocrites who are holding elected office get found out: "Oh, Senator Whoever-you-are, your office is full of pornography, that's very interesting," and then the guy pipes down a little bit. Anyway, I'm really thinking that it has a lot still to do with religion and, following on what Lorna said, with power—who has the right to decide matters of life and death. There are so many who still will not grant that power to everyone. Only *some* people get to make important decisions.

LORNA: Religion is important, you're right about that. There's been an upsurge of people returning to religion of all kinds.

ROBIN: But the core of religious thought is who is a receptacle—a proper recipient of God's word. You mentioned priests. Okay, that's something that no woman can be, at least for a lot of religions. But that's also involved with class as well as with gender. Who is a subject, who is an agent, who gets to choose?

JEANNIE: It's not the people who are religiously opposed to abortion that I'm thinking about, it's the people who had abortions or their family members.

ROBIN: I've always regretted that we had to throw away the names, that we couldn't come back in 90 days, or a year, and say, "could you consider helping us now?"

JUDI: But it was the right decision.

ROBIN: It was right. I just have those regrets.

LORNA: But one could make a national call, if the movement really got started again, for all women and men who benefited since *Roe v. Wade* to come forward to go on the streets.

JEANNIE: Whether—you could couch it in such a way—you've personally benefited or not, step forward and be on the right side of the decision.

ROBIN: But in the climate that has been created—and I became well aware of it from doing telephone calls for Tapestry—people are really afraid of being targeted by the righteous.[7] Now it's an awful lot harder. I think that we've been really torpid since 1972.

LORNA: I also think that there are all these women that were helped by having access to counseling, both pre- and post-*Roe v. Wade*. Now [women] are not getting that.

I think that a lot of women are, in fact, making decisions against having abortions out of fear and ignorance because the counseling and the positive spin of having a right to make your own decision is no longer out there. What's out there are the religious fanatics and the violent fanatics.

JEANNIE: Also, nobody much likes doing abortions. So now there's just a very small handful of doctors who are willing.

JUDI: This is kind of an aside, but it came to me as we've been talking—we used to call it "problem pregnancy" and we tried to give people choices. You referred to the woman with the daughter who made the decision to keep the baby—we really did push all the choices. And then when Family Planning began to do the counseling, they did the same thing, gave all the options.

ROBIN: But since we haven't told our own story, it's being given the negative spin of "*those people* always wanted you to have abortions." It gets characterized as so crude and so cruel.

PAT: I remember when I worked at the clinic, a woman called at ten of five in the afternoon—bordering on desperate, she's fourteen [weeks], and really needed an abortion. We got her in. We squeezed her in the next day, and I don't know who counseled her, but she had her abortion. Then three or four years later, the same woman was going around saying that she had been *coerced* into having this abortion. In her mind, she felt that she had been coerced. Listen, we went out of our way to *help* her! That kind of stuff really irks me.

ROBIN: You know, it irked me, too. I was such a skeptic at the beginning about an awful lot that the psychologists say, which I now accept. I really did not take into account any of the mechanisms of denial. I was operating on a much simpler view of human psychology than I use now—if somebody got help, she would be grateful, she would help us.

JUDI: Or at least not turn around and say that she'd been coerced or that we'd talked her into it.

ROBIN: Right, not *lie!*

Looking Back: "We Made Abortion no Longer a Secret"

LORNA: I think we did a remarkable job both before and after *Roe v. Wade*. But what I remember most was Robin calling me at seven in the morning to tell me about *Roe v. Wade*. How the hell did you know about it at seven in the morning is what I want to know! Robin said then, and it was very astute: "It's a surprise. We didn't think we would get it through the judiciary. It's too bad. We'd be better off if it came through the legislature." Because if we'd gone through the legislature—and we knew it would take much longer—we would not be in the position we're in today about access.

ROBIN: Because we're [now] getting nibbled to death.

LORNA: Right. And I kept thinking, "but Robin, it's over, it's legal!" But Robin knew better.

JEANNIE: I think we did a remarkable job. I think perhaps outreach might have been different or better, but it was amazing. One of the things I think we all felt was that some sort of counseling component was really essential for provision of abortion services—to talk to people in advance about their decision to have an abortion. Our group helped to put pressure on clinics in New York and then on Amherst Medical and the HGA doctors. They actually hired the people recommended by the Abortion and Birth Control group to provide counseling services.

LORNA: The other thing we did is that we really worked toward making physicians more sensitive to women's needs beyond just pregnancy and termination of pregnancy. Doing all those interviews made them aware of the fact that women had a right to ask questions and to determine their own lives. I think we did a very good job at that. I think that maybe now it's fallen away a bit, which is too bad.

ROBIN: We made abortion no longer a secret. Now, there are a lot of downsides to that. But it was so striking to me when I was living in California in the mid-1960s, before I came here, I saw a poster which asked, "Is your mother a secret criminal?" And of course, that applied to *me*. *I* was a secret criminal. I had never dealt with criminals before I had to have an abortion. And that was only because of the culture of secrecy around it. It was secret as to why some women were in the hospital and it was secret if that's how they died, and so on. So it has changed.

I believed in it so strongly, it was like . . . I'm sorry, I will confess it first: it was like a rush. "I am doing something illegal, and it feels great!" I think there was an awful lot of righteousness to it, a crusade part of it that drove us. Furthermore, if I can refer to denial again, it did not occur to me that snipers would hang out and target people.

LORNA: Because there had not been any violence at that point, I think that the fear we had—or whatever paranoia it was—was not about violence being directed at us. It was more about getting entangled in legal issues. I think the ingredient of violence changes the picture.

PAT: When I think back, one of the things that I come up with a lot is that we're being nibbled to death [now] and it disturbs me. And I keep thinking—I've been out of that stuff for a while and I don't have the energy to go back into it—we need some younger women to pick up the pieces and go forward, and I'm convinced that that's not happening.

JUDI: Well, I've seen younger women in the last year. I was impressed when I went to the consortium of groups the Massachusetts NARAL project put together to try to see if Cooley-Dickinson Hospital would do abortions in-house. There was a woman from all the five colleges there and there were some other younger women. That was really good to see.

TWENTY

Springfield Women's Health Collective

The Springfield Women's Health Collective (SWHC) sprang from an unnamed women's consciousness-raising group that began meeting in Springfield in the later 1960s. In early 1970, some of the members turned to abortion and birth control activism and began providing problem pregnancy counseling and abortion referrals from an office at 115 State Street in Springfield. The seven initial members of the SWHC staffed the drop-in center that, according to their 1971 information brochure, offered "a service especially for women which will meet their needs for information and support. Beyond this we think it is important that women working together can take responsibility for improving and controlling the quality of their lives." The SWHC volunteers provided general parenting, birth, and birth control information, offered birth control and abortion counseling, and gave referrals to doctors and abortion providers. In addition, some volunteers reviewed out-of-state abortion clinics and sometimes drove patients across state lines for their abortions. The SWHC drop-in office on State Street apparently became known as the Springfield Women's Center in 1973, though by that point all of the original members interviewed here were no longer active in this sphere of feminist activism, and later relocated to Worthington Street and eventually morphed into the Springfield Women's Union.

Joyce Berkman and Susan Tracy interviewed "Mary Doe," Ann Meeropol, Sherri Oake, Betty Wright, and Alice Zaft on December 1, 1999.

Origins

ALICE ZAFT: I'm Alice Zaft. I'm an attorney. I do a mix of about half discrimination law, focusing on sexual harassment, and about half general personal injury.

BETTY WRIGHT: I'm Betty Wright, and I'm a nurse clinician in women's health.

MARY DOE: I'm Mary Doe.[1]

ANN MEEROPOL: I'm Ann Meeropol. I work in special education. I'm the chair of the Department of Special Education at Longmeadow High School.

SHERRI OAKE: I'm Sherri Oake. I work in disability claims management. We started the abortion work probably in 1970.

ALICE: We were already living together when we formed the Health Collective. It was an offshoot of the general, political, demonstrating kinds of things [that we were involved in]. And when women's issues and feminist issues were coming out, we had a consciousness-raising group.

MARY: That's all that it was for a very long time [a women's consciousness-raising group]. I don't know if this is accurate, but my memory is that at some point, when we'd processed just about everything there was to process about being a woman in those days, we all kind of came to the sense that we needed to *do* something, needed to take some kind of action.

ANN: That's my memory, too. There was a larger group of women. I remember an early meeting—it seemed like there were women everywhere—up the staircase, all around. We had that brown itchy sofa in the living room. That was the only chair. It was the beginning of groups getting together, and a core group came out of it that wanted to set up the counseling service.

ALICE: We didn't want to just talk, we wanted to *do*. We also liked the idea of teaching women about themselves, about their bodies, about their own health. It was not confined to [abortion]. There were whole areas of things that we were talking about.

ANN: I remember a self-examination evening early on.

BETTY: Yeah, I do, too. We had somehow found a speculum.

ALICE: We were doing things [like that] for a while before we formally incorporated. I remember when we started off we were actually helping runaway women for a while, and then it focused into these things.

ANN: There was a woman in another state who had her own one-woman abortion counseling work. She ran an ad in the paper, and my memory is that she was the one who used the phrase "Problem Pregnancy?" She did her own work individually, but she was somebody that we knew. We then thought that we should organize a broader group and do something similar.

SHERRI: She had found herself in a difficult position [i.e., pregnant] with no help, and later on, said, "I don't want this to happen to other women. I'm going to do something about it." She was about 19 at that point, because she was a year younger than I. I knew her well. She had already started doing research and stuff.

ANN: I felt for me, it was an impetus. I considered it very brave. She was a part of the larger consciousness-raising group. We incorporated the spring of 1970. Another impetus for me to get involved was partly based on a bad experience in New York with a very dear friend, who ended up *not* having an illegal abortion. It was going to be really terrifying and I was her closest friend. I went through every step up to the point where I said, "You can't do this; you could die." And she ended up unmarried having twins. She had had no prenatal care at all, and the twins were a total surprise at delivery. So you know that impacted me.

SHERRI: I think part of our desire to [put rhetoric into action] came out of the MDS group, Movement for a Democratic Society. Some of the women in the group were somewhat dissatisfied because we felt that as women, our position was no different in MDS than it was any place else in society; that we were relegated to the backseat, and didn't have as much of a voice as we felt we should have. I think that was pretty much a feeling that went across the entire left political movement at the time. I think most women were feeling that. And so we got together to just talk about things. I think that's where our need to do something active came from, because that's what we wanted to do in the first place. So this was perfect. Also, this affected us personally. We were all women of childbearing age at the time. It was an important issue to us, personally. At least to me.

MARY: I member the discussion phase as fairly lengthy. We were trying to decide what we should do. It didn't take us long to get to a health-based thing, because a lot of us in the group either were involved in or interested in health stuff or, as you said, at a time in life [childbearing age]. That was so mutual—raising issues and making decisions and figuring out what to do. It was just a model of the consciousness-raising stuff that we'd been working on.

ALICE: And I don't think there was ever any issue in terms of division of labor. Everybody wanted to give and worked with each other's schedules and "what are you good at, what are you comfortable with?" and everything.

Opening the Counseling Center

SHERRI: When we got an office, we started doing really in-depth counseling. We didn't feel comfortable doing it in homes. We felt like we should have a central place, where everybody felt comfortable.

ANN: We didn't pay for that office because it was a satellite to the Leukemia Society's headquarters for their fundraising. I was working part-time doing the fundraising drive, and so it was available. It was nice.

BETTY: The office was open for walk-ins, and then we had a phone, and people could call us.

ANN: The phone had a taped message that would give the appointment times when the office would be open. I think we were open every day, and we took turns. We [each] had a set time, a set day.

BETTY: I was pregnant at the time and was going to school too, so I was very busy. But I remember I would walk down from school and work in the office. I would go to the weekly meetings, but I don't remember having a lot to do with the actual paperwork. I think some other people really did the hard work in getting the office opened.

ALICE: We had a network, an underground network, and we were already in contact, with the OBs (obstetricians) in the area. They were referring people to us, and they also knew of physicians in other states [about] whom they said, "Here's a good place; here's where you can take this person." But they could not legally do [abortions] themselves.

SHERRI: It was generally known that there were some obstetricians in the area who would assist patients in getting psychiatric referrals for first trimester abortions. That was never technically illegal—you could get an abortion, but for psychiatric reasons. You had to have two psychiatrists say that you'd throw yourself out a window if you didn't have your abortion. We did sometimes put women in contact with the psychiatrists and physicians that we knew were sympathetic and would assist these women. We were doing *that* before we started sending people to New York. It was that kind of word of mouth stuff—somebody would know somebody who went to Dr. So-and-So and he was helpful. I remember taking people to psychiatrists' offices, going through this whole process. Hopefully [the women] started early enough, so by the time the process was finished, they were still in their first trimester. It was quite a circus. But the thing is—it *was* available *if* you knew what the process was. A lot of these eighteen- or nineteen-year-old girls, they didn't have a clue as to who to go to. So, at least we were able to provide them with that kind of information, if nothing else.

ALICE: In the office, the tasks would be: seeing women, referring women, and then for some of us, traveling with women out of state. Sometimes we would drive them, and we would be with them through the waiting period afterwards, hold their hand, make sure they felt okay, do the follow-up medical care with them.

MARY: There would be appointments with us after. But I also remember that before we started taking people to specific places out of state, we did some research runs, and we went and visited and learned about these places.

SHERRI: There was one hospital in New York that we absolutely would not send people to. We got negative feedback from somebody that we had sent at the very beginning. I don't think it was anything horrible; I think they were just very badly treated by the staff, and we decided that we were *not* going to put anybody through that.

ALICE: My recollection is there was also a doctor that we didn't use because *we* got very negative feelings from the doctor. We felt as if his place was a mill or something like that.

ANN: We had the sense that aftercare was really poor. I remember the recovery rooms a few times that I went—seeing this whole line-up of women lying there in recovery for three or four hours before they could get up and leave. They were really alone. I think we were acutely sensitive to that. We felt that it was essential that there be counseling right on the spot afterwards.

MARY: We did go back, also, after we'd been using these places for a while just to make sure that they were still clean.

ANN: That's right. I remember we went as a group. I think there were two or three places, then one closed. There was that very modern clinic, Eastern Women's.

ALICE: I don't remember whether the physicians required this, or whether they strongly suggested this, but every one of us was asked to actually watch a procedure so that we would know what these women were going through, and what a hard process it was. There was none of this standoffish callousness kind of thing. As far as I know, there was absolutely never a single person who wasn't able to do it because of not having money. Somehow, something was always worked out.

SHERRI: Financially, there wasn't a heck of a lot we could do, but most of the clinics had resources where, if the woman could come up with part of the money, somehow there were funds that could be dipped into that filled it out. But my recollection is there was a minimum amount that they had to come up with. It might have only been $25, but they had to come up with *something*. I think that it wasn't so much that the clinics wanted their money, but they wanted them [the women] to be absolutely sure that this is what they wanted to do. They needed to participate, so they paid for part of the service. At that time, 25 bucks was a lot to a 19-year-old.

ANN: I think sometimes we contributed money. That's my memory. Each of us contributed a small amount. It wasn't a burden, and it added up. Because we had some people who really were nearly destitute.

SHERRI: Right. That was just on a case-by-case basis. That wasn't a standard policy. But I don't think we ever said to anybody, "Sorry, no money . . . ."

ALICE: Afterwards, we required them to come back for birth control counseling. And that was when we had the strong follow up network with the doctors in the area who would then provide it to them.

SHERRI: We wanted to be able to say to the doctors, "This is a postabortion check up." We wanted them to know what they were looking at so nothing would be overlooked if there were any complications. We needed to feel comfortable that we could trust these doctors with that kind of information. One of the reasons why we wanted to see people afterwards was to get feedback on a lot of these places. It's very hard to send somebody off without knowing exactly what you're sending them to. I think we all felt this really strong need to know what was going on there. We obviously couldn't go with every single person, so we relied a lot on people to tell us what their experience was like.

MARY: I think we were really worried about the medical after-effects too. I remember being scared every time we sent somebody.

ALICE: And what if something went wrong? I think that that was part of why we had the network with physicians in this area. We had physicians lined up who would be there if something happened. They would be willing even though they weren't the ones who had done the abortion. They could not legally have done it, but they would be willing immediately to do the follow-up care. We also didn't want the woman coming back to us again and again. We would hope that for everybody it was one shot. That may be how we came up with the name [Springfield Women's Health Collective]. We wanted it to be a more generic kind of thing rather than "Women Who Take Women for Abortions" or something.

SHERRI: I think part of that, too, was that we wanted to do a lot of birth control and general women's health. Because there was so little.

ALICE: I remember there was just so much stuff going on in those days—political stuff—and people were *so* glad that somebody was doing this. We were all putting ourselves at risk. I think that after we were doing it awhile, there was a crackdown on bringing women across [state lines for abortions]. People were being stopped and arrested. I remember this heightened sense of it being like an underground railroad kind of a thing. We worried about what if the car breaks down and we get stopped, and what's going to happen, and "here's the story we're going to tell." I don't remember it being that tense when we first started, but that may also have been because we were all so young. We felt *so* invulnerable.

SHERRI: I was thinking the same thing. I had this bravado, like "yeah, just try and arrest me." I had no children to worry about—that's a responsibility that I felt years later. I would be much less likely to put myself at risk once I had kids.

ALICE: Do you know what I remember? I remember you stopping and yelling at a woman who was driving a car with a pro-life bumper sticker and she had a kid who was not seat-belted. You stopped the car and I thought you were going to beat that lady up!

SHERRI: She had this kid that was about three years old standing on the front seat, holding onto the dashboard while she's driving. And she had a Right to Life sticker on her bumper! And I said, "Why are you so worried about other people's unborn children and you're treating your own child so irresponsibly?"

ALICE: I still now get that urge to do that when I see somebody driving along with various kinds of bumper stickers and a kid not in a car seat. I feel like pulling them over and making a citizen's arrest.

Worries and Concerns

BETTY: I remember feeling that it was the right thing to do, but I remember not bringing up [my abortion work] when I was in school. I didn't talk about it to classmates. The person who ran my program at Springfield Technical Community

College was Irish and Catholic and very religious. I was [already] afraid that I'd be kicked out of school for being pregnant [so] I just never really talked about it there.

MARY: I was older than everybody else and already had two kids at the time and I remember being scared of what we were doing. I remember feeling that it was risky. But, as everybody else has said, it just seemed as if it had to be done. It *had* to be done. We were the right group to do it.

ANN: I had two kids too. I certainly felt like we were doing something risky, but I also felt—and I think this came out of discussion in the group—that if something was going to come down real hard, it was going to come down in Boston. That we were the "neglected West." That's part of how I kind of hedged my bets—that what I was doing was probably not going to get me arrested.

SHERRI: I guess I thought we were spared mostly because we were quiet. We weren't out in the streets, drumming up business. Though we ran an ad and that kind of thing, I felt like a lot of people didn't even know we were there—people who would be in a position to make it difficult for us.

MARY: I also remember a sense that the group, in a very deliberate way, wanted to be very responsible about what we were doing. So, for example, we taught ourselves a *ton* about the procedures. Also, I think that over time we learned that certain other things ought to be included in the counseling. We wanted to be very clear that we weren't pushing these people toward abortion. We wanted to make sure that *all* the choices were laid out for them, without judgment by us.

SHERRI: There were actually two nurses in our group. And I think as a group we really educated each other in a lot of respects. I think we also got kind of a schematic of the equipment that was used by the clinics. I think we got it from one of the clinics. We also went in and observed procedures and asked a lot of questions.

MARY: I remember descriptions of the three different available procedures—very detailed descriptions so that there was no mistake about what was going on, even down to the details of "now, you're going to hear this noise that sounds like a vacuum cleaner." And we would tell the women those things and be very descriptive and prepare them in advance.

ALICE: And we got literature that we all read and that we talked about in terms of what are the things to watch for afterwards.

ANN: And we did do that. We worked on that as a group. I remember doing that with every client. And we had conversations to remind ourselves how important it was to talk about birth control—to always bring that up, especially with the youngsters.

SHERRI: Later on, I think we did get information from the various clinics that we were referring to, whenever we could scavenge stuff from them. But I think at the beginning, we were really doing our own stuff [creating our own forms and literature].

ALICE: My parents [didn't know what I was doing].

ANN: I have a Catholic family. We didn't talk about it. No way. I would talk about my political beliefs with my family, have arguments, but I don't think I made an issue about abortion.

SHERRI: I don't remember talking to my family about it. I just never did. I don't remember feeling particularly uneasy about it. Certainly my husband knew, but I don't know about anybody else. I do know that for a long time—even after I did it as a profession after the law changed—I was reluctant to tell people. When I would send my resume to somebody, I'd put "Family Planning Counselor." I knew that to say that I had been an abortion counselor for ten years would get a real strong reaction from a lot of people.

The Clients

ALICE: The ages [of our clients ran] the full spectrum. I was surprised at our getting older women. It was something that I thought of as a young woman's issue. Yet, we would actually have women of all ages. We had women of all races, from all walks of life. I don't think race was ever an issue.

SHERRI: I have to think it was largely white women, though I did have a client once who was Romanian and spoke only Romanian and Polish. I found a translator who spoke Polish and English. We had a very interesting session that day, translating through all that. I think for the most part, it was white women. That's my memory.

ALICE: As well as the ads, I also think that there must have been some word of mouth. I remember one of our concerns with the ads was that somebody calling up wasn't a bona fide person looking for our services, but was somebody who might be trying to get information to bust us. So we would not give out much information on the phone. We would require them to come in and sort of get a sense of who they were. But I remember having women of color and I don't remember it ever being any issue one way or the other. I don't remember anybody ever saying to us, "You're white, middle class people" kind of stuff.

SHERRI: We saw whoever came through the door. We didn't choose our clients, they chose us. So we just saw whomever, and, for whatever reason. But I do think it was largely white clients.

Crossing the Line

BETTY: Who took people to New York?

ANN: I did.

ALICE: I did.

BETTY: And did you go alone or with someone else?

MARY: I tend to think we always doubled up.

ALICE: We always doubled up.

ANN: We didn't necessarily just go with the patient. Sometimes the patient came with somebody—boyfriend, or another friend.

SHERRI: I don't think [we drove] that many. Some of our trips were merely observation trips, investigation trips. We wanted to see these places before we actually sent people to them. I think only *occasionally*, we would drive somebody.

Going Legit

ANN: My memory is that we folded with *Roe v. Wade*. That was it. There was a mini-celebration. I don't remember how we celebrated, but I remember thinking we had a good celebration.

SHERRI: Right. And then we all went out and got jobs!

MARY: Yes, a lot of people from our group went out and got jobs in the obstetricians' offices that were now going to be able to do these things legitimately.

SHERRI: I did it for about ten years altogether. There were a number of us who did. Because we were the only ones around who knew anything about the procedures, who had been in the operating room with patients at facilities outside of Massachusetts, and knew what to expect. So when the obstetricians in the area wanted to hire people, there were very few people to choose from.

Abortion Counselors: Hidden Even from Each Other

MARY: Sherri, is this a correct memory: when you started working for the obstetricians—once it was all legit—didn't you have to sell to them the notion that they needed a counselor in the office?

SHERRI: Yes, we did.

ALICE: Yes, we did! Oh, my gosh.

SHERRI: But some of the doctors were much more open to it than the others. But their idea was, "Well, we don't counsel people for anything else." And we said, "Shame on you. You should." And so ultimately, when I worked for them, I ended up counseling people for tubal ligations, for just about everything.

MARY: I think that's really an important thing that came out of our work. In the end, it put women in a position to teach the doctors what was needed in good medical care—which is a huge contribution.

SHERRI: You're right—it was. How *little* credit we gave ourselves! It's amazing. We did have contact with the women in New Haven. I remember there was a lot of friction over the issue of counseling. They felt that by providing counseling, we were setting women apart from—you know, that it should be just considered another surgical procedure. Our contention, if I remember correctly, was that the solution was that *every*body should get counseling for *any*thing they ever have done medically; this was the first step in having somebody sit down with them to talk about the procedure and the possible consequences.

ALICE: But what's funny is that we had fairly close ties to the Northampton-Amherst community in terms of lifestyle and things that we did, but we just had absolutely no knowledge [of the groups there].

ANN: I think there is a disconnection between the North Valley and the South Valley. Springfield is an insular community. I know Northampton is as well. Northamptonites are not interested in coming to Springfield, and vice versa. That probably plays itself out in other areas as well. I think we operated our group very independently and didn't look [further from] home.

SHERRI: My memory is that back then the Northampton-Amherst area was seen as very academic and the Springfield area was seen as very working class, and that there was a lot of tension between those two groups. I think in Springfield there was a lot of "you're reading about it, but we're doing something about it." And a lot of self-righteousness of the "I know the working class." I come from an upper-middle-class community where my family was working class and one of the poorer families in the community; suddenly I was exalted because my father was a truck driver! You know, that was "real working class." It was great! But I think there was a lot of that kind of tension of Northampton-Amherst not being the "real world." Springfield was the real world. Holyoke was the real world.

MARY: Yeah, I think that's right. In the Springfield group there was a real sense of *doing* and not being part of an elite. I also had the sense—maybe it was just because I looked so hard for a group and couldn't find one until I found you guys—that we were the only thing that was going on.

SHERRI: And we were trying to be a secret about it!

ALICE: I came from the Northampton area, having gone to school there. I remember still having friends, still having contacts there who said, "Why would you want to live in Springfield?" I think we were all very aware of what was going on in Boston. But Boston, at least in my perception of it at that time, was not out to really help women on a personal basis, but [wanted] to make a political statement. Everything was designed to be very public, and very challenging to the status quo. That wasn't what we were about at all.[2]

Looking Back (and Going Forward)

ALICE: We talked before about whether at the time we had discussed this with our families. We now all have children. How many of us have told our children what we did? And what do our children think?

MARY: I have.

ANN: I have.

BETTY: I don't think I told Ben. Did you tell?

ALICE: I don't think I told Matthew. I think I told Judith, though. So maybe it's a daughter thing.

SHERRI: I told my daughter and my son, but he wasn't very interested. So maybe it *is* a daughter thing. But of course, my kids think I was this wild maniac. They're so much more conservative.

ALICE: I don't know whether I told my daughter anything specific—that it was against the law, that we would take the people out of state.

MARY: I told them in a recent discussion. What was really, really amazing to me was there were two reactions. One was disbelief that this was such a problem then. I really had to take time to set the context and create the history. And once I did that, there was this kind of open-mouthed, "My god, how did you all have the guts to do that?"

ALICE: I didn't tell *my* daughter until recently. I think that it was because it didn't seem that significant. It was really only recently that it became something that, "Oh, that might be of interest, and hey, do you know I did this? That's something important that I did." I don't know, I guess it's a sort of, if you had it to do over, would you do it? I think that I would and I think that it partly shaped my life. My becoming a lawyer was in part related to challenging the laws, realizing what laws are doing, wanting to represent people and help people. I remember our floundering around at that time, frustrated with the law and finding a lawyer. I think it's interesting how many people here went into either social services or health professions.

MARY: I agree with a lot of what Alice just said. I especially agree, that in my own mind, it didn't seem like that big a deal all this time. But I also asked myself, did I *not* talk about it with my daughter because it had to do with abortion? I really don't know the answer to that, but it is a question. I have to say that, not so much the Women's Health Collective, but the experience of being a part of a women's consciousness-raising group in the early years of the women's movement, *that* was formative for me. I can't imagine my life without it. This time in history was a wonderful time to be alive as a woman. And so much of it had to do with the feelings that we created for each other and with each other.

SHERRI: I agree. I always tell my kids that they really missed out not being alive in the late 60s–early 70s. That was just a wonderful time to be around. I think that what was wonderful about it—and what I feel bad that my kids are missing—is being part of a working group where there was that trust involved and feeling like you were working together for an important reason. I think maybe it is just in retrospect that I realize that it was important. At the time it was sort of like, "Let's just do this until it becomes legal. We have to pick up the ball, and then once it's legal, it'll be okay." So I saw it just as sort of filling a gap at the time. But, thinking about it now, the fact that we did it, and that we did such a good job! It amazes me. When people are talking about the things that we did, I'm thinking, "*Wow, we really were pretty much on the ball, there, weren't we?*" Because so many times you look back on things and you say, "*Oh, I would have done this differently, I would have done that differently.*" I think because it was a group effort and everybody contributed that we didn't make a whole lot of mistakes. We simply had enough people contributing their ideas so that we could watch out for each other. And, really, I think we did do a pretty good job.

BETTY: Well, I'd like to say that I disagree about the times [being great]. I remember when I tried to get a charge card, and I couldn't get it without a man's name on it. And I couldn't borrow money. It was so archaic! But I feel like I have a really deep kinship with women and that came out of that period. And I have some empathy for women's lives. Even now, the whole reproductive part of it still is very problematic for women, in spite of technology.

ALICE: There's a legal procedure in the courts of Massachusetts where you counsel young women. There is actually a formal training that you go through. But I had already been trained in women's health counseling. I can remember that for the first women that I represented in the court system, just being able to recite: "And this is what happens, this is the noise you'll hear, and this is what the alternatives are, and this is how you'll feel afterwards, and is anybody pressuring you?" It was this whole speech that I knew from the Springfield Women's Health Collective.

PART FIVE

The Connectors

Uniting Medical Care, Activism, and Feminism

Leslie Laurie and the Family Planning Council of Western Massachusetts

Other than the death of Nancy Kierzek from a botched abortion, perhaps the other defining moment of the birth control and abortion movement in the Pioneer Valley was the arrival of Leslie Tarr Laurie in August of 1970. A trained community organizer, Laurie met with members of the women's collectives, local doctors, Clergy Consultation Services (CCS), and other groups within weeks of moving to the Amherst area. Laurie had an M.A. in Community Organizing and Planning from Columbia University and had been Director of Education and Outreach for the Planned Parenthood of Southeastern Pennsylvania. She found it appalling that Western Massachusetts had no organized family planning services and set about to solve this. She spent several years as the Western Massachusetts representative for the Boston-based Planned Parenthood League of Massachusetts, developing programs and independent, government-subsidized family planning clinics in the four counties of Western Massachusetts. In 1973, these clinics were linked and incorporated as a new organization, the Family Planning Council of Western Massachusetts (FPCWM) and Laurie was hired as Executive Director. Renamed Tapestry Health Systems, the organization thrives today with Laurie still at the helm.

Laurie's activist nature had been honed during her graduate work at Columbia, an institution whose School of Social Work was well known for putting theory into practice on the streets. Projects rooted at the school in the 1960s helped shape the national War on Poverty's strategy of community-based reform. Leslie and her colleagues at Columbia were immersed in unraveling the government's new initiatives for Medicare, Voting Rights, and the Higher Education Action. Laurie's approach to organizing was further influenced by the Planned Parenthood system, with its emphasis on educational outreach in combination with community clinics. Though she clearly identified as a feminist and believed that reproductive freedom was an essential goal in the women's rights struggle, she believed in a medical approach to fertility care.

While at Planned Parenthood in Pennsylvania, Laurie had worked closely with the Clergy Consultation chapter in the area. It was natural, therefore, that she seek out the Western Massachusetts CCS chapters when she arrived. Elaine Fraser, then doing CCS counseling at the United Christian Foundation (UCF) offices at the University of Massachusetts (UMass), remembers that Leslie came to talk with her less than a week after she got to town. Laurie also made contact with those working at the University Health Services and with the abortion counseling group from the Amherst Women's Liberation group. While she was impressed with what each of the groups was doing individually, she could see that they were each limited in their scope—CCS appeared to alienate some who were not religious, the University Health Services only served students, and the Abortion and Birth Control (ABC) group tended to focus only on the Amherst and Northampton area. She also understood that each of these groups worked in relative isolation from one another and perceived major differences in their approaches to the issues. Coming in from the outside gave Leslie Laurie a perspective informed by her work and academic training while not entangling her in local cliques or attitudes. It also gave her a larger regional focus, as she looked to fill gaps in service in four Western Massachusetts counties, three of which had no services at all when she arrived.

While the Amherst ABC group, for example, might in some ways have been reacting to "those men in the clergy," and saw their counseling as a feminist political act, Leslie sought reform rather than revolution. She was willing to work within government and medical structures, adopting and adapting their strategies and networks for her own work while building strategic alliances. Equally skillful in gaining the support of these establishments as well as the support of the women's groups and clergy, she was able to navigate and even negotiate alliances between them. She exercised what one researcher has termed "pragmatic radicalism."[1] Moreover, Laurie saw pregnancy counseling as only one piece of a much larger picture of comprehensive family planning; the best way to address the overall family planning needs of the community, she believed, was through the development of reproductive health clinics, especially for poor women.

Laurie was aided in her efforts by new Federal Legislation and Funding. As part of the War on Poverty, new and revised government programs, including Medicaid, funded health exams and birth control for poor women in both rural and urban areas. President Richard Nixon's Title X Public Health Act, signed into law in 1970, mandated that "no American woman be denied access to family planning assistance because of her economic condition." Title X provided funding for health clinics established according to its set rules for "comprehensive family planning," which included providing complete physical exams, family planning counseling, birth control provision, and outreach and educational programs.[2] The Planned Parenthood League of Massachusetts (PPLM) used some of its Title X funds to implement reproductive rights education and find partners to start clinical delivery services in Western Massachusetts. PPLM wanted to stay out of the clinic creation business and hoped to use Title X funds to support clinics within existing agencies. Laurie's job was to connect with these agencies and try to build clinic programs within them.

Since she worked far from Boston and spent most of her time on the road working with local communities, Laurie was largely free from the constraints of an established bureaucracy and was "able to be much more responsive to what was happening locally. It became a community-based effort." Being far from the watchful eye of PPLM headquarters and state government perhaps allowed Laurie and the clinics, once they were established, to take some risks they might not have taken had they been closer to Boston. These risks included giving abortion referrals—the names of providers in legal areas like New York most likely came from Laurie's CCS contacts—while doing so was still illegal under the Comstock laws in Massachusetts.

She began organizing in Berkshire County in 1972 and over the next two years helped establish clinics there and in Hampden and Franklin Counties. In each case, she located a local host organization and created a community advisory group. In this way, the clinics were community projects and not purely the result of an outside organization, Planned Parenthood, or the influence of an outside organizer, Laurie. In August of 1972, she was working on a grant to fund a clinic in her home county, Hampshire, when President Nixon vetoed a bill that would have increased funding for programs, including Title X programs, in the Department of Health, Education, and Welfare. This veto meant that there would be no new grants funded in the area, and thus no money for separate clinics in Hampshire County.

Laurie, with funding and consulting aid from the Massachusetts Department of Public Health, conceived of a way to expand services into Hampshire County and beyond even while operating under the new funding restraints. She convinced her partner organizations, each of them operating under a separate grant, to turn the grants over to a new, combined, regionalized organization to be called the Family Planning Council of Western Massachusetts. By creating one central location for administrative functions such as billing and scheduling with the clinics operating then as satellite service providers, there would be more money with which to create and offer additional clinics and services. The partner organizations relinquished their individual Title X grants, a new Title X grant was given to the new regional organization, and FPCWM launched on September 1, 1974.

The organizational headquarters, as well as a new clinic, were opened at 16 Center Street in Northampton, finally bringing services to Hampshire County. Leslie Laurie was hired as the Executive Director, and Merry Boone, who had been in charge of the Franklin County-based family planning clinic at Wesson Women's Hospital, became the Vice President. Ellen Story was soon hired in a clerical role, and within a year had risen to be the Coordinator for Hampshire County services. Ellen Story worked with the Council for 17 years before running successfully for the Massachusetts House of Representatives in 1992. She has held that position ever since and serves the Third Hampshire District, which includes Amherst and Granby in Hampshire County.

In 1998, the Family Planning Council of Western Massachusetts became Tapestry Health with ten locations throughout the Pioneer Valley. Tapestry Health continues to provide family planning and community health services such as gynecological care, birth control, emergency contraception, screening for sexually transmitted diseases, and pregnancy testing and options counseling. Tapestry also provides a range of other services: HIV/AIDS testing, counseling and education/ prevention outreach programs (including one of four needle exchange programs in Massachusetts), sexuality education outreach programs on contraception, puberty, and AIDS, and a Special Supplemental Nutrition Program for Women, Infants, and Children (WIC) offering food and nutrition services for low-income women and their families.

Tapestry Health also works to advocate for health policies at the state and national levels, many times in the person of Leslie Laurie who has continued as Executive Director. In addition to this lobbying work, she has played several high profile roles in the reproductive health care movement and profession, including serving two consecutive terms as President of the National Family Planning and Reproductive Health Association, and serving on the Executive Committee and Board of the Alan Guttmacher Institute.

Counselors' Cooperatives

While Leslie Laurie was employed by Planned Parenthood and was organizing for provision of reproductive health services in Western Massachusetts, she was also, on her own time, organizing those people who had already been active in the area around provision of abortion referrals. Laurie's new clinics included or would eventually include options counseling in their work, but rather than compete with the clergy and feminist volunteers who had already been making referrals, Leslie tried to unite them. While individual groups like the Springfield Women's Health Collective and the Amherst Women's Liberation's ABC Group and the two Clergy Consultation chapters all individually improved women's access, they did not work together in a focused way until Leslie Laurie organized the Western Massachusetts Counselors' Cooperative in 1971.

The groups Leslie helped to unite had each individually been working both effectively and illegally to secure access to problem pregnancy options. The reproductive rights activities of both the Springfield and Amherst women's collectives were deeply rooted in their commitment to redefining American women's access to information. The women of these organizations fit the pattern recognized by historian Ruth Rosen: "Most of the original health advocates were college educated, middle-class and white: women's liberation activists, nurses, a few male doctors and research scientists, all of whom saw their greatest problem as lack of information rather than access to medical care, which was the barrier faced by poor women."[3] The founders of these groups, although generally of a different social class than those they sought to serve, made access to information by poor and minority women a key goal. Leslie Laurie and the Family Planning Council would extend this goal to access to actual local services for poor women. This is not to say that local groups limited their services just to providing education and contact information. The Amherst group established the Lucy Fund to help those who could not pay for abortions and the Springfield members often contributed out of their own pockets. On the UMass campus, students helped establish the Medical Emergency Loan Fund, a thinly veiled abortion loan project. But it took the arrival in the area of an experienced community organizer and reproductive health educator, Leslie Laurie, to create a structure that would allow the various groups to combine their collective strength to the advantage of poor women.

The problem pregnancy groups at the Valley Women's Center and Springfield Women's Health Counseling both joined Laurie's Western Massachusetts Counselors' Cooperative. Both local chapters of the CCS were also very involved in the Cooperative and Ruth Fessenden, from the UCF chapter, served as co-convener of the group.[4] (Returning the favor, Laurie served as co-chair of UCF's CCS Task Force during 1972.) During this period, Laurie was helping to open family planning clinics throughout the region, and the Counselor's Cooperative statistics provide a good record of this growth.[5] In April 1973, eight groups are listed as part of the Cooperative; by November twelve groups belonged, including the new clinics Leslie had helped to establish.[6] All the groups in the Cooperative shared resources such as the names and information on abortion providers who had been thoroughly checked out and approved.

The Western Massachusetts Counselor's Cooperative changed its name to the Western New England Counselor's Cooperative (WNECC) in 1973, reflecting Laurie's effectiveness in uniting counselors throughout the region. While the Cooperative functioned initially as simply a way for counselors to be in touch with each other and share information, it soon evolved into a pressure group by which the various groups could push the New York clinics to discount their services or provide free abortions for indigent women. The groups sent women to local hospitals for therapeutic abortions and to clinics in New York State for legal abortions. After *Roe v. Wade* went into effect, the Cooperative began referring primarily to two clinics in Springfield and Amherst. The WNECC negotiated deals with the abortion providers, such as for every five patient referred, the sixth would receive their abortion free of charge.

In this way, "credit" was built up with the providers that would allow the clinics to refer indigent women to receive free abortions.

The Cooperative also played an essential role in convincing local abortion providers to include the feminist practice of involving female counselors as part of their service. This direct influence of the women's movement upon the health care system survives to this day in many clinics that provide abortion procedures.[7]

Through their work with both the FPCWM and the counselors' cooperatives, Leslie Laurie and her staff and allies united those who had been working toward reproductive health access during the illegal years and moved them toward sustained access and practice post-Roe. In the story of Pioneer Valley reproductive-health work, she and her allies are truly "the Connectors."

TWENTY-ONE

Merry Boone

Meredith "Merry" Boone was born Meredith Gage in Boston, Massachusetts and grew up in West Hartford, Connecticut. She earned a BA in Economics at Goucher College in Towson, MD, and then settled in Springfield, MA in 1968. She worked in City Planning and Health Planning before becoming the Director of the family planning program serving Hampden County, MA in 1972. Merry Boone helped to found the Family Planning Council of Western Massachusetts in 1973, and held management and administrative positions there over the next two decades. Boone left women's health to seek an M.Ed. in Elementary Education in 1995 and has taught first grade in Springfield, Massachusetts public schools since 1997. She is committed to city living, neighborhood building, and community activism. She and her husband Jim are the parents of two sons. Merry enjoys Victorian house restoration and gardening.

Merry Boone was interviewed by David Cline on February 12, 2004.

My name is Merry Boone. I was born Meredith Gage and grew up in the suburbs of Hartford, Connecticut. My dad worked for the insurance industry. I don't fit into my family politically. I stepped out and even today, with my remaining sister and my 87-year-old mother, we try hard not to have those political conversations. So I can't attribute my values to the politics that I grew up with.

I was a middle child of three girls, and I don't think I had ever thought of myself as a leader [until] high school. I really arrived in high school. I went to a private girls' high school, which for me was really a life-changing experience because it allowed me to kind of discover myself. It was also a tumultuous time—Kennedy was shot during my senior year, when I was president of the Student Council.

Probably the life changer for me, though, was a summer religious series at Northfield-Mount Hermon School in Massachusetts with William Sloane Coffin.[1] I went a couple of summers, and it was just completely eye-opening. It had a religious context, but it was all about progressive politics. I remember sitting around in a beautiful setting with nothing else going on other than picking other people's brains about important matters. The combination of those two things made me start thinking about women as people too, and that continued in college. Then I went to a women's college, Goucher in Baltimore, Maryland, and majored in Economics. I was politically active in the sense that I did things in Washington and worked for Spiro Agnew, who was the better of the two candidates at the time.[2] I went door-to-door canvassing. Then Martin Luther King and Bobby Kennedy were shot my senior year in college and there were the riots after King's assassination. So there was a lot going on around me then that drew me in. But I think it was high school that really started to make me look at the world in a different way, and at myself as a human being with potential. And then that probably led me to women's issues.

Making a Difference: From City Planning to Health Planning to Family Planning

I finished college in June of 1968 and got married that December. I settled in Springfield, where my husband was going to school. My job at that time was in city planning in the suburbs of Hartford. Something I've said to people throughout my life is that whatever I do with my time has to be important work. And I always chose carefully.

Then my husband was drafted, in the middle of the Vietnam War—very efficient draft board out of Maryland—and he went off to Basic Training. I moved back in with my family in the Hartford area and continued in city planning. Jim ended up in Fort Benning, Georgia, and it looked like he was going to be there long enough for me to join him. So I traveled to Georgia, rented an apartment and got a city planning job down there. Then he finished his military duty in Korea—which was lucky in the middle of Vietnam. When he returned in 1971, we once again settled in Springfield where he pursued graduate school and I shifted to the Model Cities Program in Springfield as a Health Planner. It was in that capacity that I started to develop a relationship to family planning. I wrote a Title X grant application and was successful in securing funding to begin the delivery of women's health clinical services at what was then Wesson Women's Hospital.[3] And once the grant was awarded, I turned around and applied for the job to direct the program and was hired on. That was lucky for me. So I left the Model Cities job and became a department head, because there really wasn't any other place to put me, at Wesson Women's.

We began delivering contraceptive clinic services in Springfield, not only out of the Wesson Women's outpatient department, but also at Brightwood Riverview Center in the North End, serving a predominantly Latino population. We also began to look at suburban services in Palmer and Westfield. The hospital generally supported whatever I was trying to do, as long as I could accomplish it and it wasn't going to ask a lot of them. There didn't seem to be a lot of controversy at the time with initiating services.

Forming the Family Planning Council of Western Massachusetts

Leslie Laurie came and found me soon after. She was a Planned Parenthood organizer and she was looking for a way to get services initiated in Hampshire County. She was told that no new Title X grants were going to be issued by the U.S. Department of Health Education and Welfare (HEW), and that the best way for her to get services into Hampshire County would be to talk me or my hospital or some other organization that was already receiving money into expanding into another county. And so Leslie was shopping around and she came and introduced herself to me and we got to know each other. She also looked at Berkshire County and Franklin County, because they already had services.

Leslie pulled all of us together. This was a group of very young women and we kind of worked outside of the machinery of the hospitals. We started to meet and think about how we could organize services throughout the region.

There were five of us who were the players at that time: Barbara Blakeney, a nurse; Sybil Howe, a social worker; Carol Dalrymple, who was an administrator at Holyoke Hospital, myself, and Leslie. It seems to me we got some help from HEW. We worked with some consulting groups out of New York because it wasn't always smooth sailing and we weren't always in total agreement. We'd get together for a weekend retreat and try to put together an overarching program and a grant proposal. We then went back to our various employers and came up with a proposal that they could support. We went to HEW and ultimately dissolved the programs at our various organizations and created what became the Family Planning Council of Western Massachusetts [FPCWM] [now Tapestry Health Care Systems]. That started in

September of 1973. So, I was really only an employee within the Wesson Women's Center for a little bit more than a year before this changeover occurred.

That was a pretty exciting time for us. We were amazingly successful at talking our grantees, our employers, into literally giving up the grants. I think the reason that it was appealing to them was that they weren't heavily invested in the services; this was just another outpatient clinic as far as Wesson was concerned. They weren't territorial about it at all as long as we could promise that services would continue to be delivered. And they were aware of the fact that the reporting requirements were starting to increase. There were four organizations: the Holyoke Hospital, the [Office of Equal Opportunity] OEO-funded agency, the Berkshire County social service agency, and Wesson Women's Hospital. Everybody but Holyoke Hospital ultimately turned their grants over to us.

All of us who decided to go after jobs within the new nonprofit found employment there. I was the Assistant Executive Director, the number two deputy to Leslie. And Barbara was the middle manager, overseeing the services in Franklin County. And as I recall, Sybil retired at that point and didn't follow us into the new organization. We hired Ellen Story at that time in a secretarial job. Ellen ultimately shifted from a secretarial and administrative role to a middle management role overseeing the services of Hampshire County as the County Coordinator.[4]

There was a central administrative staff and then the service delivery staff. Many of the service delivery people were already in place and they simply changed employers and started to draw paychecks from us. They were the same people, the same secretaries and nurses who were already staffing the clinics. Counselors and nurse practitioners stayed on, at least in Springfield. And we were able to extend services to Hampshire County, which had been an unserved hole in the middle of the region. In Hampden County, we initially stayed at Wesson Women's and continued to use their outpatient department, but ultimately we created a Hampden County office that was an administrative office, which was not housed in the hospital. We also started to develop new locations throughout the Western Massachusetts region to make birth control services more available.

It was hard to keep doctors. In Springfield, Bay State [formerly Wesson Women's] is a teaching hospital so we were pretty successful in tapping OB-GYN residents who needed the money and were young, supportive, and sympathetic. But we couldn't hold onto them for very long. Sam Topal was someone who came and stayed for a long time, not so much in direct service but certainly in supporting the organization and in supporting Leslie's goals and objectives and what she wanted to get accomplished.

As soon as I met Leslie I thought that she was going to be successful. I felt right from the beginning that she would be able to do this, but I also felt that she understood that she wasn't going to be able to do this alone. She was a great community organizer in that respect. She's very tenacious, very politically savvy. She knew how to work the crowd in a lot of different venues and could appreciate what point of argument would appeal to what particular group. I also think she was very good at "using," in the best positive sense of the word, the people around her. She was able to tap the talents of people and win them over in a way that was pretty selfless and very focused, very sharply focused. She never lost sight of the prize. She knew what she wanted and she knew that she needed us to get her there. She never came across to me as aggressive, but rather as tenacious, persistent, very clear-headed, knew what she wanted to accomplish. So, I didn't think of her as a bulldog. She was also more far-sighted than the rest of us and able to see how we could get things to happen. And we were young! I was 25 years old when I met her. Within a year-and-a-half we were running a big organization by ourselves, not beholden to any hospital bureaucracy. And that was fabulous.

I don't think it was purposeful that the administrative staff was all women at the beginning; I think it happened to be that the players, the people in the leadership positions in family planning, were women. I never had it in my head that we needed to be an exclusively female group, we just happened to be. I didn't think of the group as part of a formal women's movement—we had something we wanted to accomplish and we knew it would benefit women. I really came at it from city planning, health planning, and then hooked into family planning. And I believed in it! I chose the work of family planning because it was so empowering for people. I was never in direct service, so I never had the unbelievably powerful experience of changing someone's personal life by giving them access to choice or giving them access to birth control, but even one step removed I could appreciate just how important it was.

Doing the Work of Family Planning: Outreach and Involvement

As far as my personal involvement, my home, my employment, and my social community was here in Springfield. It really wasn't until I was working in the Family Planning Council in Northampton that I began to meet and get to know and have both social and work relationships with a lot of women who were involved in the women's movement in the Valley. But, because I didn't live in Northampton and would drive home to Springfield at night, there were fewer opportunities. I could have sought them out, but there wouldn't have been those natural opportunities to go to a meeting together. I was less aware of women's groups, if they existed, here in Springfield in the early Seventies.

We certainly had an agenda—I did and then the Council—of reaching people who were underserved. It seemed almost a very secondary issue whether they were people of color or whether they were lesbians. That seemed pretty natural to me. I guess that's because I came at it through Model Cities, and that was a Community Action Program (CAP) agency, which was funded specifically to target neighborhoods of the city that were poor and underserved. So that had been my frame of reference and my orientation [from my days at Wesson]. Going immediately to Brightwood Health Center simply said these are populations that aren't getting care through the private sector, so we need to serve these women and their families. I guess it was kind of color blind. But we certainly were committed to making sure the board and staff reflected the makeup of the population we were tying to serve. That was not so common in those days, but it didn't seem very revolutionary. It just seemed pretty obvious. I don't think of it as something where we sat and had a conversation or had a series of goals and one of them was let's make sure we get to this particular group.

At that time [early 1973], birth control was fully legal but it was still controversial, and very controversial for minor women. The reasons that it seemed relatively easy for us to get so-called controversial services funded, why Wesson was willing to be the original grantee when I was the health planner and writing the grant, was (a) it was legal, and (b) Planned Parenthood wasn't around. Planned Parenthood hadn't set up clinics here as it had in other parts of the country because it had been illegal here [for so long].[5] The only clinic that really existed was at Wesson Women's Hospital and they didn't call it a birth control clinic, they called it a maternal health clinic. It was just one more piece of the puzzle. And the hospitals were pretty slow to come to realize what they needed in the way of providing people who spoke other languages. And there was not very much sensitivity in terms of bedding people together who were in the hospital for different kinds of reasons—women coming in with miscarriages or ectopic pregnancies were placed in rooms with others. It was mostly a male-dominated world. I think that was part of it—they didn't have a lot of women in administrative or oversight roles. During my one short year at Wesson, I think I was the only woman department head, and certainly the youngest. The men didn't know exactly how to treat me. When we would have staff meetings, they would ask me to fix the coffee. So it was a world that wasn't very sensitive to how much courage it would take for a young woman to go to a place that she had never been before and admit that she was sexually active, that she was worried about getting pregnant, and that she wanted some help.

Certainly birth control services for minors were more controversial and there was more resistance to that from within the hospital setting in the days that it was the grantee. Wesson wasn't a place where a teenager would be caught going—your mother's friend might see you there because she was there for a postpartum visit. But it wasn't heavily publicized. We didn't do a lot of bus advertising in the days the hospital was the grantee. The things that tended to be more controversial were the educational aspects because those did take the message out into the community—whether it was in a school setting or a church setting or with a youth group. Those were the hotter areas, and it was much harder to find places that wanted us to come [out and speak]. Public schools wanted to know what the message would be all about and what kinds of consents would be required. I think Family Planning Council made much more of a goal of reaching sexually-active minors. That was a more articulated area of emphasis and was potentially more controversial too.

There really wasn't any straight-ahead sex education in the public schools and there still isn't in a lot of it. It might have been offered as part of a health education curriculum, but it was really danced around. But Tapestry is doing a lot of health education with educators in different settings. And health education has broadened to include AIDS and a lot of other gay action and gay activism kinds of things that were just unheard of back in the Seventies.

Meeting the Controversies Head On

When *Roe v. Wade* came down, I was still employed at Wesson Women's. And it's intriguing that it doesn't stand out as one of those "I-remember-exactly-where-I-was-when" moments, like JFK being shot. I don't have an image in my mind of driving in the car and turning on the radio and discovering that that had just come about even though I was working in out in the field at the time—although not directly with terminations, but certainly with women who might be in need of terminations.

Abortion is not something that anyone feels neutral about. It is something that you have powerful feelings about one way or the other. You're marching or acting or working on behalf of access, or you're marching or writing letters to the editor or raising money or going to dinners with Citizens for Life.[6] It continues to be an extraordinarily powerful public debate. And once again I think it should come down to free choice, without the interference of religion.

I don't think we [at FPCWM] actively talked among ourselves about becoming an abortion provider, certainly not in the Council's first ten years of organized life. We did various kinds of advocacy and support, but we didn't consider becoming an abortion provider ourselves because there were clinics in the western part of the state, certainly for women of the age of majority. It was more making sure that women who needed to have terminations had access to the services, and making sure that we could be the linkage to available services for many of our clients. In those days, age was an issue so we had to help them get out of state. For the women below 18 years old we found ways through other organizations by coordinating with them, making referrals to them, or by making sure transportation or support was available. I think that Clergy Consultation was the lead organization. It was kind of like the Underground Railroad. And they weren't huge, they were just effective.

But there were times before I left the Council in the mid-1980s when we did more actively consider whether or not it made sense to begin to provide abortion services in competition with other providers. We thought we could do it better, more sensitively and [make it] more geographically accessible. But [we also considered] what would we lose in terms of becoming a focal point for hostile action. Would we put ourselves personally at risk? There were those kinds of discussions in the Nineties.

Reflections

It was an amazing time; when I look back on it and think about how young we were and how suddenly powerful we were, relatively speaking, with our own kingdom.

And how important the work was. And all of that stuff coalescing at the same time, from the age of 25 to 40. I left FPCWM in 1986 when I thought I'd done everything I could have done and I didn't feel fresh anymore. Also that's when children came into my life. And so there was this natural segue to say, okay, I'm going to take some time now with family stuff. When I went back in 1990, I oversaw the writing of medical policy protocols and educational materials. It was intellectually stimulating and kept me current. But that four or five year stint when I was away was a time when the organization changed quite a bit and moved more heavily into breast health, lesbian health, AIDS, and street work. And I went back in a different role. I think I was less invested and I also now had family obligations. I knew that I just needed to be doing something different, and fell into teaching. I went back to school, got my Master's degree and became a teacher. Also important work, but just in another area.

I still feel a lot of ownership, a lot of pride in the Council. A lot of me was there and is still there. I feel that there's a piece of me that's still there and left as a gift. It's a nice legacy.

I got a postcard in the mail for the March for Women's Lives in 2004 and I said to my husband, "You know, I'm going to that." And I haven't marched in a long time. I think at some level there's something kicking in. It kind of moves up a gear, to say, there's too much of this going around and I was too complacent in assuming that the right guys and women were going to prevail. We're seeing erosion in so many areas of public policy, but certainly in women's issues. And the erosion is starting to move into a mudslide. It makes you feel like you've got to stick your foot in the ground—to keep the analogy going—and start to become active again, when you haven't felt in a long time that you really needed to do that.

TWENTY-TWO

Ellen Story

Ellen Story was raised in Texas. She has a B.A. from the University of Texas and a Master's degree from Cambridge College. She moved to Massachusetts in 1970 and in 1972 moved to Amherst. Where her husband Ron Story is Professor of History at the University of Massachusetts-Amherst. She worked with the Family Planning Council of Western Massachusetts, later Tapestry Health, from 1973 to 1990, when she ran for the Massachusetts State House. She still serves as State Representative for the Third Hampshire District, and is known as an effective crusader for women's issues, public education, labor, the environment, and human service programs. She was recognized as 2001 Legislator of the Year by both the Women's Bar Association and the Parent/Professional Advocacy League, and as Legislator of the Year in 2002 by both the National Alliance for the Mentally Ill and Girls Incorporated.

Ellen Story was interviewed by David Cline on January 23, 2004.

The Family Planning Council of Western Massachusetts

I moved to Amherst with a husband and two little boys in August of 1972. My husband's first job was teaching in the History Department at the University of Massachusetts in Amherst [UMass] and he has taught there since. The first year that we were here I stayed home with the two little boys. But one year was enough! The second year Leslie Laurie, the wife of another history professor, Bruce Laurie, was starting up the Family Planning Council of Western Massachusetts. I decided that I wanted to go to work part-time and at the last minute I applied for a job and I started with the agency on September 4, 1973.

The Family Planning Council covered the four counties of Western Massachusetts and there were four county sections. Each county had a County Coordinator and my first position for the first year was as assistant to the Hampshire County Coordinator. And then the second year I became the Hampshire County Coordinator. I worked, I think, 32 hours in the beginning at Family Planning and I also had these two little boys. The Family Planning Council was my women's group! Women's rights was *the* issue when I moved here. My main issue growing up had been civil rights. I lived in Texas from the time I was nine until I graduated from the University of Texas. The university was integrated, but not the dorms, not the restaurants, movies, etcetera. So I spent much of my four years there picketing and sitting in and standing in. And reproductive rights seemed to me like a logical extension of my interest in civil rights. It had to do with being fair, so that people who didn't have any money would have the same kind of medical care that people who were wealthy had. [It had to do with] preventing discrimination either on the basis of age or on the basis of income. So it seemed to fit the categories that I had for doing something: that it was socially progressive and that I considered it to be worthwhile.

It was quite an exciting time. A lot of radical, interesting people were drawn to this agency. And this topic attracted a very interesting group of the smartest, most committed people. One of the real plusses of working there was the colleagues that you got to know. In some ways it's the same way that there were wonderful people attracted to the civil rights movement. It's a social issue that has the potential to change things. So it's worth your time and energy and it is a vital critical issue. And if you spend time on it, you might make a difference. It's worth doing.

People were nervous about us, even in the traditional social service establishment, because this was an agency run by women, young women. I was 30 then, Leslie was about 24. There were a few men, but all the management were women and by far the greatest number of staff were women. We were talking about two issues that are the most sensitive to talk about—we were talking about sex and we were talking about money. Because we had a sliding fee scale we had to ask people how much money they made and the fee would be based on how much money they had. And then we would talk about birth control, did they need a pregnancy test, or whatever the issue was.

The Family Planning Council never did abortions and never has done abortions. There were a few people who were able to make that distinction—that if you are against abortion, then you ought to be in favor of family planning. That's the way that you prevent unwanted pregnancies in the first place. Silvio Conte, the Republican Congressman from Massachusetts' first Congressional district from 1959 to 1991, was extremely anti-choice, but he also was a national leader in terms of funding for family planning. He stood out because he was one of the few to make that connection. But both subjects are equally taboo for some parts of society here. People in other parts of the country think of Massachusetts as very liberal and it is on some issues, but not on anything that has to do with sex. In August of 1966, Massachusetts became the last state in the country to legalize contraception for married people. And until 1972 it was illegal to teach "the techniques of conception control." So if someone was teaching birth control in a school, in a class, they could be fired. I think anything that has to do with reproduction has been very, very suspect, both because of the Puritan background here and the very strong Roman Catholic presence. You do not use artificial methods of birth control if you are a practicing Catholic. Although, of course, that's never been true. Many Catholics do use birth control and some do have abortions but the official line is that artificial methods of birth control are out of the question. And of course abortion is out of the question. So for some people the two are slightly different, but they both are equally frowned upon.

We did do pregnancy tests at Family Planning Council. If a pregnancy test was positive, you explained to the woman what her choices were. And her choices were not very many. One was to continue the pregnancy and to keep the baby, to get married if that's an option, or put the baby up for adoption. The other was to terminate the pregnancy. And that's it! Basically, those are the choices, and it was the feeling of the Family Planning Council that of course you had to explain all of those options. If the person chose abortion, then we would tell her where her choices were in Western Massachusetts, where she could go to terminate the pregnancy, and give her the phone number.

I was doing some of the counseling myself. The sessions were quite easy going. We did not have fancy office space, but people felt at home as soon as they came in. We had a door that shut so there was some privacy. You would either explain methods of birth control if someone was interested in birth control or if somebody came for a pregnancy test you would talk to her. Every once in a while it would be couples, but it was mostly the woman by herself. People were tremendously relieved to have a place that they could go, where there were people who looked like them and did not have on white coats and stethoscopes, and where it was confidential and where they could afford it. You paid if you had enough money to pay, and if you didn't have money you didn't pay anything. It was just tremendously appreciated by the people who came.

I stayed for 17 years, from 1973 to 1991. I was the Associate Executive Director for the last few years. I stayed until I ran for public office. Part of running for state office was to be able to deal with some things that were not about reproductive rights, because that's what I'd been doing for seventeen years. So it was nice to think about funding for the university or some other things. But this issue is part of my bones. It has kept being very, very important to me and it's still a live issue, in this state and in most states. Some states are even worse off than we are. I have an acquaintance who is a state representative in Missouri—every single bill that they have has some sort of antiabortion rider tacked onto it. It's just a much more constant struggle than we have in Massachusetts.

Taking the Issues to the State Government

As a State Representative, I've been the chief sponsor of a number of bills that have to do with reproductive health. For example, having health insurance pay for contraception for women. What finally got that off the ground, since we'd been filing that bill for years, was that it became public that insurance companies were paying for Viagra but not paying for birth control pills. So that finally got passed a few years ago. And I was a chief sponsor of the "Buffer Zone Bill," trying to have a space outside of abortion clinics so that women going in for abortions were not manhandled by zealots, who were thrusting pictures of aborted fetuses in their face. That was a huge struggle but that bill finally passed as well.[1] The Speaker of the House, Thomas Finneran, is extremely anti-choice and very much against this bill, as was the Catholic Church, although not all Catholics [were against it]. There were a number of Catholics, or at least one or two, who signed onto this bill and who said, "These are the crazies who give us a bad name. We don't want this to be happening outside of abortion clinics."

The way the Speaker keeps things from happening is the [bills] never come out of committee. It finally passed because we were able to get more than 81 legislators (a majority in the House) to sign a letter to the Speaker of the House asking him to bring this bill to the floor for debate and for a vote. When he realized we had a majority, the bill finally did come to the floor. We also attached it to the budget! At the last minute the Speaker prevailed on the other chief sponsor to take it out of the budget and promised we would have a vote on it. I would not have taken it out because I would not have believed his promise. But it eventually did come to a vote because we got this letter with all these signatures and it passed by a large majority. That was a major victory. But we actually vote on issues of abortion very, very rarely.

As of 2004, the Massachusetts Legislature was 75 percent Catholic. There are 200 legislators and it's 75 percent Catholic in both branches. A couple of years ago the Senate, with 40 people, was 85 percent Catholic. That doesn't mean that they're a voting bloc, because they don't agree on anything. And some of the strongest pro-choice legislators are women whose entire education has been in parochial schools, who graduated from Regis College, a Catholic college, and who go to mass at least once a week. And they are absolutely out front about being pro-choice. Some choose to go to mass outside of their district, because if they went to mass in their own districts, they would be criticized from the pulpit. That happens to people. Their name and phone number will be given out in church for people to call and try to "straighten out" and make sure that they vote the "right way." The two issues that the Church takes the strongest stand on are the death penalty and abortion, and they are strongly against both. And the Catholic legislators do not follow the Church's line on either of those issues. There are many who are strongly in favor of the death penalty, and a number who are strongly pro-choice.

Many other churches are very, very committed to reproductive freedom. I have no doubt that if there were some imminent threat, people from the religious community could be mobilized overnight to be very, very public about this. There just hasn't been the need for that the way there was 30 years ago.

Remaining Vigilant

It was always clear to me that we had to be extremely vigilant. Some people thought that after the Roe decision, we could relax now that we've got we wanted. I thought, thank goodness that this decision has happened. But it became clear pretty quickly that this was not something that we could take for granted. When I worked at Family Planning I did a lot of education in high school and college classes and I would talk to very bright young women students at Smith or at Hampshire College, or at the university who had no idea at all how recent abortion had become legal and how much in jeopardy it was. And that some schools would not allow sex education classes. That's still a very, very controversial subject. There are some schools that feel very strongly that this is for parents to talk to their kids about and not for the school to have any role in.

I think the majority of people feel very, very strongly that abortion needs to be a legal right. And that includes people of all religions. I personally don't think that Roe will ever be overturned. But that's not something that I say publicly because I think people need to pay attention to this. And in fact they do.

You have to keep people involved. You shine the spotlight on this when you can. Every year you have some sort of celebration. You make sure that people are conscious of who's potentially being appointed to the Supreme Court. You have bills like the Buffer Zone bill. You make sure this is in the press so people don't relax and think they can dust off their hands and say, well, we won that one, we can move on.

We have Martin Luther King Day every year, thank goodness, so that young people can hear the stories of what it was like before abortion was a legal right. And that's what people need to hear about reproductive rights. That it is not something that you take for granted. That there is a very, very strong movement in the country to try to stop this; to try to overturn Roe, to try to make abortion, any kind of abortion, illegal. It doesn't matter if it's for the health of the mother—anything to make abortion illegal. And there are also people who think birth control should not be as easily available to unmarried people. It is a right that has not always been there and may not always be there, although I think that people are so used to it now that if they felt it were really threatened, they would mobilize really quickly. But it's just something that has to be in your consciousness that there are many, many people, well funded, absolutely zealous people who have this as their only issue. They don't care about any other issue. They are waiting to pounce and take this right away from men and women.

TWENTY-THREE

Leslie Tarr Laurie

Leslie Tarr Laurie grew up in Great Neck, New York and attended Buckley Country Day School. She received her B.A. from Chatham College and an M.S. from Columbia University. She was Director of Education and Outreach at Planned Parenthood of Southeastern Pennsylvania. She moved to the Pioneer Valley in 1970 and began working as the Western Massachusetts coordinator for the Planned Parenthood League of Massachusetts. She helped found the Family Planning Council of Western Massachusetts, now Tapestry Health, in 1973 and remains the President of Tapestry Health. She served two consecutive terms as President of the National Family Planning and Reproductive Health Association and is also a past president of the Massachusetts Family Planning Association. Leslie has testified many times before Congress in support of reproductive health measures and was one of five women in the United States Delegation to the First International Conference of First and Third World Women on Reproductive Health. She resides in Pelham, Massachusetts, with her husband Bruce Laurie, Professor of History at the University of Massachusetts Amherst. Their daughter Rebecca Laurie is a student at Sarah Lawrence College. Leslie continues to find inspiration from her family, including mother Elvira Tarr, Professor Emeritus at Brooklyn College, New York and her brother Lawrence Tarr, a lawyer who is Commissioner of the Workers' Compensation Commission for the Commonwealth of Virginia.

Leslie Tarr Laurie was interviewed by Kris Woll on February 20, March 28, and April 17, 2002.

As Much Social Reformer as Feminist

So much of who I am and what I believe comes from my mother. I hope that I can be as positive an influence on my daughter as my mother has been for me. I think that I always have thought of myself as a feminist. To me that is a very positive description of a woman. In my case it was genetic as my mother was a feminist. I am as much a social reformer as a feminist.

Family planning and abortion have always been key issues for me. I was in college in the late '60s and very involved in the anti-Vietnam War effort, but as a white woman I felt there were some causes that I could be especially effective working on to promote social justice. Reproductive freedom was that primary cause. When I was a sophomore in college—and this was pre-Roe—the most poignant thing was my roommate got pregnant. That was one of the defining events for me in coming to believe that abortion must be a protected right. She came from a very affluent family in the Northeast, and she didn't want anybody to know she was pregnant. We needed to figure out what to do and how to get her an abortion. It was really eye opening for me. We were able to find a local doctor in Pittsburgh who would see her, but after lots of intrigue it ended up that she did tell her parents and she was sent to Puerto Rico for the procedure. She got an abortion over a vacation, so nobody would know. She graduated from college, became a significant lawyer doing good work, and had a family. Her life went on undisturbed really despite her unwanted pregnancy. At that same time, I was tutoring in the Hill District of Pittsburgh, which was a poor area where a large African-American population resided. A young woman who I was tutoring got pregnant. And here was my roommate and this young black student, and it was so clear what was going to happen. There wasn't a choice for my student. The class difference between my student and my roommate afforded access to different choices that would fundamentally influence their entire lives. It seemed really significant for me that if a woman couldn't control her own fertility, she wasn't really free. Margaret Sanger said it and it really made a whole lot of sense to me.

Then, during the time I was in college, I was sent to Malawi in the eastern part of Africa during their celebrations of becoming an independent nation. While it was so exciting to witness a nation's independence, I also saw just how oppressed women were by the lack of control over fertility in an international setting. It was really inspiring to be in that place where a republic was being born, but yet it didn't feel that everybody was going to be equal. When I graduated from college I considered going to law school and doing [useful] work that way, but I decided that it really made much more sense to be a community organizer. I went to Columbia University. I wanted to start working in family planning, but Columbia wouldn't let me do it initially, so I worked with a community health center on the Upper West Side of Manhattan and basically got to see family planning in the context of health. The second year I was there they did let me do a concentrated placement in family planning, and I went to Philadelphia and was able to really get in the middle of the freedom struggle for abortion. We challenged the Pennsylvania law while I was there. So I think it just felt like I had found a real work match. It just felt right.

Before moving to Western Massachusetts in 1970, I worked for Planned Parenthood in Philadelphia. I directed the education and outreach department and wrote their first Title X federal grant that initiated family planning services in Chester, Pennsylvania. I also worked on the legal challenge to the Pennsylvania abortion law, and was very involved with the Clergy Consultation Service for Abortion [CCS] in Pennsylvania. So both issues, abortion and family planning, were of concern to me.

Planned Parenthood of Southeastern Pennsylvania was based in Philadelphia and was one of the largest Planned Parenthood affiliates in the United States. Planned Parenthood at that point was an organization led by the Philadelphia elite. They recognized in terms of their mission that they needed to reach out more than they were doing. We were able to organize a health clinic in Chester, Pennsylvania. Chester is very close to Philadelphia and yet was a place that was just enormously, enormously needy. That was when I really understood just how important access to voluntary family planning services is to the health of women and the community at large.

At the time, Planned Parenthood wouldn't allow people who were unmarried and younger than 21 to get family planning services without parental consent. It seemed ludicrous. I remember saying, "I can't even come here'." I was working for them but didn't meet their criteria to receive service. I was a little bit of an upstart, and after much internal work, the policy was changed. So it was almost fun to be able to help change these regressive internal rules at a Planned Parenthood. But the idea that you couldn't get services because of age or marital status was just appalling. People were forced to go to New York for birth control services. You could get your birth control pills but you just had to go over the state line to get them. If you didn't have money, you couldn't get the birth control. How'd you pay for your transportation out of state to get the birth control? How'd you know the doctor who'd be willing to do it, or how'd you have the money to pay for the service if you could get someone to give it to you? So the class differences were just really out there at every turn.

Organizing in Western Massachusetts

We moved up here because my husband, Bruce Laurie, got a teaching position at the University of Massachusetts in 1970. I was appalled to learn that there were no subsidized family planning services in Western Massachusttes. The Planned Parenthood League of Massachusetts, which was based in Newton Centre at the time, wanted to be a statewide organization. They hired me as the community organizer for Western Massachusetts. From a 100 miles away I became PPLM's community organizer/grant writer for Western Massachusetts.

I was just really appalled at the lack of any services for poor women here in Western Massachusetts as compared even to Philadelphia, especially as related to family planning. There were some very interesting and committed women who were involved [in reproductive rights work], especially in Amherst. For abortion, there was an active Clergy Consultation Service in the Valley, and because I had been involved in challenging the abortion law in Philadelphia and was very involved in the Clergy Consultation Service there, it was just natural for me to gravitate to that same community. But I was secular, always secular. What brought me to abortion was not anything related to faith-based concerns. While I was respectful of that endeavor and really felt it was wonderful to have the legitimacy of cover of the church, that wasn't what brought me to this cause—feminism not religion brought me to that issue. But since I had ties to Clergy Consultation and was very active in the women's movement, I really became a link between the clergy and some of the more activist women. Because I had come from the outside, it was easier for me—not having a troubled history with any members of either group.

It seemed to me that even though Planned Parenthood hired me as an organizer, they weren't committed to providing family planning services. It was almost like they hired me so they could say they were doing something in Western Massachusetts. Even though it was frustrating, Planned Parenthood's lack of commitment turned out to be a blessing in disguise by allowing the development of a locally based and controlled service. I also learned that there was new federal money available for Title X family planning services.

The first organizing and grant writing that I did in this area was in Berkshire County. In 1969 I helped found a community advisory group in Berkshire County that was interested in the issue of providing subsidized family planning services. This was a challenge because it meant finding allies who were so committed to family planning that they would help establish a service in a skeptical, often hostile community. I also needed to find an organization that was willing to administer a family planning program and I did—Berkshire Family and Children's Services. I wrote the grant and we received funding to start a family planning program. We delivered services, including services to minors without consent.

The network of people who were interested in this kind of work was very small and there was a lot of misinformation about Family Planning. Many people didn't believe it was even legal for married women to have birth control in Massachusetts. Although we were the last state that allowed that to happen, it was legal at that point. The advisory board helped people to understand the need for family planning services. It was wonderful for me because I really got to know the area well. I was seen as the expert, because I had a Master's degree, even though I was much younger than those I was working with. We did a lot of good work in North Adams, Pittsfield, and Great Barrington. There was a nurse, Dorothy Kazam, who is retired now and lives in Amherst. At the time, she worked for the Massachusetts Department of Public Health and was very interested in family planning. Her support gave our effort the institutional blessing of the state government. She already had contacts in the social service sphere in Berkshire County, so that also opened many doors.

What I thought was really good about Family and Children's Services and the Berkshire County project was that it was very focused. I mean, with the availability of grant money from the federal government, some of the usual turf fights were minimized and we could unite behind the goal of initiating service. And that's what ended up happening. You needed, in a sense, a community buy-in for the delivery of service, and we felt we really did [have it]. Again, it wasn't an organization that I was running. Planned Parenthood, my employer, didn't want that. It was an organization that I helped start, and then turned over to another organization to administer.

The plan was that they were going to start in Great Barrington, Pittsfield, and North Adams. But doctors in North Adams organized against having their town in the program. So initially only educational efforts, not medical services, were available there. The reason that many of the doctors who had migrated to northern Berkshire County did so was to, quote, "avoid socialized medicine." The federal family planning program stipulated that you can't discriminate based on age or marital status; that birth control services needed to be available [to all]. And that's why I really loved the construction of Title X. The family planning program is required to have a sliding fee scale. But in North Adams the doctors saw the sliding fee scale as some sort of conspiracy for socialized medicine. So it took it a little bit longer in North Adams to actually start delivering medical services, but that did happen after about two years. Initially we did have to hire a doctor from another community. That was actually an advantage for us, because of the pressures that were put on local doctors, who might provide this kind of service. Sometimes you really needed an outside doctor.

In 1973, I began doing similar organizing in Franklin County. There was an Office of Economic Opportunity Community Action Program [OEO-CAP] agency, which is now called Franklin County Action Commission or FCAC. There was a nurse, Barbara Blakney, in the leadership of FCAC who was also interested in family planning services. She is now head of the National Nursing Organization. I helped organize a similar advisory group—that's what we really needed—and again got a cross section of people. With the help of Barbara and Mark Berson—a young upstart lawyer—and some longtime community people on the advisory board, we wrote and received a federal grant and were able to initiate a Family Planning program.

So we then had two separate programs, one in Franklin and one in Berkshire County. By that point I had much more of a sense of what was really happening in Western Massachusetts. I could see that each county had similar but separate needs. Unfortunately, the people making the decisions in Washington D.C. or Boston didn't see any difference. I began to appreciate Western Massachusetts' lack of power; that decision making really happened far from here, and that if Western Massachusetts was going to have any clout, we were going to need to develop a broader program.

I also did some work in Hampden County, with what had been a small OEO-CAP program at Baystate Medical Center, which at that point was called

Wesson Women's Hospital. Merry Boone was working in that program and she shared my view that we needed a larger delivery system and the ability to have a more comprehensive family planning program. We were also able to get a grant. That afforded us the ability to have three programs.

But I was living in Hampshire County and it really seemed to me that we also needed service there. As we were trying to organize services in Northampton, in Hampshire County, there was an interesting twist we hadn't counted on. When we were about to submit our federal grant for Hampshire County, we learned there was a doctor in Northampton—and this is where you get to understand small towns— this doctor felt threatened that he was going to lose all this business. It turned out that this doctor's wife was the president of the board of Children's Aid and Family Services, the agency that was going to be the grantee. At a board meeting, the board deferred going forward with the grant. The timing was awful because by the time they untabled the motion to proceed with a family planning service, President Nixon had put the hold on funding any new grantees.

So here we were with a need for services but a freeze on federal funds. It seemed to me that our only option was to use the economies of scale—that if we had one administrative structure instead of four of them—we could spend a lot more on services. And so from 1972 to 1973 we basically "regionalized" the family planning programs in Western Massachusetts. This was a tremendous process for the people involved because they had to sacrifice for the larger good—the good being to extent services to an unserved county within Western Massachusetts. The federal government actually ended up helping too—they gave us a small grant to help us regionalize so that we could finally provide services to Hampshire County in addition to the other three counties.

One of the people who was a tremendous help was Jane Zapka, who started the Health Education Program at University Health Services [at UMass]. Jane had a really deep and abiding commitment to contraceptive access and she was able to work out a system where as long as a student would go through a contraceptive educational session then the University Health Services would actually provide birth control. Jane was a local Hatfield girl but yet very, very committed to family planning services. It was great for me to see this because I then really understood Massachusetts in a different way. First of all, being far from Boston, people could do different things that people in power in Boston might not be aware of or things that people were willing to overlook because Western Massachusetts was not in the same media market. In Boston, you would have had the archdiocese close by and the *Boston Globe* ready to do a story. I recognized that there were people here who were willing to have different interpretations of the law, even in public institutions. So in fact at UMass there was access to birth control services despite the fact that the law hadn't changed. Here was a state university, it was "against the law" to do this; nonetheless, UMass was providing contraceptive services to undergraduates who were unmarried. I really give a lot of the credit for that to Jane Zapka.

Two of the other primary women who were involved were wives of Amherst College professors. One was named Britt Guttman and the other was Robin Dizard, who is still here in Amherst. Now Robin is a professor in her own right! As wives of Amherst College professors they were willing to use the reflected institutional authority of the college to further reproductive rights. They were part of a group called Amherst Women's Liberation. They did some pregnancy counseling and support. But the different groups here were often comprised of the same people, so if tonight it was Thursday night then it was Amherst Women's Liberation, then Wednesday morning it was Clergy Consultation Service. At that point people really were very committed to reproductive freedom as part of what was seen as women's liberation. I felt very close to this group and they were very supportive of the work that I was doing. They primarily focused on the abortion issue and I was primarily focused on the initiation of family planning services. Over time there were surely tensions or disagreements about policy or tactical discussions. Why can't all the services be free? Or that we should only deal with Amherst Women's Liberation, not with those men in Clergy Consultation Service. But these were not significant enough to impede the development at a service.

I also need to mention two other women who were really involved through an organization on campus at UMass, the United Christian Foundation—a woman named Ruth Fessenden who's now recently retired from Everywoman's Center and a woman named Elaine Fraser, who died recently. Her husband was very helpful, too. He was the editor of the local paper, and made sure these issues were covered in a fair way. Elaine was initially doing counseling for Clergy Consultation at the UCF office, and then at UMass Health Services. So toward the end of her tenure she was actually doing that counseling as a paid state worker. Speaking of the clergy, I think the other really important person was a man named Dick Unsworth. I liked him from the moment I met him and he has been a consistent help, often under difficult circumstances. He was the chaplain at Smith [College], and then became the head of Northfield [Mount Hermon School]. Because the institutions he represented were so powerful in the area, it kind of gave him cover or great latitude. I so appreciated his using his local leadership to further and legitimize this controversial service.

These people were doing their own things in Hampshire County, but it seemed clear that we could better serve our clients if we had a wider delivery system. I wanted to get the Planned Parenthood League of Massachusetts involved, but there was a problem. Planned Parenthood, historically, had refused to provide direct medical services. Instead of delivering services they chose to be evaluators. They decided that they wanted to be, in a sense, above service. I know that from an organizational development standpoint, it would have made a whole lot more sense for Planned Parenthood to be involved because we could have used their national clout. This "non-service" policy didn't make a whole lot of sense to me, but in the end it didn't really make a difference either because we were delivering quality services without them. And because there wasn't a statewide or a national organization behind us, ours became much more of a community-based effort. We were able to really be much more responsive to what was happening locally.

Planned Parenthood did agree to temporarily fund a family planning clinic in Worthington in Hampshire County until we were able to get funding from the federal government. There was this really wonderful clinic there with a doctor, George Scarmon. He was part of a bunch of people who had purposely moved to Worthington so they could go back to the "country." But they also wanted to provide medical services to locals and they were interested in providing family planning services. We just really hit it off. And I'm sorry to say this really sounds sexist, but George Scarmon was really gorgeous looking—a wonderful young hippy doctor. He was a very charismatic figure and I really believe that was why people came. The Worthington Health Center at the time was George Scarmon's private practice. It is now a Health Center Program funded by the federal government.[1] Someone from the community had donated a building so that's why it was called the Worthington Health Center, but it was his practice and the rest of the week he provided just regular medical services, not exclusively family planning services. The woman that he was living with was the clinic receptionist, music played, and so it was a very nice, warm atmosphere. People would hitchhike and travel miles to see this doctor. It was kind of a hippy mecca at the time.

Planned Parenthood's funding allowed the Worthington clinic to provide a broad range of family planning services, and it really was an entrée to health care, because for many this was the first interaction they had with the health care system. The beauty of Title X is its commitment to comprehensive family planning, not just the medical services. Comprehensive family planning included counseling, education, and an entrée to the health system. That was pretty much our goal from the beginning, to create the whole infrastructure to provide those services.

The guidelines of Title X were pretty detailed in regard to the plethora of services we needed to provide. Specific goals were set out by the federal grants, and we needed to meet their numerical goals in order to keep getting support. I loved Title X because, for all of the criticism of family planning, if you looked at what we were attempting to do, it was really to raise the health status of individuals. Someone could say, "oh all you were doing was giving out birth control pills," but in fact anyone who came and used our service needed to have their health status determined. So they also had laboratory tests and medical exams. What we could really do was move them into the medical system or social service system. So, I would say that was a big piece of how we determined if we were really being successful or not.

Establishing the Family Planning Council of Western Massachusetts

September of 1973 was a very significant time because the federal government had frozen funding that would have allowed us to have a program in Hampshire County.

And so in September of 1973, the smaller federal grants were combined into one and the Family Planning Council of Western Massachusetts was established—by creating one regional organization, instead of separate programs, we could then serve Hampshire County as well. A regional board with members from all of the four counties was formed and they conducted interviews for an Executive Director. I was hired and in September 1973, I officially left Planned Parenthood and began as the Executive Director of the Family Planning Council of Western Massachusetts.

The Family Planning Council has an organizational structure for service delivery that has become the standard. It uses a team approach to medicine, where doctors were part of the service delivery system, along with counselors and nurses, all with the responsibility of helping and answering questions. That may not seem like much now but back then it was a new idea. This was something that people who came to the service really appreciated. We did lots of surveys about why people came to the service, and often times the referral came from another client who had said, "they'll treat you decently there," or "someone there will answer all of your questions."

Western Massachusetts is a very diverse area and one of the biggest questions initially was how we would deal with ethnicity and religion, especially with the large Polish Catholic population in this area. We needed to show all our clients, but especially our Roman Catholic ones, that we were consistently nonjudgmental; that if you were someone who was a practicing Catholic you were welcome to come and use our services. It was really important that our clients knew that we were committed to strict confidentiality—that no one would know who used our services.

Even though it was a regional organization spanning the 3,000 square miles of Western Massachusetts and there also was an outreach component, we were located centrally in Northampton. The whole organization was envisioned as a model of centralization—one administrative office—and decentralization—service through a number of local community clinics. I'm sure there are some academics who would challenge that as not being a good business model. I certainly don't recommend it to everyone. It was a challenge having to manage everything from so far away, but for us, it really made sense to do it that way. And we hired local people at each of the clinic sites. The word spread in a very different way if there were local people working at a clinic. I think language and cultural sensitivity have also been important features of our decision making related to staff—hiring local people helps us to try to mirror the community. For example, in Franklin County there's now a growing Latino community, and we need to make sure that our staff is able to communicate with the people who use our service. Quite a number of years ago it wasn't important to have bilingual staff or bicultural staff in Franklin County. It was more important to have it in Holyoke or Springfield. And there's now a growing Russian population in Springfield, so we also need to be able to accommodate their needs. So that was what we attempted to do—as much as we could—to hire local people who were committed to the work that we were doing

But even to this day, we need to make sure that someone who works with us can deal with the mission of the organization. Recently we were interviewing for a new chief financial officer and one of the issues was what are the candidates' positions on "choice." And there are some nurses who started to work with us before emergency contraception.[2] Because we don't provide abortions, this is my "litmus test" about whether they believe in the mission of this organization: can you say, yes, I'm really pro-choice, and I support the ability of the woman to make a decision [about terminating a pregnancy]. So we have had issues with some nurses who do not want to participate with emergency contraception. These continue to be really important conversations that we have as we hire people. But there are many staffers who have worked with us for many, many years. I give 20-year awards and 15-year awards.

We tried to do our best in selecting a medical director. We really wanted to make sure we had a "premier doctor," a board certified OB-GYN. Sam Topal was loved in the area, so that also added legitimacy to the medical work that we were doing.

I think the hardest part of what I did was to find a way of balancing time, because Western Massachusetts is a large area. It's not like I was going to one office. I needed to be publicly visible. In addition, a lot of the work that I needed to do initially was actually based in Washington.

Because so much of what we do is focused on Western Massachusetts, I think many people don't appreciate the role that the state and federal government plays, particularly through the grant process. One of the things people find surprising is how much effort has to be made away from Western Massachusetts. I have been fortunate to serve as President of NFPRHA [National Family Planning and Reproductive Health Association] and also served on the Executive Committee and Board of the Alan Guttmacher Institute. I have worked closely with Cory Richards, the Vice President for Public Policy and head of Guttmacher's Washington Office. This national perspective has helped put my work in Western Massachusetts in context. Through these efforts I have been able to work on important policy issues. Whenever I go to Washington, D.C., I am reminded of one of our unsung heroes, the late Congressman Silvio Conte. On paper no two people could be more dissimilar than Conte and me in terms of how we feel about abortion. Yet we managed to bridge the cultural and political differences, effectively work together, and become good friends. Representative Conte was strongly anti-choice, but it is not well known that he worked long and hard for family planning. I miss his good work and his friendship. As the ranking Republican on the Appropriations Committee, he was instrumental in expanding the national family planning program and saving it from vicious attacks from some in his own party.

Difficulties and Challenges

Whenever I am asked what was the greatest challenge that I had there is only one answer and it may surprise you. It's not the federal government. It's not the local politicians, or even attracting clients. By far the greatest challenge really came from the doctors. They were especially significant in Franklin County. Although we were almost always able to best him, one of our strongest adversaries was a Franklin County doctor named Percy Wadman, who was head of Franklin Medical Center's OB department and was opposed to what we were trying to do. Fortunately, we had stronger advocates in the form of a local nurse and lawyer.

After the doctors, the biggest challenge came from, of course, the Catholic Church. The Church did not want us to succeed and tried its best to block us at every turn. One thing I have learned is that the Church often does not speak with one voice and even within the Church are forward thinking individuals who understand reproductive freedom. And there actually was a Catholic priest who was informally part of the Clergy Consultation Service though he wasn't on call like the others. But if you really wanted to talk to a priest, you could; there was a priest, who was willing to do that. For some Catholic women, it was so important to feel that they could talk to a priest about this. A religious person has a really different ability to soothe or heal or help someone work through a problem. So it felt really important that there were some renegade Catholics who understood the importance of this issue of reproductive freedom, too. Overall, I tried not to fight very publicly with the Church.

Early on—pre-Roe—I spent a lot of time debating the abortion question, but it got to be pointless. Abortion is one of those issues where very few people are willing to change so I stopped accepting invitations to debate the topic. I got tired doing it because it felt like it was going nowhere. Initially it was really important that we provide what was called at the time "natural family planning"—the rhythm method. That was our way of being able to provide the full range of methods that were available and some, like the rhythm method, that were endorsed by the Catholic Church. After we had a number of clients who had already received our services, we were able, not so subtly, to speak to the problem of the position of the Church as far as whether Catholics really used and wanted birth control. Our client population mirrored the community. In a community that was 50 percent Catholic, 50 percent of our clients were Catholic. It was really important from the beginning that we got good data, so that we would be able to document that what we were saying was true. Also, the federal government wanted to maintain that information too.

There was a period of time in the late '70s where there had been issues related to genocide and family planning, especially in regard to race. There had been some irresponsible reporting on not-very-well-documented cases in this area about sterilization abuse. Although we did not provide sterilization services, it really became very important that people saw me fighting against sterilization abuse and for health services for low income people in addition to reproductive health. So, in terms of the issue of race, I think we dealt with that well.

The Family Planning Council had, I would say, a very interesting relationship with the Planned Parenthood League of Massachusetts. As I mentioned earlier, I had come from a Planned Parenthood in Philadelphia and thought that the Planned Parenthood in Massachusetts should be the one to organize and run the clinics much like the one in Philly. But this Planned Parenthood did not want to be in the business, as they said, of running medical services.

A few years ago, however, PPLM hired a new Executive Director and bought an abortion clinic in Springfield. So now there is a Planned Parenthood of Western Clinic in Springfield. Even though they are primarily an abortion clinic and only in Springfield, Planned Parenthood is now doing private fundraising in other parts of Western Massachusetts. So now we're in a position where, sadly, we'll need to compete with them for private charitable dollars. With Planned Parenthood's name recognition it feels like Walmart or Starbucks coming into an area where a local independent store has been for years. While I welcome Planned Parenthood providing needed abortion service for our area, I don't welcome their soliciting the very limited number of private donors interested in reproductive health in Western Massachusetts.

Providing Universal Service

It wasn't prohibited for someone from the colleges and university in this area to use our services if they didn't really trust the confidentiality of records at their health services. And in some places that was a really reasonable concern—to trust that there might not be sharing of information. Especially in the early years and especially in regard to the issue of abortion, many [students] didn't want to go to their health services if they didn't think the issue was really confidential. It may seem silly now, but at the time, for a young undergraduate who wasn't married, there could be issues about how she would feel about a professor knowing she was using birth control. We always opened our doors to anyone. It didn't matter if you were a student or not. But we tried to work with those institutions so that they would recognize that their students were, in fact, sexually active and needed birth control. In places like Smith [College] it took longer for them to acknowledge that. Right now, we actually do all the HIV counseling and testing for Smith. In much the way that students wanted confidentiality about birth control and abortion now the greatest concern seems to be to protect the confidentiality of HIV testing. So if a student doesn't want to have her records enmeshed in the regular medical records at the health services, they'll be in our records.

Right from the beginning, teenagers were a very big issue. To provide services to minors, we rely on the Civil Rights Act of 1964, whereby you couldn't discriminate based on, among other things, age. There were some people who didn't believe that was a good thing. But we needed to provide the service in the interest of good public health. There continue to be, even to this day, parents who don't think what we're doing makes a whole lot of sense. What we try to do in those situations is to have the parent come in and talk with a staff member and help them see how responsible their child in fact is for wanting to seek this kind of care. Some really important research has now been done which documents that it's approximately nine months *after* a teenage girl is sexually active that she first comes to a family planning clinic for contraception. Typically, the teenager comes because she is afraid she's pregnant. I think we're not doing our job well enough if in fact it's that long a time that someone is sexually active before they seek birth control. We need to do better than that.

I feel very good now about what we've accomplished for teenagers in this community. Years ago, we were the only place where many teenagers could go, because they couldn't go to their private doctors. Now there are adolescent medical specialists who also include family planning. I'm not taking credit for this change, only saying that this community is adaptable.

We've always tried to offer universal service. What that means is that we've tried to be as deeply respectful as we can about someone's financial situation. And we want to be trusting too. We've never asked people to bring in pay stubs in order to get totally free service. Now, some may say that we then get taken for a ride because some people won't be honest and will say that they make less money than they really do. We've always had clients paying almost all that is asked of them based on our sliding fee scale.

The Counseling Cooperative

I started the Western New England Counselor's Cooperative back in 1973 as the contact point for women who needed abortions. Referrals were then made to the clergy or laywomen for counseling and then on to the clinics and doctors. The idea of this was that some women felt very comfortable dealing with clergy, and others thought they weren't necessarily a positive life force. After the law changed, then the New England Counselor's Cooperative (the name changed as we grew and expanded) negotiated prices with the abortion providers in the area. That meant that if you were referred from this co-op you could get a reduced fee and no one would be denied access to abortion services because of inability to pay. This later became what's called the Abortion Fund of Western Massachusetts. So, if we sent five people to, say, Hampden County OB-GYN for abortions, then we would get credit for one free abortion. Over time there were enough credits that you didn't have to say, "wait let me see if there's credit." Unfortunately, there used to be a number of providers, but there ended up being fewer and fewer. That hurt our ability to negotiate. This work had nothing to do with my work with the Council or with any Title X dollars.

Most of the abortion services were in Amherst and Springfield. The Family Planning Council of Western Massachusetts referred people through the Co-op and did all of the pre-abortion laboratory work. We were the primary referrer, but there were other places, like Everywoman's Center, that also used the Counselor's Co-op. It was a system that was really working, as long as there were counselors. We had a model in our minds as to what was a good service and we tried to enforce our vision. We tried to insist that abortion providers have a counseling component.[3] Amherst Medical Associates and Springfield and also the place in Berkshire County cooperated with our policy of not referring to places or agencies that had no women counselors. The underlying threat in all of this was that if they didn't do it right, then the Family Planning Council of Western Massachusetts was going to start abortion services and the clinics would lose clients and money. And we never really needed to do that because we were able to have this parallel system, which worked.

A Vision Shared

One of the things that attracted me to Western Massachusetts was that there was a small progressive community, a core of local people who I could rely on. Many people who helped start the organization have stayed with it all these years—Ruth Fessenden, Mark Berson, Judi Fonsh, Jack Stone—and many more have joined through the years—Ellen Story, Lucy Hartry, Helen Caulton-Harris, Betsey Selkowitz—and many, many, more. So it doesn't feel like an individual pursuit .One of the real satisfactions and benefits of working in an organization that has stayed pretty stable for all these years is seeing the thousands of people who have benefited from the service and working with the many good people who share my vision.

I have come over the years to appreciate the importance of like-minded people working together toward a goal. It has been critically important that I was part of the national family planning and reproductive health movement. There were national meetings and there were people who I was seeing and talking to all the time. There was a great flow of information.

I was president of the NFPRHA during the Reagan period. We were really the ones who were standing up and saying don't "block grant" the family planning program.[4] I had to testify in D.C. while I was still needed to run our local organization, so there were many times when I would catch the 6 a.m. flight from Bradley with all the insurance guys and I would come back at ten at night. But it afforded me the ability to feel like I was able, in a personal way, to make a contribution to fight for something I believed. And it was very empowering because we won! We beat Reagan, and it was one of the only discretionary programs that wasn't block granted at the time that most programs were. And Tapestry still has a relationship with the federal government. That was important.

I still get a kick out of the fact that even now—now that Tapestry has more than 150 dedicated staffers that serve all of Western Massachusetts in four counties—even now whenever I am at a restaurant or at the movies or just about anywhere, inevitably someone will come up to me and ask me something about contraception or STDs or family planning. It's a good thing my husband and daughter are so at ease with the subject by now! Sometimes, though, people think of *me* as family planning. Even now people call me up at home and say, "When are you open?" This actually happened just this past weekend. Someone didn't realize his daughter was sexually active and she said, "Oh, my God, Dad, guess what the, condom broke." I was glad he thought to call me. I'm really happy to try to find emergency contraception—and we did. It is great that people ask. I am now at the stage of life where you look back and see if you really did make a difference. And its gratifying to know that after so many years of struggle, I know that I have done my part to make sure that young women and poor women have the right to ask and that there are services to help them here in Western Massachusetts.

Acknowledgments

I must first thank all of those who consented to interviews for this project and who became collaborators in the end result. Just as an oral history interview is in itself a collaborative process, so too has this book been from its very origins. The Valley Women's History Collaborative had already focused on reproductive rights as an area of inquiry and begun interviews long before I came on board. I am grateful to the founding members of the collaborative, Kaymarion Raymond, Joyce Berkman, and Susan Tracy, and to Marla Miller for inviting me into their dynamic investigation of local social history. Joyce Berkman and Susan Tracy in particular have been the guiding lights of the collaborative while I have been with it and they have also served as wonderful mentors and "guidance counselors" to me as this process has unfolded. They approach local history with an effective combination of sensitivity, eager inquisitiveness, and a keen comparative sense of how local events interact with an unfolding national history.

I also wish to thank all of the other volunteer interviewers who have been with the collaborative on this and other projects, but specific thanks go to those who performed the interviews that make up this book: Judi Fonsh for her work with Elaine Fraser and Amherst Women's Liberation; Susan Tracy and Joyce Berkman for their work with the Springfield Women's Health Collective; Susan Tracy for her work with Amherst Women's Liberation; Marilyn Smith for her work with Amherst Women's Liberation; and Kris Woll for her work with Leslie Laurie.

My involvement with the collaborative began as a the result of graduate work with Marla Miller and Joyce Berkman at the History Department at the University of Massachusetts at Amherst (UMass), specifically through their fine Public History program. Marla Miller has been an invaluable teacher, coconspirator, and cheerleader for me over the course of many years and I am truly grateful to her. In the same vein, this book owes a large debt to Kris Woll for both her excellent oral history skills and for the vivacity and intellectual sharpness she brought to both collaborative meetings and late nights at coffee shops. If she were less sane, she would have agreed to be coauthor; as it is, she must make do with my thanks.

The staffs at the Sophia Smith Collection at Smith College and the Special Collections and Archives at the W.E.B. Du Bois Library at UMass were terrific in guiding me through their collections. Special thanks to Michael Milewski at the Du Bois Library, and to Marlene Fried and her staff at the Civil Liberties and Public

Policy Program at Hampshire College for access to their materials from past years of the "From Abortion Rights to Social Justice" conferences, especially the tapes of early speakouts on abortion. Thanks, too, to Dr. Jaquelyn Dowd Hall and everyone at the Southern Oral History Program at the University of North Carolina-Chapel Hill.

I am also grateful to James Loewen, author of *Lies Across America* and *Lies My Teacher Told Me*, for supporting this book when it was just an idea over lunch and for all of his advice on navigating the publishing world.

My father set out to produce three doctors to follow in his footsteps and somehow managed to produce two historians and an internet entrepreneur. Even more surprising, to him at least, is how he has become editor to all of us. I am indebted, in all definitions of the term, to Dr. Martin Cline for the great care and effort he spent in helping me fine tune the preceding pages. Thanks are also due to my brother, Dr. Eric Cline of George Washington University, and his family, and to my sister Avril and nephew Max.

The incomparable Shelley Nichols deserves tremendous praise for her thoughtful guidance, support, and great humor during the oft-exciting creation of this manuscript. Shelley, you have my enduring love, respect, and gratitude. Thank you. And many thanks to the entire Nichols clan for keeping me happy and well-fed!

I also wish to acknowledge the Oral History Association and the National Council on Public History, which have given me supportive communities as this project has developed. In particular, thanks to National Council of Public History and Historical Research Associates for presenting me with the 2004 HRA New Professional Award, which enabled me to attend the 2004 NCPH conference.

Finally, my thanks to the series editors, Linda Shopes and Bruce Stave, for their contributions to the field of public history and for their fine and sensitive work on this and the other volumes in the series.

Notes

Introduction

1. *Daily Hampshire Gazette*, September 11, 1970; September 22, 1970. The newspaper coverage of this event did not include the outcome of the case and the records in Holyoke District Court cannot be accessed, therefore the legal fate of Mr. Day is not known by the author.
2. The movement for women's suffrage is commonly seen as the first wave of the women's movement, with the second being the rise of feminism in the later 1960s and early 1970s.
3. Planned Parenthood web site, www.pplm.org/Mission/pplm1.html.
4. Linda Gordon. *The Moral Property of Women: A History of Birth Control Politics in America*. University of Illinois Press, Chicago, 2002. p. 299.
5. C. Thomas Dienes. *Law, Politics, and Birth Control*. University of Illinois Press, Urbana, 1972. p. 324.
6. Ibid., p. 322.
7. Ibid., p. 322.
8. The Alan Guttmacher Institute reports that estimates of the annual number of illegal abortions during the decades of the 1950s and 1960s range from 200,000 to 1.2 million. Since *Roe v. Wade*, legal abortions have averaged in the 1.3 millions. For statistics see the Guttmacher Institute web page, http://www.agi-usa.org.
9. Recent works have investigated those individuals and groups that defied the law to provide family planning information and abortion referrals, and in one case, abortions themselves. Historian Rickie Solinger was the first to write an in-depth investigation of modern illegal abortion in *The Abortionist* (1994) and sociologist Carole Joffe contributed to the body of knowledge on illegal providers in her 1995 book *Doctors of Conscience: The Struggle to Provide Abortion Before and After Roe V. Wade* (Beacon Press, Boston, 1995). Joffe's book highlights how abortion, though now legal, is still very marginalized from the mainstream of U.S. medicine, and therefore many abortion provides experience isolation from their colleagues.
10. Although the *Roe v. Wade* decision that finally and definitively legalized abortion came from the Judicial Branch, ten state legislatures in the decade prior to Roe had enacted significant abortion law reforms, many of them based on the American Legal Institute's Model Penal Code.
11. Major works on the subject of illegal abortion in the United States are Leslie J. Reagan's *When Abortion Was a Crime: Women, Medicine, and Law in the United States*,

1867–1973 (University of California Press, Berkeley, 1997) which uses court records instead of oral histories, Laura Kaplan's *The Story of Jane: The Legendary Underground Abortion Service* (The University of Chicago Press, Chicago, 1995), which is essentially one woman's memoir of a feminist collective in Chicago that began performing lay abortions, several works by Rickie Solinger, and Carole Joffe's *Doctors of Conscience*. An essential text on the legal history behind the Roe decision is David J. Garrow's *Liberty and Sexuality: The Right to Privacy and the Making of Roe v. Wade* (Maxwell Macmillan International, New York, 1994). However, much of the existing historiography does not emphasize the related battle for legalized access to birth control that in some states preceded and in many states coexisted with the fight for abortion rights.

12. Alessandro Portelli. *The Death of Luigi Trastulli and Other Stories: Form and Meaning in Oral History*. State University of New York Press, Albany, 1991.

13. The stories of Meredith Michaels and Susan Tracy were originally recounted at an "Abortion Speakout" at Hampshire College in 1989 the scripts of these interviews served as the basis for additional oral history work by Michael and Tracy with the author.

14. *Daily Hampshire Gazette*, November 20, 1970, p. 12. Interestingly, the campus newspaper, *The Massachusetts Daily Collegian* did not cover this event.

Part One   The Women: Survivors of Illegal Abortions

1. Patricia Therese Maginnis and Laura Clarke Phelan. *The Abortion Handbook for Responsible Women*. Contact Books, San Francisco, 1969, p. 62.

2. Janet Farrell Brodie. *Contraception and Abortion in Nineteenth-Century America*. Cornell University Press, New Haven, 1994. pp. 5–6.

3. James C. Mohr. *Abortion in America: The Origins and Evolution of National Policy, 1800–1900*. Oxford University Press, New York, 1978. pp. 15, 26–27; Leslie J. Reagan. *When Abortion Was a Crime: Women, Medicine, and Law in the United States, 1867–1973*. University of California Press, Berkeley, 1997. p. 13.

4. Reagan, *When Abortion Was a Crime*, p. 43.

5. Ibid., p. 13.

6. Mohr, *Abortion in America*, pp. 54, 56.

7. Nanette Davis. *From Crime to Choice: The Transformation of Abortion in America*. Greenwood Press, Connecticut, 1985. p. 42.

8. Reagan, *When Abortion was a Crime*, p. 201.

9. Davis, *From Crime to Choice*, p. 73; Sam Topal interview, VWHC archives, Special Collections, W.E.B. Du Bois Library, University of Massachusetts Amherst.

10. Davis, *From Crime to Choice*, p. 27.

11. See Rickie Solinger's excellent biography, *The Abortionist: A Woman Against the Law*, The Free Press, New York, 1994.

12. Davis, *From Crime to Choice*, p. 66; Elaine Fraser transcript, VWHC archives, Special Collections, W.E.B. Du Bois Library, University of Massachusetts Amherst.

13. Reagan, *When Abortion was a Crime*, p. 205.

14. Calderone discussed not only the numerous illicit abortions, but also the thousands of legal "therapeutic" abortions performed annually in some states.

15. According to the Boston Women's Health Book Collective website, "in 1969, as the women's movement was gaining momentum and influence in the Boston area and elsewhere around the country, twelve women met during a women's liberation conference. In a workshop on 'women and their bodies,' they talked about their own experiences with doctors and shared their knowledge about their bodies. Eventually they decided to form the Doctor's Group, the forerunner to the Boston Women's Health Book Collective, to research and discuss what they were learning about themselves, their bodies, health, and women. The fruit of their discussions and research was a course booklet entitled Women and Their Bodies, published in 1970, which put women's health in a radically new political and social context. The Boston Women's Health Book Collective formally incorporated in 1972 in order to publish commercially its renamed underground success, *Our Bodies, Ourselves*. The result was an expanded 1973 edition that became a national bestseller."

16. Springfield Women's Health Collective transcript, Amherst Women's Liberation transcript, VWHC archives, Special Collections, W.E.B. Du Bois Library, University of Massachusetts Amherst. See also, e.g., Ruth Rosen. *The World Split Open*. Penguin, New York, 2000.

17. Rosemary Nossiff. *Before Roe: Abortion Policy in the States*. Temple University Press, Philadelphia, 2001. p. 81.

18. Ibid., pp. 64–72.

19. Laura Kaplan. *The Story of Jane: The Legendary Underground Abortion Service*. The University of Chicago Press, Chicago, 1995.

20. Cynthia Gorney. *Articles of Faith: A Frontline History of the Abortion wars*. Simon & Schuster, New York, 1998.

21. Ibid., pp. 48–49.

22. Ibid., p. 71.

23. Ibid., p. 85.

24. Ibid., pp. 92–93.

25. See, e.g., Ellen Messer and Kathryn E. May's *Back Rooms: Voices from the Illegal Abortion Era* (St. Martin's Press, New York, 1988), Gloria Feldt's *Behind Every Choice is a Story* (University of North Texas Press, Denton, 2002); Laura Kaplan's *The Story of Jane*, and Angela Bonavoglia's *The Choices We Made: Twenty-Five Women and Men Speak Out About Abortion* (Four Walls Eight Windows, New York City, 2001).

26. Reagan, *When Abortion was a Crime*, p. 213.

One   Elizabeth Myer

1. State Representative David T. Donnelly, Democrat, from the 10th Suffolk representative district, is Chairperson of the Joint Committee on the Judiciary for the Massachusetts House and Senate.

2. She has chosen to use her birth name in this interview out of concern for her privacy and safety.

Two   Dr. Robin Dizard

1. This name has been changed.
2. Dilation and curettage (D&C) is a procedure in which the cervix is opened, or dilated, and a hollow tube, a curette, is inserted into the uterus. Fetal tissue is either scraped out or removed by suction.

Three   Jean Baxter

1. Abortions were not in fact legal in Puerto Rico but they were performed very openly there with little fear of prosecution.

Six   Dr. Susan Tracy

1. *Our Bodies, Ourselves* was published by the Boston Women's Health Book Collective under the original title *Women and Their Bodies* in 1970. It has gone through numerous editions and is still in print, most recently as *Our Bodies, Ourselves: A New Edition for a New Era* (Boston Women's Health Collective, Boston, 2005).

Part Two   Providers of Reproductive Health Care: Doctors, Health Educators, and Illegal Abortionists

1. History of the Planned Parenthood League of Massachusetts, www.pplm.org, 2000.
2. "Abortion-Rights Scorned Profit: Hated by Both Sides, Bill Baird Raises Hackles, Not Funds," *New York Times*, April 14, 1993, B1 and B5.
3. Dr. Robert Gage, of the University of Massachusetts Health Services, noted one of Baird's frequent visits in a September 1970 letter to the university's *Massachusetts Daily Collegian*.
4. Ruth Fessenden transcript, VWHC archives, Special Collections, W.E.B. Du Bois Library, University of Massachusetts Amherst.
5. Lawrence Siddall, Michael A. Cann and Robert W. Gage, "Report of a Preliminary Study of Pregnancy on the University Campus," *Journal of the American College Health Association*. Vol. 19, no. 2 (December 1970): 111.
6. Ibid., pp. 112–113.
7. Davis, *From Crime to Choice: The Transformation of Abortion in America*, p. 67.
8. Ibid., pp. 68–69.
9. Ibid., p. 71.
10. Ibid., p. 69.
11. Ibid., p. 68.
12. Leslie J. Reagan, *When Abortion was a Crime: Women, Medicine and Law in the United States, 1867–1973*. University of California Press, Berkeley, 1997. p. 1.

13. Johanna Schoen. *Choice and Coercion: Birth Control, Sterilization, and Abortion in Public Health and Welfare*. University of North Carolina Press, Chapel Hill, 2005. p. 145.
14. Lorraine Florio's career as an illegal abortionist was profiled by Eileen McNamara in "Out of the Shadows of Back-Alley Days: Abortionist Recalls Frightened Women, Fast Money," *Boston Globe*, May 16, 1989, p. 1.

Seven   Dr. Merritt F. Garland, Jr.

1. Silvio Conti represented Western Massachusetts from 1959 to 1991.

Eight   Dr. Sam Topal

1. Gram negative sepsis is a serious infection resulting from a combination of Gram negative bacteria in the bloodstream with loss of blood pressure.
2. He is referring here both to therapeutic abortions in Massachusetts and to "regular" abortions in New York State, which were legally effective from July 1, 1970.
3. Hampden Gynecological Associates operated a large practice in Springfield.
4. Menstrual extraction is a method of removing the menses using a standard abortion suction machine with a flexible cannula or, more typically for the time under discussion, a homemade device using a Mason jar. While this method extracts menses from non-pregnant women, abortion can be a by-product of the procedure. The procedure was popular with women's self-help groups in the early 1970s before quickly developing a reputation for often being unsafe.

Ten   Dr. Jane Zapka

1. See Dr. Robert Gage transcript, VWHC archives, Special Collections, W.E.B. Du Bois Library, University of Massachusetts Amherst.
2. Dr. William Darity was Professor of Public Health at the University of Massachusetts, Amherst until his retirement in 1989.
3. See Ruth Fessenden interview in Clergy section (Part 3, chapter 18).
4. J.G. Zapka, S. Lemon, L. Peterson, et al., "The Silent Consumer: Women's Reports and Ratings of Abortion Services," *Medical Care* vol. 39, no. 1(2001): 50–60.

Part Three   The Clergy and their Allies: Clergy and Affiliated Lay Abortion Counselors

1. Lawrence Lader. *Abortion II: Making the Revolution*. Beacon Press, Boston, 1973.
2. *New York Times*, May 27, 1967, p. 1.

3. Arlene Carmen and Howard Moody. *Abortion Counseling and Social Change: From Illegal Act to Medical Practice: The Story of the Clergy Consultation Service on Abortion.* Judson Press, Valley Forge, 1973. p. 97.

4. Ruth Fessenden transcript, VWHC archives, Special Collections, W.E.B. Du Bois Library, University of Massachusetts Amherst.

5. Moody later wrote: "It was apparent from the start that the clergy who would be most likely to become involved in a project of this kind would be the same ones who had been most active in the school integration battle in New York, in the Civil Rights battle both there and in the South, as well as in other areas of civil liberties." (Moody and Carmen, p. 21) The history of activist clergy working in the Civil Rights movement and then the antiwar and Women's Movements parallels the general history of Women's Rights activism that has been written about by Sara Evans and others. The role of the clergy is often discounted or missing entirely from these histories and is still waiting to be written.

6. According to the United Methodist News Service, official News Agency of the United Methodist Church, January 21, 1998.

7. The minutes of only two Western Massachusetts CCS meetings are known to survive. The first is dated December 9, 1969, though it is clear the chapter has already been in existence for some time. Private collection of Reverend Frank Dorman.

8. Sherri Finkbine. "The Lesser of Two Evils," in Alan F. Guttmacher, *The Case for Legalized Abortion Now.* Diablo Press, Berkeley, 1967. pp. 15–25.

9. Moody wrote in *Abortion Counseling* that, by 1969, National CCS was its own distinct organization and that by 1972, three regional meetings were held instead of one national convention. Unsworth remembers that there may have been what he characterizes as "get-together seminars," which no one from the Western Massachusetts CCS chapters attended. But, Unsworth recalls, "That didn't mean we weren't in touch. I mean, we were on the phone back and forth, we exchanged letters when that was appropriate. But it was much more of a movement than it was a bureaucracy." (Unsworth transcript, VWHC archives, Special Collections, W.E.B. Du Bois Library, University of Massachusetts Amherst).

10. Ibid.

11. United Ministries in Higher Education (UMHE) was established in 1964, and was an offshoot of the United Campus Christian Fellowship, which had formerly represented the student movements of four Protestant denominations. The UMHE supported a number of Protestant organizations like the United Christian Fellowship. The archives of the UMHE are at Yale University.

12. Collection Group Description. Student Affairs: United Christian Foundation, 1923–1977, W.E.B. Du Bois Library, Special Collections and Archives, University of Massachusetts Amherst.

13. Record group 30/12, United Christian Foundation Collection, Special Collections and Archives, W.E.B. Du Bois Library, University of Massachusetts Amherst.

14. *The Massachusetts Daily Collegian*, November 9, 1971, p. 2.

15. Journalist Cynthia Gorney's book *Articles of Faith: A Frontline History of the Abortion Wars* (Touchston/Simon & Schuster, New York, 1998), documents lay women counselors working with the CCS chapter in St. Louis, Missouri and Nanette Davis, in her book *From Crime to Choice: The Transformation of Abortion in America* (Greenwood Press, Connecticut, 1985), claims that for the Michigan chapters she studied, "as the

movement developed, [clergy] counselors 'farmed out' routine cases to agency and lay persons, leaving only the difficult assignments for themselves." Since the only book-length treatment of the national CCS movement was written in 1973 by Howard Moody and Arlene Carmen, there is still much that is not yet known or documented about the arrangements of the individual city and regional chapters.

16. UCF Record Group, Special Collections, W.E.B. Du Bois Library, University of Massachusetts Amherst.

17. Fraser died in August 2001.

18. Elaine Fraser began a Master's program in Counseling and Education at UMass, perhaps in the fall of 1970 or 1971. As part of her degree work, she officially "trained" Ruth Fessenden to do problem pregnancy counseling during 1972, at which point Ruth had already been doing counseling sessions well over a year. From CCS task force minutes 9/6/72: "Training Practicum: Elaine is doing a training practicum under Sy Keochakia. She hopes to work with 2 or 3 people during the year, and has begun with Ruth."

19. Ruth Fessenden transcript, VWHC archives, Special Collections, W.E.B. Du Bois Library, University of Massachusetts Amherst.

20. Ibid.

21. Record group 30/12, United Christian Foundation Collection, Special Collections and Archives, W.E.B. Du Bois Library, University of Massachusetts Amherst, box 2, folder 2.

22. Record group 30/12, United Christian Foundation Collection, Special Collections and Archives, W.E.B. Du Bois Library, University of Massachusetts Amherst, box 4, folder 80; *Daybreak* (UCF Newsletter), Volume 1, Issue 5, February 24, 1970, p. 2.

23. *Daily Hampshire Gazette*, November 7, 1970. An obituary in the student newspaper, *The Massachusetts Daily Collegian*, November 9, 1970, reported that Hardy's "wife said he has been depressed for several weeks (by the frustrations he said he was having as one of the University's chaplains [*sic*]) and had been under the care of a psychiatrist for several weeks."

24. Elaine Fraser, in her interview on October 17, 1999, spoke about the stress involved in problem pregnancy counseling: "I mean, you're caring and . . . but I have a wonderful knack for compartmentalizing, and I never would take it home with me. It could have been just an incredible week, and I left on Friday, and everything was sort of up in the air, and I would not think of it, I wouldn't even remember it, the women's names, over the weekend. Monday morning it was front and center and then I was back on again. And each night, I left my work at the office. Which is the only survival technique." Ruth Fessenden explicitly saw a connection between Ron Hardy's work at UCF and his death, which she characterized as "in some ways a measure of how kind of unsettling the state of the world was at that point. That if someone had the ability to take that all in, really, it is as though you wouldn't be able to withstand what that was all about." Fraser transcript, VWHC archives.

25. Fraser transcript, Fessenden transcript, VWHC archives.

26. Figure taken from an unfunded grant proposal to the university to fund problem pregnancy counseling as a separate entity. United Christian Foundation Collection Group, Special Collections, W.E.B. Du Bois Library, University of Massachusetts Amherst, box 4, "Abortion."

27. The undated memo was clearly written sometime after the legalization of abortion in New York State since Hardy described the majority of CCS referrals as going to the

Women's Medical Service in New York City, which opened its doors on the first day of legal abortion in New York, July 1, 1970. The memo was thus written sometime between July 1, 1970 and Ron Hardy's death on November 6, 1970.

28. UCF Collection Group, Special Collections, W.E.B. Du Bois Library, University of Massachusetts Amherst, box 2, folder 2.

29. Fraser transcript, Zapka transcript, VWHC archives, Special Collections, W.E.B. Du Bois Library, University of Massachusetts Amherst.

30. The Valley Women's Center recorded 110 abortion referral interviews from January 1971 to January 1972.

31. At UMass CCS after the New York law change, less and less of the counseling was done by the clergy. The reduction in clergy staff by the fall of 1971 was a major factor in this.

32. Kriss Woll, "Organizing for Access" (unpublished paper), collection of author.

33. CCS Task Force minutes, September 6, 1972. Record group 30/12, UCF Collection Group, Special Collections and Archives, W.E.B. Du Bois Library, University of Massachusetts Amherst, box 4, "Abortion."

34. Unsworth transcript, VWHC archives; *Daily Hampshire Gazette*, November 20, 1970; Leslie Laurie transcript, VWHC archives, Special Collections, W.E.B. Du Bois Library, University of Massachusetts Amherst.

Thirteen   Reverend Richard Unsworth

1. Mary Calderone was medical director for the Planned Parenthood Federation of America during the 1950s and 1960s. She wrote in 1960 in the *American Journal of Public Health*: "Abortion is no longer a dangerous procedure. Why should illegal abortion be a public health problem?" She convened a 1955 conference on abortion, whose published proceeding marked the first major work on abortion in the modern era.

2. Moody was approached by Lawrence Lader, who, after the publication of his book *Abortion*, had begun to receive numerous requests for information on abortion providers. For more information on the origins of this relationship and the origins of CCS, see Howard Moody and Arlene Carmen's *Abortion Counseling and Social Change, From Illegal Act to Medical Practice: The Story of the Clergy Consulation on Abortion*. Judson Press, Valley Forge, 1973.

3. This is most likely Dr. Milan Vuitch, whose indictment in the District of Columbia brought abortion to the Supreme Court under allegaltions that D.C. laws were unconstitutionally vague. In April 1971, the Supreme Court in the *United States v. Vuitch*, upheld the abortion law that allowed abortions for "the preservation of the the mother's life and health" but defined health as including "psychological as well as physical well-being." Washington D.C., thus continued to be a major area of abortion practice nationally.

4. Leslie Laurie worked as a Planned Parenthood organizer for Western Massachusetts from September 1970 until September 1973, when she became Executive Director of the Family Planning Council of Western Massachusetts.

5. The New York decision was handed down on April 9, 1970 and took effect on July 1 of that year.

6. Quickening describes the first recognizable movement of the fetus.

Fourteen   Reverend Samuel M. Johnson

1. The five colleges are Amherst, Mount Holyoke, Smith, and Hampshire Colleges and the University of Massachusetts Amherst. Hampshire College did not have its first students until 1970.
2. Everywomen's Center is a resource center for women at the University of Massachusetts Amherst.
3. According to Jane Zapka, the Public Health Educator at University Health Services, an arrangement was worked out through which CCS could refer worried students to Health Services for pregnancy tests and Health Services could refer pregnant students to CCS for counseling.
4. Only one minister, Reverend Robert Hare of the CCS chapter in Cleveland, was ever charged with conspiracy to commit abortion. The case, brought by the State of Massachusetts, which was where the abortion had been performed, was eventually dropped.
5. CCS did have some involvement in helping women fund their abortions but they distanced themselves from that effort early on. Around 1969 or 1970, students and CCS counselors helped establish the Emergency Medical Loan Fund to help women pay for abortions. Initially, Elaine Fraser and others at CCS did the screening of applicants and kept the finances, but they soon realized that this was risky. It also seemed inappropriate, to Fraser, to have the counselor be the same person who came after the money. The Loan Fund was soon transferred to the Student Activities office and was managed from there.

Fifteen   Reverend Franklin A. Dorman

1. "UMass Chaplain Dies of Burns," *Daily Hampshire Gazette*, November 7, 1970.

Sixteen   Rabbi Yechiael Lander

1. *Olev ha'shalom* is Hebrew for "of blessed memory." Equivalent to rest in peace, it is said when giving the name of the departed.
2. Abraham Joshua Heschel, 1907–1972, is considered to be one of the most important twentieth-century Jewish theologians. He escaped from Nazi Germany to England and later America, where he taught at Hebrew Union College and then the Jewish Theological Seminary of America. He is the author of the books *Man is Not Alone* (Farrar, Straus and Giroux, New York, 1976), *God in Search of Man* (Farrar, Straus and Giroux, New York, 1976), and *The Prophets* (Harper Perrenial Modern Classics, New York, 2001, originally published 1962).
3. Destined.

Seventeen   Elaine Fraser

1. Dr. Robert Gage transcript, VWHC archives, Special Collections, W.E.B. Du Bois Library, University of Massachusetts Amherst.

2. CCS at UCF set it up so that referrals would only come from clergymen, so as to keep the protection of the privileged counseling. While Elaine Fraser claims here that's the way it was done, her colleague Ruth Fessenden recalls occasions when she gave referrals herself without calling in a pastor. See pp. 175–176.

3. Several of the others interviewed in this collection asserted that while follow-up interviews were ideal, most women did not keep those appointments.

4. Actually one physician and two psychiatrists.

5. Since the abortion itself would be legal, it was felt that the referral could now be given directly by someone who was not a member of the clergy; that protection was no longer necessary. At that point Elaine, and later Ruth Fessenden, did the CCS counseling at the United Christian Foundation on their own.

6. Amherst Women's Liberation transcript, VWHC archives, Special Collections, W.E.B. Du Bois Library, University of Massachusetts Amherst.

Eighteen   Ruth Fessenden

1. Community health organizer Leslie Laurie created the Western New England Counselor's Cooperative around 1970 to unite all those working in abortion counseling, including the clergy, social workers, and feminist activists. They shared information about referrals and in some cases used volume referrals to demand discounts from providers in New York and, after Roe, Massachusetts.

2. According to Elaine Fraser, she always left the room before the referral was given by the clergy person so that the referral would always have been part of religious counseling and would fall under the "answerable to a higher power" defense. Why did this change for Ruth Fessenden? Perhaps she and CCS were just more willing to take the risk at that point. But it is most likely that once abortion became legal in New York and all CCS referalls were then for legal abortion out of state, they may have felt less need to stay under the umbrella of clergy protection.

3. See interviews of Dr. Robert Gage and Dr. Jane Zapka to see how the Health Services approached this problem and instituted policies that would ensure that other students did not endure the same treatment experienced by Ruth.

Part Four   The Feminists: Feminist Lay
Abortion Counselors

1. Springfield Women's Health Collective (Alice Zaft, Betty Wright, Mary Doe, Ann Meeropol, and Sherri Oake) transcript, VWHC archives, Special Collections, W.E.B. Du Bois Library, University of Massachusetts Amherst.

2. Valley Women's Liberation transcript, VWHC archives, Special Collections, W.E.B. Du Bois Library, University of Massachusetts Amherst.

3. Robin Dizard recounted this story about fellow ABC member Mel Heath.

4. Ruth Rosen. *The World Split Open: How the Modern Women's Movement Changed America.* New York, Penguin Books, 2000. p. 238.

5. Linda Kerber and Jane Sherron De Hart. *Women's America: Refocusing the Past, Fourth Edition*. New York, Oxford University Press, 1995. p. 550.
6. Rickie Solinger. *Abortion Wars: A Half Century of Struggle, 1950–2000*. Berkely: University of California Press, 1998. p. 44.
7. Ibid., 44.
8. Springfield Women's Health Collective transcript, VWHC archives, Special Collections, W.E.B. Du Bois Library, University of Massachusetts Amherst.
9. Robin Dizard, "Speech for Flag Day," June 14, 1987, VWHC archives Special Collections, W.E.B. Du Bois Library, University of Massachusetts Amherst.
10. Valley Women's Liberation transcript.
11. "VWC Runs Pregnancy Counseling Service,"*Holyoke Transcript*, April 20, 1971.
12. "Laws Don't Prevent Abortions, Fem Writes," *Holyoke Transcript*, April 20, 1971.
13. "Judges Rule Pregnant Holyoke Woman Doesn't Need a Therapeutic Abortion: Valley Women's Center Responds," *Holyoke Transcript-Telegram*, November 18, 1971.
14. "Problem Pregnancy in the Valley," a three-page report by Britt Gutrtman, Valley Women's Center Pregnancy Counseling Service, February 1, 1972. Valley Women's Center Papers, Sophia Smith Collection, Northampton, Massachusetts.
15. Ibid.
16. Many of the women in the Springfield consciousness-raising group had been involved in the Movement for a Democratic Society, the nonstudent offshoot of Students for a Democratic Society, one of the principal anti-Vietnam War organizations of the 1960s era.
17. From *An Execution in The Family: One Son's Journey* by Robert Meeropol, St. Martin's New York 2003, p.130: "Elli had focused on Feminist issues since our move to Springfield. She'd helped to found the Springfield Women's Center and later the Springfield Women's Union, which developed Programs to meet women's education health, child-care, and political needs. She'd been active in a reproductive rights group and in a modern underground railroad of sorts that facilitated women's trip to New York where abortion was legal. After Roe v. Wade, she worked as an abortion counselor for Springfield's first abortion clinic."
18. Oral History with Liza Solomon, July 22, 2004. Collection of author.
19. Leslie Laurie transcript, April 17, 2002. VWHC archive, Special Collections, W.E.B. Dubor's Library, University of Massachusetts Amherst.
20. "Abortion and What to Expect," University of Massachusetts *Daily Collegian*,Tuesday, November 9, 1971, p. 2.

Nineteen   Amherst Women's Liberation's Abortion and Birth Control Group

1. Melanie Heath was one of the founders of Amherst Women's Liberation.
2. See Introduction for the lineup of speakers as reported in the *The Daily Hampshire Gazette*, November 20, 1970. Nancy Kierzek was actually taken to Holyoke Hospital in Holyoke, MA.
3. Members of the collective would be "on duty" at various times; the woman on duty would be responsible for counseling any clients who called during that time.
4. Eastern Women's Clinic was the first big legal clinic in New York City. It was started by CCS in 1970. The credit system meant that for a certain number of referalls for paid abortions, the clinic would do one at no charge.

5. Family Planning Council of Western Massachusetts, started by Leslie Laurie in 1973. See pp. 241–255.
6. She is most likely referring to the Springfield Women's Health Collective of which Liza Solomon was a member. The Springfield Women's Center was a separate organization, though it may have had some overlapping membership with the Springfield Women's Health Collective.
7. Tapestry Health Systems, formerly the Family Planning Council of Western Massachusetts.

Twenty   Springfield Women's Health Collective

1. Her name has been changed and her occupation not revealed at her request.
2. The main groups in Boston at that time were Massachusetts Organization for the Repeal of Abortion Laws (MORAL), The Boston Women's Health Book Collective, and the Pregnancy Counseling Service.

Part Five   The Connectors: Uniting Medical Care, Activism, and Feminism

1. Kris Woll, "Organizing for Access: Leslie Laurie and the Origins of the Family Planning Council of Western Mass," unpublished. Collection of the author.
2. Office of Population Affairs, http://opa.osophs.dhhs.gov/tflex/ofp.html.
3. Ruth Rosen. *The World Split Open: How the Modern Women's Movement Changed America*, Penguin Books, New York, 2000. p. 180.
4. Laurie remembers a certain amount of friction between the feminist counselors and the clergy, and viewed herself as a go-between, bridging the gap. Leslie Laurie transcript, March 22, 2002 interview, VWHC archives, Special Collections, W.E.B. Du Bois Library, University Massachusetts Amherst.
5. See Woll, "Organizing for Access."
6. UCF Records Group, box 4: "Abortion," Special Collections, W.E.B. Du Bois Library, University of Massachusetts Amherst. The groups were the Valley Women's Center, the Community Women's Center clinic in Greenfield, the Birth Control Information group in North Adams, the Health Counseling Service in Pittsfield, the Great Barrington Health Center, Springfield Family Planning (two clinics), Fitchburg Family Planning, Holyoke Family Planning, the Hilltown Family Planning Clinic in Worthington, University Health Services, Women's Health Counseling group in Springfield, CCS, and Planned Parenthood in Springfield, Massachusetts and Brattleboro, Vermont.
7. The WNECC also survives to this day, in slightly altered guise, as the Abortion Loan Fund of Western Massachusetts, which "focuses on ensuring access to abortion for low-income women and information on legal attacks against such access."

Twenty-One   Merry Boone

1. William Sloane Coffin is the theologian, educator, and writer associated for many years with Yale Divinity School.
2. Agnew, the Baltimore County Executive, was the Republican candidate for governor in a race against Democrat George Mahoney, whose racial platform was akin to that of George Wallace.
3. Now part of Baystate Medical Center.
4. Now Massachusetts State Representative for Hampshire County.
5. Massachusetts did not legalize strict control for unmarried women until the *Eisenstadt v. Baird* case was decided on March 22, 1972. Massachusetts thus became the last state in the nation to legalize Strict control for all women regardless of marital status.
6. Massachusetts Citizens for Life is affiliated with the National Right to Life Committee, one of the nation's largest "pro-life" organizations.

Twenty-Two   Ellen Story

1. The "Buffer Zone" bill is Bill 148 of April, 1999. The Birth Control bill, Bill 2139, was passed in January 2000.

Twenty-Three   Leslie Tarr Laurie

1. According to the Department of Health and Human Services, "the Community Health Center [CHC] Program is a Federal grant program funded under Section 330 of the Public Health Service Act to provide for primary and preventive health care services in medically-underserved areas throughout the U.S. and its territories."
2. The "morning after pill" is actually not one pill but is a special use of a high dose of certain kinds of birth control pills. The pills provide a strong burst of hormones, which breaks up the hormone pattern necessary for an egg to implant in the uterus.
3. The clinics agreed to add counseling to their services and indeed hired some of the same women who had previously been doing such work as volunteers. Once counseling was established in the clinics, CCS and the feminist counselors ceased doing the work.
4. Reagan proposed reorganizing support of federal programs by consolidating 85 categorical grants into 7 block grants. Congress revised the plan slightly for its Omnibus Budget Reconcilliation Act of 1981, consolidating 77 grants into 9 block grants. The block grants provided about 25 percent less funding than the individual grants and some programs ended up receiving smaller pieces of a smaller pie.

Bibliography

Carmen, Arlene and Howard Moody. *Abortion Counseling and Social Change, From Illegal Act to Medical Practice: The Story of the Clergy Consultation Service on Abortion.* Judson Press, Valley Forge, 1973.

Davis, Nanette J. *From Crime to Choice: The Transformation of Abortion in America.* Greenwood Press, Westport, 1985.

Feldt, Gloria. *Behind Every Choice is a Story.* University of North Texas Press, Denton, 2002.

Gluck, Sherna Berger and Daphne Patai. *Women's Words: The Feminist Practice of Oral History.* Routledge, New York, 1991.

Gordon, Linda. *The Moral Property of Women: A History of Birth Control Politics in America.* University of Illinois Press, Urbana, 2002.

Gorney, Cynthia. *Articles of Faith: A Frontline History of the Abortion Wars.* Touchstone/Simon & Schuster, New York, 1998.

Hole, Judith and Ellen Levine. *Rebirth of Feminism.* Quadrangle/The New York Times Book Co., New York, 1971.

Jacob, Krista. *Our Choices, Our Lives: Unapologetic Writings on Abortion.* Universe Star, New York, 2004.

Joffe, Carole. *Doctors of Conscience: The Struggle to Provide Abortion Before and After Roe V. Wade.* Beacon Press, Boston, 1995.

Kaplan, Laura. *Jane: The Legendary Underground Feminist Abortion Service.* The University of Chicago Press, Chicago, 1995.

Messer, Ellen and Kathryn E. May. *Back Rooms: Voices from the Illegal Abortion Era.* St. Martin's Press, New York, 1988.

Mohr, James C. *Abortion in America: The Origins and Evolution of National Policy, 1800–1900.* Oxford University Press, Oxford, 1978.

Reagan, Leslie J. *When Abortion Was a Crime: Women, Medicine, and Law in the United States, 1867–1973.* University of California Press, Berkeley, 1997.

Rosen, Ruth. *The World Split Open: How the Modern Women's Movement Changed America.* Penguin Books, New York, 2000.

Schoen, Johanna. *Choice & Coercion: Birth Control, Sterilization, and Abortion in Public Health and Welfare.* University of North Carolina Press, Chapel Hill, 2005.

Solinger, Rickie. *Abortion Wars: A Half Century of Struggle, 1950–2000.* University of California Press, Berkeley, 1998.

Solinger, Rickie. *The Abortionist: A Women Against the Law.* University of California Press, Berkeley, 1996.

Index

Printed in the United States
70119LV00002B/100-249